Contemporary Pragmatism

Edited by

Mitchell Aboulafia
&
John R. Shook

Volume 5
Number 1
June 2008

AMSTERDAM - NEW YORK, NY 2008

The paper on which this book is printed meets the requirements of "ISO 9706:1994, Information and documentation - Paper for documents - Requirements for permanence".

ISSN: 1572-3429
ISBN: 978-90-420-2485-4
©Editions Rodopi B.V., Amsterdam - New York, NY 2008
Printed in The Netherlands

Contemporary Pragmatism

Volume 5 Number 1   June 2008

Contents

Contemporary Pragmatism
Vol. 5, No. 1 (June 2008), 1–11

Editions Rodopi
© 2008

Argument-Forms Which Turn Invalid Over Infinite Domains: Physicalism as Supertask?

Catherine Legg

Argument-forms exist which are valid over finite but not infinite domains. Despite understanding of this by formal logicians, philosophers can be observed treating as valid arguments which are in fact invalid over infinite domains. In support of this claim I will first present an argument against the classical pragmatist theory of truth by Mark Johnston. Then, more ambitiously, I will suggest the fallacy lurks in certain arguments for physicalism taken for granted by many philosophers today.

1. Introduction

Argument-forms exist which are valid over finite but not infinite domains. One such was discovered by De Morgan, who dubbed it the "syllogism of transposed quantity." A particularly vivid example articulated by Charles Peirce (1931, §3.288) is the following:

Every Texan kills a Texan,

No Texan is killed by more than one Texan,

Hence, every Texan is killed by a Texan.

Common-sense suggests interpreting this argument over a domain containing (legendary state pride notwithstanding) a finite, albeit large, number of Texans. If so, the argument is valid in the sense that there is no possible world where the premises (as interpreted) are true and the conclusion false. But where the Texans are even countably infinite, there is such a possible world. The argument is an instance of the following argument-form:

$$\forall x \, \exists y \, K(x,y)$$
$$\forall x \forall y \forall z \, (K(y, x) \wedge K(z, x)) \rightarrow (y = z))$$
$$\therefore \; \forall x \, \exists y \, K(y,x)$$

That this argument-form is invalid is shown by the following instantiation:

> *Every number has a successor.*
>
> *For any three numbers, if the second and the third are successors of the first, then the second is equal to the third.*
>
> *Therefore, every number is the successor of some number.*

When interpreted over a domain consisting of the positive natural numbers, the premises of this argument are true and the conclusion false. However if the domain is restricted to any finite subset of those numbers, this does not hold.

Many logicians are uncomfortable with talk of argument forms "turning" invalid over infinite domains – they would rather say that infinite domains show that such argument forms are invalid *simpliciter*. But I believe it is worth highlighting the fact (however one refers to it) that certain argument-forms can be relied on to deliver true conclusions from true premises if one only interprets them over finite domains, while at the same time if infinite domains are considered they cannot. I wish to argue that an understanding of this fact has still not fully percolated from formal logic into broader philosophical reasoning, insofar as philosophers can be observed treating as valid arguments which are in fact invalid over infinite domains.

In support of this claim, I will first present an argument against the classical pragmatist theory of truth by Mark Johnston, where a fallacy of this form is arguably quite clear-cut. Then, more ambitiously, I will suggest the fallacy lurks in certain arguments for physicalism taken for granted by many philosophers today.

2. The Classical Pragmatist Definition of Truth and Johnston's "No Ideal Theory" Objection to it

The American pragmatist tradition introduced a new and distinctive internalist position to the landscape of philosophers' attempts to define truth. This position differs from major (non-deflationary) rivals by not characterising truth in terms of a relationship between *truth-bearers* (such as propositions, sentences or beliefs) and something else. (This "something else" is thought in the case of correspondence theories of truth to be worldly *truth-makers*, and in the case of coherence theories of truth to be *other truth-bearers*). Rather, truth is defined as what is believed by what might be termed *truth-believers* (that is, inquirers, *albeit* often idealised in some way). More precisely, as Peirce originally put it (1931, §5.407), "The opinion which is fated to be ultimately agreed to by all who investigate, is what we mean by the truth." Much more recently, but in the same lineage, Hilary Putnam (1981) defined truth as an "idealisation of rational acceptability."

This view attracted the critical scrutiny of Mark Johnston, who attacked it as follows. Johnston (1993a, 88–89)[1] takes for granted that this conception of truth is committed to the existence of an ideal theory, "T." For such a theory, surely, is what is "fated to be ultimately agreed to by all who investigate," in Peirce's terms, and is what would be ideally rationally acceptable, in Putnam's. Johnston then asks what such an ideal theory might consist in. He suggests that it would be a set of sentences from which every true sentence may be deduced. He then objects that, "[a]s a matter of simple metalogic it could not be true that something is true if and only if it follows from the ideal theory T."

Johnston's argument runs as follows. If the language of T is rich enough to express arithmetic, then it will be rich enough for a Goedel argument to be constructed within it. From this it follows that there will be truths expressible in T which are not provable within T, such as the famous "Goedel sentence" which, very roughly, says truly of itself that it is not provable. The best that can be hoped for, he writes, is an ideal *hierarchy* of theories, each closer to the truth than the last, proving to be true statements which were only expressible in the theory directly below it. Thus, instead of the classical pragmatist account of truth, Johnston favours a "Progressive Protagoreanism," which is protagorean (or internalist) merely regarding which truths one should pay attention to – so that one might avoid wasting epistemic energy on "metaphysics in the pejorative sense" – but not regarding truth itself, which he treats in classical correspondence terms.

3. Why Johnston's Objection Fails

This is a clever objection, to which it might seem *prima facie* that the classical pragmatist theory of truth must fall. It seems that "the opinion which is fated to be ultimately agreed to by all who investigate" (sometimes referred to as the "final opinion") cannot contain the Goedel sentence – but neither may it omit the Goedel sentence, surely, if the sentence is true. To conclude that this is a knock-down argument would, however, be premature.

First and most importantly, Peirce never said that every true statement had to be *provable* within the final opinion. All that is required is that the statement be *included* in the final opinion. It may be protested that this is to admit that the final opinion is not "complete" (in the logical as well as the ordinary language sense), and this seems to be a strange and troubling failing for such an idealised notion.

However, just because *any* true statement (such as the Goedel sentence and its many higher-order equivalents) would be believed if inquiry proceeded indefinitely, it does not follow that there has to be *some complete* theory in which they are all believed together. Johnston has failed to recognise that the pragmatist may commit to *any* question receiving an answer at *some* point in time, while not committing to there being any point in time at which *every* question has received an answer: just as the fact that every person has a mother who loves them does not entail that there is some particular mother who loves every person.

At this point Johnston's construal of the pragmatist theory of truth might seem to involve a simple quantifier scope confusion, and thus to constitute an invalid argument even over finite domains, as follows (letting Qx mean that x is a question and $A(x,t)$ mean that x is answered at t):

$$\forall x \, \exists t \, (Qx \rightarrow A(x,t))$$
$$\therefore \exists t \, \forall x \, (Qx \rightarrow A(x,t))$$

However, a supporter of Johnston might respond that the nature of inquiry is, when all goes well, *cumulative* (or "progressive" as Kuhn put it) so that questions which are answered at any given time tend overall to stay answered.

Indeed, the classical pragmatist's own talk of the 'final opinion' seems to demonstrate a commitment to inquiry being at least sufficiently cumulative for such an opinion to form (however haltingly).[2] This can be argued to add a new premise to the argument, so that the inference from *any* question receiving an answer at some point in time to *every* question having received an answer at some point in time should nevertheless be valid.

Consider the case where every mother loves not just the child she has just brought into the world, but (in a burst of new maternal affection) all other children brought into the world previously. In such a case it seems that we may infer: if every child has a mother who loves them, then there is some mother who loves every child – the last mother to give birth. Formalised (letting Qx mean that x is a mother, $A(x,y)$ mean that x loves y maternally, and $B(x,y)$ mean that x was born before or simultaneously with y), the argument-form may now be represented thus:

$$\forall y \, \exists x \, (Qx \rightarrow A(x,y))$$
$$\forall x \, \forall y_1 \, \forall y_2 \, (B(y_1, y_2) \rightarrow (A(x, y_2) \rightarrow A(x, y_1)))$$
$$\therefore \exists x \, \forall y \, (Qx \rightarrow A(x,y))$$

In other words:

> *Everyone is loved by some mother.*
>
> *For any two individuals, if the first is born before or simultaneously with the second, then any mother who loves the second also loves the first.*
>
> *Therefore there is a mother who loves everyone.*

Johnston's argument is isomorphic except for a reversal of the inequality:

Every question receives an answer at some time.

For any two times, if the first is before or simultaneous with the second, then any question which is answered at the first time is answered at the second.

Therefore there is a time at which every question is answered.

These arguments are valid *only over a finite domain* (of mothers and children, or questions and times at which they are answered). The arguments' validity depends upon the existence of a "last" member of the domain. As Peirce put it:

> We must look forward to the explanation, not of all things, but of any given thing whatever. There is no contradiction here, any more than there is in ... saying that any future time will sometime be passed, though there never will be a time when all time is past. (1931, §1.405)

Given that the set of questions to be answered, and future times at which they might be answered, is greater than finite, then, Johnston's argument fails. And surely this is the case.[3]

4. Further Consequences for Physicalism

Physicalism is widely believed in contemporary philosophy. It is often put forward as the natural philosophical heir of the scientific naturalism which provided such spectacular explanatory successes in the physical sciences from the seventeenth century onwards. Such successes often lead physicalists to argue for their position (*albeit* often implicitly) by way of an optimistic meta-induction along lines such as the following. Given that physicists were so successful explaining planetary motion, the behavior of gases, the paths of projectiles, and so on, therefore sooner or later they will achieve similar explanatory successes with respect to all other phenomena.

As an example of this optimistic meta-induction, physicalism is particularly popular in current philosophy of mind, where it is often defined in terms such as the following:

> All mental properties, states, and events can be wholly explained in terms of physical properties, states, and events.

What is not often drawn attention to is that this definition of "philosophy of mind physicalism" is ambiguous between two interpretations:

(P1)   Any mental property can be given a physical explanation in some physical theory.

(P2)   There is some total physical theory which explains every mental
        property.

Philosophical physicalists tend naively to assume the stronger (P2). Consider for
instance, the following remark in Jackson and Braddon-Mitchell (1996, 13),
"The physical story that explains each and every physical happening may very
well have irreducibly probabilistic elements." Jack Smart goes so far as to
suggest that that physical story is current "physics of ordinary matter" (1978,
339–340). In many other cases (P2) is not explicitly stated but is implicit in a
definition of physicalism as the denial of *emergentism* (see for instance, Pettit
2003 and Stoljar 2001). For it is only against the background of a total physical
theory that phenomena can *be* emergent, rather than merely explained by a
different physical theory to the theory one is presently considering.

    However, induction over the history of explanatory successes in science
arguably only establishes (P1) at best. One might attempt to argue that (P2)
follows from (P1). An argument such as the following (letting *Mx* mean that *x* is
a mental property and *E(x,y)* mean that *y* provides a physical explanation for *x*):

$$\forall x \, \exists y \, (Mx \rightarrow E(x,y))$$
$$\therefore \exists y \, \forall x \, (Mx \rightarrow E(x,y))$$

would of course constitute another straight-out quantifier-scope fallacy. Once
again, therefore, one might seek to add a further premise to make the argument
valid.

    A consideration which often occurs to physicalists who make use of
Ramsey sentences is the following. Physical explanations can simply be
concatenated *via* logical conjunction. If a physical theory (*T1*) explains one
mental property (*m1*), and a different physical theory (*T2*) explains another
mental property (*m2*), then (*T1* ∧ *T2*) will surely be a "theory" which explains
both *m1* and *m2*, and so on for every theory and every mental property until (P2)
is satisfied. One might formalize the argument like this:

$$\forall x \, \exists y \, (Mx \rightarrow E(x,y))$$
$$\forall x_1 \forall x_2 \forall y_1 \forall y_2 \, [((Mx_1 \wedge E(x_1, y_1)) \wedge (Mx_2 \wedge E(x_2,y_2))) \rightarrow \exists y_3 \, (E((x_1$$
$$\wedge x_2), y_3) \wedge (y_3 = (y_1 \wedge y_2)))]$$
$$\therefore \exists y \, \forall x \, (Mx \rightarrow E(x,y))$$

    This suggestion flies in the face of much careful work in the philosophy
of science regarding scientific theory-holism following, for instance, Quine
(1953, 1960), arguing that scientific terms such as 'force' and 'electron' do not
have a theory-independent meaning that would be interpretable across the
conjunction of two very different theories jammed together. As an example, try

to imagine a vast conjunction composed of all the claims made about gravity by Newtonian mechanics and Einstein's general relativity. What would such a set of statements mean? What would it "say about gravity"?

If such holism is denied, and theories are considered as nothing but sets of individually-interpretable statements, a further issue arises. What if certain statements in *T1* and certain statements in *T2* are logically inconsistent? Obviously the conjunction of the two theories would then give rise to a contradiction, which would arguably not constitute a very good explanation of anything. All explanatory virtue might not be lost if one dipped into some form of relevance logic allowing the isolation of contradictory theory-components from one another, and adherents of paraconsistency would most probably see precisely this kind of case as grist for their mill.

Alternatively, defenders of theory-concatenation might wish to argue that, given the principle of excluded middle, one cannot have a logical inconsistency in a group of statements without having at least one true and one false statement. (In other words, for a contradiction one needs something of logical form p and something of logical form $\sim p$). However, all successful physical explanations are *true*. (For surely it is a necessary condition for successful explanations that they be true?) Thus two statements of differing truth-value will not be found anywhere in T1 and T2, and thus there will be no contradiction. This reply seems to involve quite a leap of faith however, particularly when one notes that one must claim not only that all successful physical explanations are true but that all *parts* (i.e. component propositions) of all successful explanations are true. How many real-life physical theories could live up to that?[4]

Even leaving that thorny issue aside, however, once again, the argument-form above is not valid. Consider the following instantiation of it:

> *For every natural number there is a number larger than it.*
>
> *For every two pairs of natural numbers (a1 and a2) and (b1 and b2) for which it is the case that the second number is larger than the first, there exists a number which is larger than (a1 + b1), namely (a2 + b2).*
>
> *Therefore, there is a natural number which is larger than all natural numbers.*

To sum up then: there is no largest number (due to the infinity of the domain over which the successor relation is defined), there is no last moment in time (due to the infinity of the domain over which the 'later than' relation is defined), the number of different phenomena which might require physical explanation is arguably infinite[5] and thus the potential emendations of physical theory are infinite, so why should we think there is *a* theory which explains everything?

The physicalist may wish to argue at this point that talk of "the" physical theory which would explain everything is a benign *idealisation*, as harmless in epistemology as the concept of the frictionless plane is in physics. Physical law ensures that we never encounter such a thing as a plane with utterly zero friction. Nevertheless, to assume that such a thing exists greatly simplifies certain physical equations. What harm does it do to assume that all explanations come together in a single theory?

Well, first of all, we have already noted that Johnston was led into a fallacious argument by it. More generally, however, an intriguing literature is emerging concerning so-called "super-tasks," pointing out that once we idealize a process to infinity, the properties possessed by the limit of the process are not always what we would expect given its finite instances. For instance, Thomson's lamp, which switches from 'on' to 'off' and *vice versa* at ever-halving intervals of time, is neither 'on' nor 'off' at the end of its infinite series of switchings, in apparent violation of physical law.

A recent short exchange in *Analysis* (Friedman and Black 2002) provides an even more nicely counterintuitive example. Friedman describes a supertask involving an infinite number of numerically labeled balls, as follows:

Step 1:   Place balls '1' and '2' on a table. Discard the ball numbered '1'.

Step 2:   Place balls '3' and '4' on the table. Next, interchange numbers '2' and '3'... Finally, discard the ball that is now numbered '2'.

Step 3:   Place balls '5' and '6' on the table. Next interchange numbers '3' and '5'. Finally, discard the ball that is now numbered '3'....
            (p. 344)

If this process is idealised to infinity, the number of balls on the table tends to infinity while the number of labels on the balls tends to zero! In response to this apparent paradox, Black cheerfully notes (p. 346), "you can only think this is a problem if you think the equinumerosity of [the balls] and [the labels] has to be carried over to the limit sets, and it doesn't."

A number of standard challenges to physicalism in its many guises and versions exist. For instance, it has been complained that physicalism is in principle unable to explain qualia (Chalmers 1996), and intentionality (Kripke 1982), and that physicalists illicitly convert what should be a methodological into a metaphysical claim. However as far as I know this particular criticism has not been raised.[6]

One might complain at this point that there is an odd structure to the dialectic of this article. It would appear that the very same considerations have been used to defeat both Johnston's argument that can be no final physical theory, and the physicalist's argument that there is. Can one really have one's cake and eat it too in this way?

However, though the two views are indeed opposites:

~∃t ∀x (Qx → A(x,t)) (Johnston)

∃t ∀x (Qx → A(x,t)) (the physicalist)

neither one of these two views is the contradiction of Peirce's view:

∀x ∃t (Qx → A(x,t))

I conclude that despite a certain popular "fast-and-loose" image which pragmatism seems to have picked up, a proper understanding of the classical pragmatist theory of truth requires an exact appreciation of modern logic.

NOTES

1. See also an almost identical discussion in his 1993b, p. 318.

2. Of course the possibility must be faced of inquiry not just *slowing down*, but *backsliding*, such that inquirers stop believing certain true things which they once believed, and start believing certain false things which they did not believe before. Taking this possibility duly into consideration would add more bells and whistles to the formalization which follows, but not alter the objection I am about to make.

3. Further assumptions are of course implicit in the classical pragmatist definition of truth as the end of inquiry, such as that rational beings will continue to exist and to inquire, which may be taken issue with. However this would be a further discussion.

4. Consider Newtonian mechanics once again. According to this theory there is no upper bound on the speed of a moving mass, and an object's acceleration cannot alter its size, but neither of these claims is true according to best scientific theory today.

5. As an argument that the universe's phenomena are infinite not merely in quantity but also in kind consider the infinite number of different kinds of thoughts which arguably might be entertained by the human mind. If however this argument is felt to be too swift, and that the possibility should be left open for some kind of finitist discrete theory of space-time, it may be argued that at least one's philosophical naturalism should not beg such an empirical question.

6. Crane and Mellor (1990) do discuss a worry that the key claim of physicalism is crucially ambiguous – but they identify the ambiguity as holding between the claim that an explanation can be given for any phenomenon by *current physical theory* and by *future idealised physical theory*. Both of these options seem to be conceived as unitary theories. Nevertheless there are probably interesting links to be drawn between the two discussions.

REFERENCES

Black, Robert. 2002. "Solution of a Small Infinite Puzzle," *Analysis* 62: 345–346.

Chalmers, David. 1996. *The Conscious Mind*. New York: Oxford University Press.

Crane, Tim, and Mellor, D. H. 1990. "There is No Question of Physicalism," *Mind* 99: 185–205.

Friedman, K.S. 2002. "A Small Infinite Puzzle," *Analysis* 62: 344–345.

Hookway, Christopher. 1985. *Peirce*. London and New York: Routledge.

Jackson, Frank, and Braddon-Mitchell, David. 1996. *The Philosophy of Mind and Cognition*. Oxford: Blackwell.

Jackson, Frank. 1997. *From Metaphysics to Ethics: A Defence of Conceptual Analysis*. Oxford: Oxford University Press.

Johnston, Mark. 1993a. "Objectivity Refigured: Pragmatism Without Verificationism," in *Reality, Representation and Projection*, ed. J. Haldane and C. Wright (Oxford: Oxford University Press), pp. 85–130.

Johnston, Mark. 1993b. "Verificationism as Philosophical Narcissism," *Philosophical Perspectives* 7: 307–330.

Kripke, Saul. 1982. *Wittgenstein on Rules and Private Language: An Elementary Exposition*. Oxford: Blackwell.

Laraudogoitia, Jon Perez. 1996. "A Beautiful Supertask," *Mind* 105: 81–83.

Lombardi, Olimpia, and Labarca, Martín. 2005. "The Ontological Autonomy of the Chemical World," *Foundations of Chemistry* 7: 125–148.

Misak, Cheryl. 1991. *Truth and the End of Inquiry*. Oxford: Clarendon Press.

Moore, Adrian. 1991. *The Infinite*. London and New York: Routledge.

Peirce, Charles Sanders. 1931. *Collected Papers of Charles Sanders Peirce, vol. 1: Principles of Philosophy*, ed. Charles Hartshorne and Paul Weiss. Cambridge, MA: Harvard University Press.

Peirce, Charles Sanders. 1976. *New Elements of Mathematics*, vols. 3 and 4, ed. Carolyn Eisele. The Hague: Mouton.

Pettit, Philip. 1993. "A Definition of Physicalism," *Analysis* 53: 213–223.

Putnam, Hilary. 1981. *Reason, Truth and History*. Cambridge, UK: Cambridge University Press.

Quine, Willard Van Ormand. 1953. "Two Dogmas of Empiricism," repr. in *From A Logical Point of View* (Cambridge, MA: Harvard University Press), pp. 20–46.

Quine, Willard Van Orman. 1960. *Word and Object*. Cambridge, MA: Harvard University Press.

Smart, J. J. C. 1978. "The Content of Physicalism," *Philosophical Quarterly* 28: 339–341.

Stoljar, Daniel. 2001. "Physicalism," *Stanford Encyclopedia of Philosophy*, http://plato.stanford.edu/entries/physicalism/. Accessed 26 March 2008.

Thomson, James F. 1954. "Tasks and Super-Tasks," *Analysis* 15: 1–15.

Catherine Legg
Senior Lecturer
Department of Philosophy and Religious Studies
University of Waikato
Private Bag 3105
Hamilton
New Zealand

Contemporary Pragmatism
Vol. 5, No. 1 (June 2008), 13–38

Editions Rodopi
© 2008

Wittgenstein's Question and the Ubiquity of Cultural Space

Joseph Margolis

Wittgenstein's question about agency in *Philosophical Investigations* §621 provides a fresh way of addressing the analysis of the distinction between physical nature and human culture, featuring the artifactual, hybrid, second-natured, enlanguaged and encultured transformation of the members of Homo sapiens into selves; and a third model of the cultural between the hermeneutic and the reductive: including the cultural "penetration" of the physical, internal and external Bildung, the sui generis features of the culturally emergent, and the new unity of the human and natural sciences.

1.

Somewhat more than thirty years ago, Charles Taylor sketched a very plausible line of argument against what he then called "naturalism." He was drawing our attention to a systematic animus among analytic theorists of the human sciences against invoking anthropocentric attributes in explanatory contexts. His objective was just the reverse of the purpose of "naturalists" like the Wilfrid Sellars of the well-known essay, "Philosophy and the Scientific Image of Man."[1] Taylor wished to illustrate what would need to be secured (against naturalism's presumption) in mounting an acceptable philosophical analysis of what belonged to what, in a relatively unmarked way, we would now name a "culture" or "the cultural world" – meaning by that the *sui generis* human world, the world of human persons or selves, uniquely formed by cultural and enculturing processes – which, against Taylor himself, would rightly fall within the boundaries of a more generous reading of "naturalism." In effect, Taylor missed the mark of his own objective. For one thing, he never rightly identified what distinguished the cultural from the natural; for a second, he wrongly supposed the cultural could not conceivably be brought under the range of what he called the natural; and, for a third, he was mistakenly convinced that the materialist reduction of the cultural world would, if successful, eliminate whatever was distinctive of the cultural or the mental. He was in error in all of this.

Taylor almost always focuses on the most problematic "cultural" phenomena, but he hardly ever addresses their distinction in a philosophically robust way: he hardly ever contrasts the "cultural" and the "natural" frontally, which one might have thought was the essentially contested issue in working out the right relationship between the so-called natural and human sciences. Even in his huge recent book *A Secular Age* (2007), Taylor features distinctions that already fall entirely within the boundaries of the cultural itself, without ever isolating what we should mean by the cultural. "Our understanding of secularity [occupied with the question of the presence and absence of God in our thoughts and practices] is [he says] in terms of public spaces."[2] His entire discussion – it's as true of his earlier, more easily recognized philosophical forays as it is here – is invariably focused on what is interior to the cultural world, more often "civilizational" than cultural: so that when he signals a general allegiance to Aristotle, he speaks in an idiom that touches on Greek *paideia* construed within the (apparently) adequate space of an ample biologism.

By a strained use of terms similar to Taylor's – well, following the usage of John McDowell, which without analysis of any kind permits the Aristotelian conception of *paideia* to incorporate Hegel's and Gadamer's conception of *Bildung* – I would be willing to treat Taylor's use of "civility" as a version of what might be called "internal *Bildung*." By that I mean a version of enculturing education that never ventures to theorize about the "metaphysical" nature of the cultural world or its evolutionary sources prior to and approaching the true emergence of the encultured competences in question. The lesson to be gained, as we shall see, is simply that the needed decisive distinction rests with what may be called "external *Bildung*" or what, explicating external *Bildung*, governs our understanding of what falls within the scope of internal *Bildung*, and why.

Hard as it may be to believe, this distinction is all but inaccessible prior to the advent of Darwin's evolutionary theory, though it is present in Vico's contrast between God's "manufacture" of nature and man's "manufacture" of the distinctly human world. It is noticeably lacking or inchoate in Herder, Hegel, Marx, Heidegger, and Gadamer – as, indeed, it also is (more bafflingly!) in figures like Taylor and McDowell, who favor one or another author like those just mentioned or, more distantly still, a puzzlingly attractive figure like Aristotle, who had no sustainable inkling at all about what we now would feature in the analysis of human culture. Thus:

> Renaissance "civility" [Taylor says], is the ancestor of our "civilization" and has much the same force. It is what we have, and those others don't, who lack the excellences, the refinements, the important achievements which we value in our way of life. The others were the "savages."
>
> The city, following the ancients, is seen as the site of human life at its best and highest. Aristotle had made clear that humans reach the fullness of their nature only in the polis. "Civility" connects to the Latin word which translates "polis" (civitas); and in fact derivations of the Greek

word were also used with clearly related sense: in the seventeenth century, the French spoke of an "état policé" as something they had and the "sauvages" didn't.[3]

This counts, I judge without the least hesitation, as a brief for invoking no more than the doctrine of internal *Bildung*, which makes no sense *philosophically* when separated from external *Bildung*. You cannot then go beyond Aristotle's biologism (which Taylor favors) or Kant's formalism (which McDowell favors, usually as if it were somehow, inexplicably, hospitable to the internalist thesis). We cannot make progress here unless we provide a picture of the "metaphysical" distinction between nature and culture, which is not to treat the contrast itself as essentially disjunctive. It is, rather, emergentist in an evolutionary sense, but the sense indicated is not and cannot be Darwinian.

The matter is too easily obscured, however, in admitting that much, because the evolving process depends on the Darwinian process and on the revolutionary innovations made possible by what I am calling external *Bildung*, which marks biology's initial enabling, but also, its remaining inability to generate the routines of internal *Bildung*. There's a conceptual puzzle there that, I suggest, is profoundly focused in our time by Wittgenstein's famous question at §621 of the *Philosophical Investigations*. In any case, you cannot find the contrastive pair in Taylor's sustained analyses of Hegel,[4] even in the Conclusion to the *Hegel* volume, where Taylor actually mentions Marx's pertinent thesis, namely, "the self-creation of man through the fashioning of an adequate external expression as the 'objectification [*Vergegenstandlichung*] of man's species life [*Gattungswesen*]."[5]

Here, as we may anticipate, Marx's perceptive grasp of the "internally" self-transforming powers of the human world (internal *Bildung*, bridging Aristotle and Hegel on the artifactual side) argues the need to explain the original emergence of that capacity from animal sources (external *Bildung*). The natural answer invokes the Darwinian contribution: a fortiori, the fortunes of the post-Darwinian metaphysics of culture – as, promisingly, in the decisive convergence (in this respect) between American pragmatism and Marburg neo-Kantianism, most notably in the work of Charles Peirce and Ernst Cassirer. The nerve, for instance, of Cassirer's criticism of Hippolyte Taine's "Darwinian" zeal for classifying cultures as if they were much like animal species may be guessed from the following remarks:

> The theory of evolution [Cassirer says] had destroyed the arbitrary limits between the different forms of organic life. There are no separate species; there is just one continuous and uninterrupted stream of life. But can we apply the same principle to human life and human *culture*? Is the cultural world, like the organic world, made up of accidental changes? – Does it not possess a definite and undeniable teleological structure? Herewith a new problem presented itself to all philosophers whose starting point was

the general theory of evolution. They had to prove that the cultural world, the world of human civilization, is reducible to a few general causes which are the same for the physical as for the so-called spiritual phenomena. Such was the new type of philosophy of culture introduced by Hippolyte Taine in his *Philosophy of Art* and in his *History of English Literature*.... But if we examine the explanations which these theories were designed to give, the unity of human nature seems extremely doubtful.[6]

My own conviction is that man is indeed a "second-natured," hybrid, artifactual entity – a "natural artifact," as Marjorie Grene very prettily puts it[7] – not a merely "natural-kind" entity at all, though our evolutionary biology appears to prepare us for our encultured second nature. We are transformed by cultural forces (enculturation), and culture itself manifests a *sui generis* evolution that reaches back into biological evolution in a long "preparation," but then exhibits a "metaphysics" of its own. That is what I find missing in Taylor (hence, also, in McDowell), though Taylor is indeed one of our most perceptive discussants of what we mean by "culture" and the "human sciences." The trouble is that, not unlike Aristotle, who, some twenty-five hundred years earlier, lacking the modern conception of the cultural world and historicity, effectively fell back to the adequacy of his biologism, Taylor does much the same (not unlike Taine), despite his command of the post-Hegelian tradition. For his part, McDowell is forced to be more daring than Taylor, because he is wedded to the adequacy of the analytic canon; but that, precisely, keeps him from grasping the more alien themes of the cultural world. The quarrel at stake – which is bound to seem a minor matter at first – introduces and helps to resolve an important paradox: how to explain how human beings "produce" themselves as persons and how, as a result, we may distinguish perspicuously between the natural and the human sciences.

Let me introduce here, without preamble, Wittgenstein's splendid question (at §621):

> Let us not forget this: when "I raise my arm," my arm goes up. And the problem arises: what is left over if I subtract the fact that my arm goes up from the fact that I raise my arm?
> ((Are the kinaesthetic sensations my willing?))[8]

Here I have in mind acknowledging the parallel pairing of human persons or selves and the members of Homo sapiens and the pairing of human culture and physical nature – and the illuminating match of subtractive questions formulated in terms of these latter pairings. Wittgenstein does not answer his own question directly; but I would say that it cannot be rightly answered without invoking something like the distinction between internal and external *Bildung*, which Wittgenstein does not implicate, unless by the cognate joke of "willing" and "kinaesthetic sensations." I myself suggest that the paradigm of all these linkings is that between speaking a language and uttering mere sounds. Wittgenstein, I suggest, is signaling the ubiquity and distinctive invisibility of the cultural world, which classic analytic philosophy (think of the Vienna Circle) was prepared to acknowledge only reductively.

Biologism and physicalism are no longer adequate to our philosophical needs, however, though it is startling to learn (and rather symptomatic) that a self-styled "hermeneut" like Taylor speaks (almost exclusively) of what – in treating Aristotle's conception of education as pertinently similar to Hegel's (and perhaps to Hans-Georg Gadamer's) account of *Bildung* (a usage, as I say, John McDowell has somehow entrenched without supporting argument)[9] – may be rightly confined to internal *Bildung* (in a sense I shall want to contrast with "external" *Bildung* more carefully). The idea is that the "cultural," or, better, the "civilizational" paideutic, is thought by Taylor and McDowell (and *a fortiori* by Aristotle) to be adequately captured as internal to the distinctive biology of the human. But that cannot be right *if*, as seems indisputable, the phenomena of language and speech cannot themselves be (have never been successfully) formulated in terms confined to the merely biological – as Noam Chomsky once famously thought was true but is now unable to confirm.[10]

The same complaint applies to historicity and (to what I am prepared to name) the "second-natured" powers of the human person or self: self-reference, self-description, spontaneous linguistic facility and understanding, and, above all, the second-natured "penetration" of all human perception, experience, thought, agency, and the like by the concepts and embedded theories of a home language. Taylor *has* all such competences in mind when he avows his "hermeneutic" commitment. But for some inexplicable reason, he seems to believe that the mere enumeration of these competences instantly defeats "reductionism" – which is indeed what *he* means by "naturalism."

But that is clearly and importantly false. Taylor rightly mentions his list of the principal hermeneutic competences.[11] But he's completely mistaken in thinking that the mere enumeration of these anthropocentric powers defeats reductionism on its face. The reason is entirely straightforward: a resourceful reductionist *welcomes* the hermeneut's enumeration, because *he* believes he *can* replace the anthropocentric idiom with a "neutral" materialism that eclipses all undesirable vestiges of an earlier philosophical innocence, in the interest of science itself. We cannot claim to know the relevant "necessities" *a priori*, though it's true enough that *no* sustained reductionism has ever been found to be fully convincing. Schizophrenia, for instance, was originally described almost entirely in cognitive, affective, and behavioral terms, but the malady is now largely confined in terms of specific brain and biochemical disorders. This sort of change profoundly affects the question of what to regard as ineliminably anthropocentric. The *a priori* itself is perhaps no more than the *a posteriori*: the full contingency of what, at one historical moment, we may have found ourselves incapable of paraphrasing in reductive terms.

This is not an ordinary quibble. To adhere to naturalism on Taylor's terms – to be what Taylor sometimes calls a "radical naturalist" (that is, a reductionist) – "we must [he says] avoid anthropocentric properties" (properties sometimes also awkwardly called "subjective"[12]). But the caveat is more than misleading. It's true that B. F. Skinner did "avoid" certain anthropocentric properties having to do with the "black box" of unobservable mental life: he was brilliantly caught out of course by Noam Chomsky's decisive review of his argument in *Verbal Behavior*. Chomsky, you may remember, demonstrated that Skinner's linear logic (ranging over stimulus and response) could not possibly cope with the feedback processes of natural-language behavior.[13] This is part of the genuine force of Taylor's account of the irreducible explanation of action, in *The Explanation of Behavior* (which appeared in 1964), on which the argument I'm now reviewing very much depends.[14] But it is not true in any standard sense that reductionists need avoid anthropocentric properties. It's closer to the truth to say that they have always failed to validate the reductive paraphrases they've proposed. The point of Taylor's early innovation is, precisely, that he introduced a "non-standard" model of causality suited to the analysis of human agency. That's to say: if (as I suppose) the human self is, conceptually, as "alien" as it is, then it would hardly be surprising that the form of causality we assign it – agency, in the least contested sense – may not be at all reducible to any of the canonical forms of causality (inspired, I would say, however distantly, by Hume's intuition of the "external" relationship between cause and effect) assigned the natural sciences. You cannot help glimpsing there the linkage between the analysis of the human and the unity of the sciences.

Effectively, Taylor misconstrues the essential issue – that is, *his* issue. He conflates behaviorism's having "tried to ignore purpose and intentionality, indeed [as he adds, its having] tried to side-step consciousness [and] what [he] call[s] 'significance'" – "the common meanings embedded in our institutions and practices," "the phenomena of intelligence," all of which we "have in common ... a certain metaphysical motivation" – *with* the objective the champions of a reductive "scientific language [favor] which essentially aspire[s] to [a distinctive form of] neutrality ['disengagement' from the anthropocentric]."[15] But the fact is, the true reductionist (Taylor's naturalist) need never ignore anthropocentric *properties*; he seeks only to describe them (or their successors) in terms of *non*-anthropocentric *predicates*. The honest reductionist has no intention of dismissing what Taylor marks as the hermeneut's "metaphysical motivation." And this simply means that the analysis of the cultural or human world may proceed with the use of such anthropocentric terms quite independently of any reductive intent or the would-be essentialism Taylor assigns his own hermeneutic alternative. It's not the elimination of "hermeneutic" properties, but their reduction, that counts. Taylor misidentifies the metaphysical question; McDowell barely escapes it; Aristotle has no inkling that it's in the offing; Kant precludes it; Wittgenstein, I would say, reclaims it as the decisive question that it is (against, say, Russell, Frege, the Vienna Circle). My own suggestion is that the adequate answer to Wittgenstein's question requires an analysis of what it means for culturally emergent qualifications to *penetrate* the merely natural world. (That, as I say, is what external *Bildung* signifies.)

The skewed picture will have to be righted before we can hope to define the natural and human sciences – or the arts and the sciences – within the space of the cultural. Put more directly: reduction's threat applies to the physical sciences as much as to the human sciences, and to all of these as much as to the fine arts. (That is, in fact, the deepest thrust of Sellars's eliminativism.) We miss what's essential if we restrict the threat's intended scope, but the threat itself is entirely negligible at the present time.

I agree that it's perfectly reasonable to believe that the elimination of anthropocentric *predicates* from any would-be science or serious inquiry aspiring to analyze and explain whatever is central to the human or cultural world signifies that important *properties* may have been dropped from the purview of this or that science. But that hardly shows that the "neutral" paraphrase of selected anthropocentric predicates is impossible (without "metaphysical" loss); and apart from that, we know no way at the present time to cast any would-be human science entirely in non-anthropocentric terms. Taylor's way of putting things distorts the relationship between the *Naturwissenschaften* and the *Geisteswissenschaften* and the arts – but it has its point.

On the view I favor, it is more promising to collect Taylor's important intuitions in accord with the idea that the cultural is *emergent* from the merely biological world (the theme of what I am calling internal *Bildung*); that the cultural is real or actual (within the boundaries of nature) in a sense noticeably more generous and of greater weight metaphysically than Taylor's rather narrow use of the term "naturalism" would allow; and that accordingly the entire cultural world is rightly characterized in terms of certain *sui generis* properties that qualify the whole of discourse (and more), whether reductionism succeeds or not.

2.

There's nothing inappropriate about reductionism's would-be "neutrality." Its conjectures are admittedly premature, possibly futile; but, then, we are not obliged to demonstrate, hands down, that reductionism is an impossible dream. That's neither here nor there; in fact, it can't be shown. Under foreseeable circumstances, there will remain an important difference, hardly a disjunction, between the natural and the human sciences and between the sciences, morality, and the fine arts. However, there will also be a common ground that joins them ineluctably, namely, the history and experience they share through the lives of the community of persons who shape the inquiries in question. Here, then, you begin to glimpse the possibility of a unity of science very different from the reductively motivated unity the early logical positivists were drawn to. For what I shall argue is that the common ground of the sciences is the agency of human selves: that selves are cultural artifacts, second-natured hybrids generated by embedding their culturally emergent *sui generis* powers in, and thus transforming, the biological gifts of Homo sapiens; that this view of selves yields the best solution to Wittgenstein's question (and cognate questions); and that such an answer specifies the metaphysical difference between nature and culture and fixes the difference and linkage between the human and the natural sciences. Quite an economy.

I don't really agree with Taylor therefore in defining the human sciences in terms of the anthropocentric. I suggest instead, in the name of the new sort of unity coming into view, that a better strategy would insist that all the sciences are human sciences, precipitates of the same evolution of culture that depends on, and serially reproduces, the unique second-natured artifacts we call persons or selves. Ultimately, the differences between the natural and human sciences reflect a difference in descriptive and explanatory interests, not an insuperable metaphysical divide of any kind.

If you still suppose the issue is no more than a quibble, let me add another bead to our string. On the argument being advanced, you will find it impossible to deny the following two theorems which are currently under siege: first, that exclusively in cultural space there are *kinds* of causes that depend on "significant" or "significative" factors (insults, say, that cause the insulted's face to redden) or that are causally effective in a way "logically" different from merely physical causes (human agency); and, second, that the well-known thesis of "the causal closure of the physical" must be false or indemonstrable on grounds confined to the empirical confirmation of instances of the externalist or relational kind.[16] Within the space of the cultural world, the analysis of the natural and the human sciences and the arts cannot fail to be a single seamless undertaking – within which (to be sure) we admit different models of causality and different scientific interests in explanation and interpretation – not always of a causal kind.

I'm attempting to clear away certain entangling prejudices from both the "hermeneutic" and "reductionist" sides. It comes as a surprise to see how little reductionism has changed, from 1985 (the publication date of Taylor's *Philosophical Papers*) and, indeed, from 1964 (the publication date of *The Explanation of Behaviour*) and even from the heyday of logical positivism and the unity of science program: which is to say, through most of the twentieth century.

Let me offer a counterweight, then, to Taylor's thesis drawn from a successful textbook ranging over the philosophy of "the social sciences," which, because of its instructional purpose, is particularly candid about the advantages of the doctrinal stand it favors – a canonically correct commitment from the materialist point of view, whether moderate or reductionist. Alexander Rosenberg, the author of the successful *Philosophy of Social Science* (now in its third edition, 2008), introduces (very early in his account) a certain proposition [L], rightly read as a *ceteris paribus* approximation to a causal or covering law –

which turns out (on Rosenberg's reading) to be indeed an incomplete version of "the leading principle of [the whole of] folk psychology" – namely,

If any agent, *x*, wants *d*, and *x* believes that *a* is a means to attain *d* under the circumstances, then *x* does *a*,

where, of course, as Rosenberg is quick to admit, [L] can never cash in all of its innumerable *ceteris paribus* claims, though *that* (he assures us) need never "undermine our confidence in [L] as a causal law." Extraordinary – perhaps even preposterous. [L] "is just what the *naturalist* needs [he explains] to vindicate a scientific approach to explaining action. Scientific explanation is essentially causal. Therefore, any scientific approach to explanation in social science should attempt to establish a causal connection to underwrite its explanations. That will be the function of [L]. It is a causal law or a precursor to one."[17] I take this liberty, in citing Rosenberg, precisely because I've already laid out the essential issue I wish to clarify and because Rosenberg is so transparent in adopting the canon I'm contesting – whether from the side of its usual champions (Hempel, Davidson, Sellars, Churchland, Kim) or from the side of its Anglo-American detractors (Taylor, McDowell, most notably). Rosenberg himself is well known for his own efforts in bringing biology and economics within scientistic terms.[18]

It follows at once, you realize that, on Rosenberg's account (and on most canonical views), a proper science presupposes and entails there being suitably strong explanatory laws in every sector of inquiry open to scientific treatment. In fact, Rosenberg champions a view of science, human science in particular, that is effectively the perfect contradictory of Taylor's views. On Rosenberg's account, the natural sciences have always experienced considerable difficulty in reaching good approximations to the exceptionless laws of nature until, as "*spectators* of the phenomena they sought to discover," their champions "realiz[ed] that our commonsense descriptive categories needed to be changed because they [the categories themselves] were a barrier to discovering [the essential] generalizations [needed]." Why then shouldn't the same be true of the human sciences, Rosenberg asks, in spite of the fact that the social scientist is himself not merely a spectator – he's actually "a participant, an agent, a player in the human domain"?[19]

The trouble with Rosenberg's optimistic way of reviewing matters (which is not, I assure you, sold short because it's drawn from a partisan textbook) is that it ignores too many of the deeper questions that must be answered. For instance, if human agency is a form of causality, then, on a suitable theory of perception (*not* a merely phenomenal theory in anything like Hume's sense), causality *can* sometimes be discerned perceptually (which Hume famously denies). Accordingly, what may be thus discerned need not conform to the relational (or externalist) model of causality favored in the natural sciences (as, by counterexample, in producing speech by speaking – which, initially, is not *relationally* defined at all, though it can indeed, and must, incorporate the usual "externalist" models of physical causation). Hence, at least provisionally anthropocentric concepts do have a significant role to play in the social and human sciences; and, of course, it must also be true that "beliefs, desires, expectations, preferences, hopes, fears, wants that make actions *meaningful* or *intelligible* to ourselves and one another"[20] must have a descriptive and explanatory role in the human sciences that cannot be restricted to the causal, or to any variant of the "relational" model of causality that builds on Hume's intuition.

If, then, paradigmatically, cognitive distinctions implicate the active role of a human or surrogate subject or agent (whether functioning perceptually, experientially, productively, analytically, interpretively, or reflectively in some other way), it is far from obvious that anthropocentric concepts are eliminable in principle or that in accord with the Kantian and post-Kantian achievement there can be a principled disjunction between the objective and subjective aspects of knowledge. Furthermore, there is no compelling *a priori* argument to the effect that causality implicates exceptionless or invariant laws of nature or that any argument can be shown to bear such a burden on the strength of admitting the human subject's mediation. The "laws of nature" appear to be constructivist posits fitted to selected generalizations, possibly even deformed or modified for systematic purposes.[21] Substantive necessity, strict universality and the like are literally beyond the human ken: causality and nomologicality do not actually entail one another; and the appearance of (synthetic) "conceptual truths" is itself subject to the evolving history of inquiry and understanding.[22] The "natural necessity" of genuine causal laws cannot be shown to be more than an artifact of our theories of the logic of causal explanation itself.

Rosenberg rather incautiously affirms – inadvertently, he helps us plumb an essential difficulty that might have been instinctively obscured – that

> the human being is subject to all the forces natural science identifies and those of psychology, sociology, economics, and so forth.[23]

> Why then, [he asks] models, generalizations, and laws? It's pretty clear that technological control and predictive success come [he answers] only through the discovery of general regularities. For only they enable us to bend the future to our desires by manipulating present conditions.... The only way that is possible is through reliable knowledge of the future, knowledge of the sort that only laws can provide.[24]

You cannot fail to see that Rosenberg risks self-contradiction here, as a result of the extremely lax way in which he allows himself to shift between empirical "regularities" and nomological universalities construed in the strictest way. The logical contrast Rosenberg needs is, finally, no more than a formal imputation that cannot be crisply made out on the basis of empirical facts. There is no empirical confirmation of the exceptionless validity of would-be covering laws; prediction does not require the assumption. The artifactual nature of the human world itself, which is not demonstrably reducible to any "merely physical" order, seems to be the emergent yield of certain very complex, decidedly contingent evolutionary confluences of biochemical enabling that offer no prospects of their own of being able to support the physicalist reduction of the cultural world (for instance, by way of the resources of the relatively late appearance of significant concentrations of proteins on the surface of the earth).[25]

My own conviction is that, in the practice of science, we never actually require the use of strict laws fitted to all regions of the world; and all approximations specifically fitted to the actual world are, for that very reason, inadequate to the purpose at hand. Also, strict nomological universals require a degree of assured predicative constancy ranging over contingently encountered instances that human discourse could never confirm. Hence, to continue Rosenberg's line of argument (which, as I say, is a reliable version of the canonical view) is to be ideologically loyal to the materialist canon or to accept a blackmail argument.[26] There need be no detectable formal differences between "accidental" constancies and would-be nomological regularities. *We* elevate ("for good reason") our provisional preferences to the status of approximating the laws of nature; there's nothing else to fall back on. Mendeleev's pioneer efforts at formulating a primitive table of the chemical elements shows the way. The result is that we *cannot* compel the analysis of the human sciences or the arts to submit to a model of description and explanation (fitted to the physical sciences) alleged to be necessary *there*. The ubiquity of the informalities of the cultural world colors all of our inquiries together.

When you think of Mendeleev's empirical success in predicting the qualitative and quantitative properties of certain as yet unknown elements, based on what we now know to be a seriously mistaken causal theory and a more than doubtful arithmetic conjecture, you realize that our usual presumption that *any and every* science is governed by the search for exceptionless causal laws is an artifact of predictive success, and not the other way around. But if so, the objective standing of the human sciences, the arts, morality, non-causal questions of interpretation and the like are entirely open to more favorable conceptions – wherever needed.

3.

All this is probably busier than it needs to be. I've said no more than that an adequate reductionism in the sciences is beyond our present competence and that it may be impossible as well. Furthermore, there is bound to be some informal system of anthropocentric (or hermeneutically favored) properties that will serve as a conjectural ground for any would-be human science at least as well as any now-proposed reductive model. Accordingly, the human and natural sciences may need to be quite different methodologically and metaphysically, despite the fact that they will undoubtedly share an ineliminable bond between them, namely, the presence of human inquirers and the culturally formed aptitude that ensures the viability of what they separately do.

To admit this much is already to admit the presence of something alien to the usual analysis of the "physical" among the physical sciences. You must consider that even if you extend the term "physical" to include the mental and the cultural, you do not thereby eliminate what is so familiarly distinctive about their – very possibly irreducible – role among the sciences. There's the lesson reductionism obscures.

I take the analysis of our two notions to be essentially intertwined. The first is the notion of certain exceptional entities (persons) who come into existence serially by the transformative processes of the second, activated primarily through the artifactual agency of already existing entities of the first kind; the second, of predicables that mark the unique powers of entities of the first kind and the unique properties of what (*qua* agents) they are able to "utter" (deeds, artworks, technologies, speech, institutions and traditions), which account for the distinctive causal history of all that belongs to the world of the second. I take the human self to be a hybrid of some sort: a unique cultural transform of the biologically gifted members of *Homo sapiens* into something that can no longer be explained in biological or physical terms alone – an artifact that has a natural life. Count that the *ur*-site of a potentially very large conceptual innovation.

I recommend, therefore, that we take time enough to review the unmatched power of Wittgenstein's famous question at §621 of the *Investigations* – and any spinoff questions that may be fairly regarded as derived from that. For example, consider the question formulated very early by Arthur Danto for very different reasons (in fact, for an incipiently reductive purpose), who, having written a book of his own on the theory of action that goes completely contrary to Wittgenstein's splendid query, saw at once the application (supporting his own analysis of the fine arts) of an objection to Wittgenstein's hint – which appears as a central thesis of the "Artworld" paper and *The Transfiguration of the Commonplace*[27] – a lax variant of reductionism. For another example, there is my own version of the original question, which I dare suppose is even more strategically placed than Wittgenstein's or Danto's – because, simply enough, it locates what seems to be the best clue we are likely to draw on in accounting for the transformation of the members of *Homo sapiens* into human selves (subjects, persons, agents, or the like), hence in accounting for actions and the fine arts as matched modes of human "utterance" viewed through the lens of speech itself. The clue's plain enough: you cannot admit the *perception* of speech without admitting the cultural "penetration" (the metaphysical transformation) of sound into legible discourse. In a precisely analogous sense, to the encultured eye one of Giotto's painted surfaces in the Arena chapel is transformed into the Betrayal. Similarly, "Wittgenstein's arm's raising" is converted into "his raising his arm" and a specimen member of *Homo sapiens* into a self. Danto balks at this because he balks at the idea that sensory perception could be so altered, culturally so transformed, that what emerges becomes our spontaneous and unshakeable second nature. There you glimpse the nerve of the conception of the human I have in mind – still too fragmentary for the story to be taken up directly. The point is, we have no idea how to answer if answering would eliminate or obscure our presence as persisting selves; and yet the theory that begins to dawn regards the self as an artifact as much as speech and painting.

Wittgenstein does not answer his question explicitly at §621 – it wouldn't accord with his expository style. But he does signal a line of speculation opposed to any response of the reductionist sort. For one thing, there's the light-fingered joke of the final parenthesis; and, thereupon, we are made aware that the standard answer fashioned by a large swath of analytic philosophy is, simply, No! It's the answer explicitly and implicitly given for instance (in different ways) by figures like Wilfrid Sellars, Donald Davidson (whose views Rosenberg clearly follows but alters in his analysis of [L]), by Arthur Danto and by very different means by Jaegwon Kim. But Wittgenstein's lesson, I surmise, is that a more positive and promising answer, eclipsing the reductionist's and the dualist's options, would require the acknowledgement of the reality of the cultural world (perhaps, then, a *Lebensform*, which would certainly not be a "theory" in the sense Danto favors in "The Artworld" paper), and could (for that reason) already have been Yes. That is, on a thoroughly fresh reading of the original question.

This much shows that reductionism and dualism are basically the same doctrine, once we resist anything like Cartesian metaphysics: dualism is, roughly, what remains when reductionism fails. That is indeed my reading of Sellars, Davidson, Danto, and Kim: admirable exemplars of a scandalous choice, which Taylor eludes with the least effort by way of his noticeably under-developed "hermeneutics." Taylor never quite commands the "third" option that his own inexplicit intuition (akin to Wittgenstein's) draws him to. I'll call it "emergentism" to mark in a plain way what appears to be the only remaining line of viable analysis left to us (between dualism and reductionism) if we suppose (as I suggest) that the human self is a hybrid artifact of certain enculturing processes irresistibly applied to the infant members of *Homo sapiens*. I may perhaps be forgiven, then, if I hurry to say we seem to share the distinct impression that the *Natur*- and *Geisteswissenschaften* must be linked through the common agency of the human subject in a sense not alien to the ground that links a bodily movement and a human action. For an action is an "utterance" of a human self adequated to its "nature" as the second-natured artifact it is. If you concede this much, you may be inclined to be hospitable as well to the idea that persons and the gifted animals of the human species are similarly linked; that paintings and mere painted canvases and uttered words and uttered sounds must be similarly linked; and, therefore, that the generic answer regarding the link between physical nature and human culture must lie there – in the same conceptual vicinity.

The answer to Wittgenstein's question is the key to answering the strategic question of how to construe the metaphysical and methodological relationship between the natural and human sciences. In fact, the competing options (briefly noted) expose just how doubtful the accepted truisms are regarding what a science finally is – for example, the presumption that a science must be committed to causal explanation; that only an externalist or relational model of causality is viable and capable of the requisite rigor; that scientific explanations confirm "the causal closure of the physical"; that explanation and prediction presuppose exceptionless laws of nature; that the human sciences are not sciences at all if they flout any of these constraints. I would say that all these claims are false or indemonstrable.

Consider a small sketch of the needed argument. Linguistic competence is so important to our picture of the human condition that we cannot resist admitting that we hear and understand speech spontaneously and that hearing speech and hearing mere sound cannot (for us) be one and the same thing! We couldn't be persons or selves if the difference weren't palpable. Speech is the motor of our "second nature." No reductionism can petition our assent compellingly if it cannot provide a convincing reduction of speech to sound – or to something of the same sort, possibly of a kind even more extreme. But there is no known reduction of speech: Skinner failed abysmally; Chomsky has withdrawn his biologisms and has no alternative to offer; Sellars and Churchland offer empty promises. If you agree, then the better answer to Wittgenstein's question falls into place at once: *any* serious Yes that rejects dualism requires the conceptual space we call a "culture." What's "left over" is nothing but *that* by which we distinguish between what belongs entirely to the physical and biological world and what *in addition* belongs to the cultural world.

It may seem easier (though it is not) to think of actions as mere bodily movements than it is to think of speech as mere uttered sound. Yet the analysis of speech and action rests on an underlying structure common to both. Consider only that you cannot greet me in the street with a wave of the hand if you are not an apt "speaker" of some natural language (not necessarily one we share). Of course, if you speak in sign language, then uttering an unvoiced piece of language *is* a way of speaking; but then voiced speech is also a kind of action. You have only to add the possibility that if you ask me where your copy of Kant's first *Critique* is, I answer aptly enough by simply pointing to the tattered paperback you let me borrow. There, pointing is linguistically significant, though not (or not necessarily) verbal: I would say it's "lingual," meaning by that that nonverbal modes of purposive action presuppose linguistic competence without yet being forms of speech themselves; they *are* semiotically significant, of course, as in dancing, making bread, making love. But then speech itself is in part inherently lingual; that is, speech itself succeeds because part of its linguistic meaning is grasped through certain closely associated nonverbal actions in which it is characteristically embedded. Also, I daresay, the pointer's well-known pose beside a dropped pheasant is incipiently cultural though it is not speech – and thus not lingual either. A certain fine-tuning is obviously needed here.

In any case, if you treat the question about speech as a perspicuous way of testing Wittgenstein's original question – *a fortiori*, Danto's opposed argument fitted to action and the fine arts – you see the sense in which the question can be answered in the affirmative: viz., "You must suppose the presence of a distinctive world," *not* a mere *façon de parler*, *not* a "theory" in Danto's sense. There's the "third" solution: the emergence of a person, an artwork, a word, a deliberate action – a hybrid, contingently indissoluble artifact belonging at once to the physical and cultural worlds, which exists only in the space of human culture. Rejecting any such possibility with regard to artworks and actions, Danto faces a flat contradiction since he does not deny the existence of persons; for, on the argument being sketched, artworks and actions are "uttered" by persons in accord with the causal model we call agency.[28]

Now then, at least three further interlocking questions remain to be addressed: for one, how, *sui generis*, human selves are "emergently" related to the members of *Homo sapiens*; second, what the "second-natured" nature of the transformed entities that thereby arise is; and, third, what the unique or distinctive marks of the new beings we become are. An adequate answer obviates reductionism and dualism; yields the essential clue to the unity of the *Natur-* and *Geisteswissenschaften*; provides a fair account of the metaphysical novelty of the cultural world; and suggests how to characterize all other kinds of entities belonging to the cultural world. Quite a windfall. Mind you, I draw these themes entirely from the proprieties of answering Wittgenstein's original question against the reductionists and even against Wittgenstein's animus against conventional metaphysics.

The human infant's ability to master any and every natural language (and every associated culture) by prelinguistic means – by merely living among apt speakers – is staggeringly efficient, swiftly exercised, reliable, effortless, autonomous, and assuredly mysterious. This ability marks a unique achievement of unmatched difficulty. It transforms a gifted prelinguistic animal into an apt self, a creature now competent (but not before) in speech, self-reference, self-interpretation, informed choice, the reporting of its inner mental life, understanding and communicating with other members of its species similarly transformed.

The change is radical and regular enough to be deemed unprecedented, "metaphysically" *sui generis*, artifactual and "second-natured": the constituting of a new sort of "hybrid" being that remains in part a specimen of a would-be "natural-kind" species but is so modified by enculturing means that it tends thereafter to favor its artifactually acquired (its lingual) interests (involving belief, desire, action, norms and the like) that can no longer be described or explained in terms confined to the supposed biology of natural kinds or of any of the would-be well-formed laws of nature to which "natural kinds" are said to conform. Even a committed neo-Darwinian like Richard Dawkins admits that the "memes" of encultured human life (Dawkins's deliberate fiction) play a causal role that cannot be construed as linked in any obvious way with the evolutionary role assigned our genes.[29] I press the difference more forcefully than Dawkins: the emergent – culturally penetrated – processes cannot, as far as we understand matters, be reductively recaptured; *and* the mode of causality that we name agency is itself penetrated – significatively, semiotically, in terms of cultural meaning – in such a way that (against Kim and Sellars, for instance) it cannot be counted on to conform to the essential regularities of the externalist account of causality. In fact, agency cannot serve explanatorily at all apart from meeting prior constraints of hermeneutic or interpretive pertinence and objectivity. The mere bodily movement of a forefinger's pressing a certain piece of metal cannot account in any causal way for the Archduke's assassination unless the bodily movement in question can be shown, first, to count objectively *as* the deliberate firing of the pistol (in hand) in an effort at assassination. Entire library shelves of analytic theories of action are defeated by that single constraint.[30] No science that invokes agency can separate causal and interpretive questions.

For related reasons, there are no "laws of nature" that apply to language that are of the strict sort claimed for the physical sciences. Chomsky's ingenuity shows that one ought not rule out the possibility too casually. But there is no argument to show that there must be strict causal laws for the physical world itself, and the failure of Chomsky's theory draws attention to the enormous differences between linguistic and "merely" physical phenomena. The very idea of the evolution of physical nature suggests the unlikelihood of "the causal closure of the physical" and the startling discovery that (on recent estimates) we may not be able to perceive more than a very small part of the "matter" that must fill the universe in order to account, on currently favored grounds, for discrepancies involving the perceived rate of expansion of the known universe and discrepancies between the age of the universe and of star clusters within the universe itself.[31]

4.

In philosophical parlance – whether with Aristotle or Rosenberg – to speak of *Homo sapiens* as a "natural kind" invariably signifies (so it is claimed) a vision of nature "carved close to its joints," a model that begins to approximate to the underlying laws of nature by which we expect to identify the explanatory regularities of the human world. But, at best, our second-natured regularities seem to be no more than immensely variable, diverse, historically labile, fluid, open-to-continual-change (though not chaotic), fluxive (as an obsolete term has it), contingent – in effect, idealized – regularities of artifactual sources that "penetrate" our biological gifts and thereby transform aggregates of apparent habits into institutions, traditions, and idiosyncrasies. The classic behaviorists were led to their own extreme views by the troubling truth that the anthropocentric categories of human desire, belief, action and the like (involved in "folk" and "hermeneutic" explanation) could hardly be said to "name" any natural kinds.[32]

Of course, if you view the laws of nature as artifactual *Grenzbegriffe* – valid only for an uncertain season but useful for that purpose – then the seeming discrepancy between the natural and the human sciences will surely fade and the unity of science will come to rely not on the ubiquity of strict causal laws[33] but on selected salient episodes, causal *or* predictive, singular *or* general, that conform with the obvious (the "anthropocentric" or pragmatist) interests of human selves on which Taylor himself insists. But against Taylor, it will require abandoning any principled opposition between naturalism and hermeneutics, without denying that the "cultural" introduces entities (persons) and attributes (linguistic and *sittlich* fluency) that appear nowhere else in the known world or appear more than merely incipiently. There's the "missing" factor that bridges the "two sorts" of science, once we admit the problematic standing of the "laws of nature." For if you concede that we have no realist grounds for supposing that we are always trying to *approximate* to the actual exceptionless laws of nature, it becomes well-nigh impossible to distinguish on formal or evidentiary grounds between general regularities that have some predictive power and regularities that are bona fide approximations to invariant laws.

Taylor gives as false an impression of his own opposition to reductionism as the reductionists do with regard to hermeneutics.[34] Very possibly, Taylor gives his clearest and least tendentious account of the "hermeneutical view" in the Introduction to his *Philosophical Papers*:

> an individual [a human person or agent] is constituted [Taylor affirms] by the language and culture which can only be maintained and renewed in the communities he is part of. The community is not simply an aggregation of individuals; nor is there simply a causal interaction between the two. The community is also constitutive of the individual, in the sense that the self-interpretations which define him are drawn from the [aggregated] interchange which the community carries on.... [Hence,] language does not only serve to *depict* ourselves and the world, it also helps *constitute* our lives.[35]

The trouble is, this scants the idea of *human agency* as well as the distinction between internal and external *Bildung*. What Taylor says is equivocal in a sense already too late (in his own century) to be useful: the term "constitute," taken in the internalist sense, is essentially Aristotelian or Gadamerian or the like – a kind of "paideutic" sharing of an entrenched ethos, *not* the "originary" constitution of a human subject by way of transforming the very nature of the members of *Homo sapiens*, not the "first" appearance of a new kind of being.

There's no evidence that Taylor's treatment of the "hermeneutical" is meant to exceed the limits of a biologism of Aristotle's kind, although it construes the intended instruction in a manner influenced by the hermeneutic treatment of *Bildung*. In fact, Taylor treats Aristotle's view as congenial to the views of figures like Herder, Humboldt, and Hamann (the authors of what he calls "the triple-H theory": the Romantic theory that emphasizes that it's human activity, primarily the activity of speaking, that explains linguistic competence best and, because of that, the "expressive" use of language and culturally "penetrated" thought and affect by which an ethos "constitutes" historical beings like ourselves.[36]

Taylor's theory is confined to the question of "internal *Bildung*," in the narrowest of senses. The processes of "external *Bildung*" remain a mystery until at least the advent of Darwinism and the possibility of tracing the continuity of the proto-cultural life of primates and other species and the fully articulated cultural life of humans.[37] (External *Bildung* remains a mystery for Taylor.) On my reading, the myth of the Platonic forms, the medieval articulation of the Biblical theory of Creation, universalism and essentialism, early modern forms of inherently privileged cognitive faculties, Kant's transcendentalism, innatism, and all the post-Kantian treatments of Mind or *Geist* that match and inform the limited competences of human *Geist* are heroic but failed approximations of the artifactual evolution of human language and what language makes possible: viz., the reflexive and free powers of the forms of culturally induced agency that Darwinian evolution facilitates but never captures.

Taylor never supposes a human society without language of course, but he also never considers (as far as I know) the evolutionary possibility of a human species (*Homo sapiens* or Neanderthal) that has not yet achieved a true language. So he thinks of what is biologically essential to human nature – and therefore, potentially, what is normatively appropriate to the moral and political life of mankind. That is, he thinks of the human *self* and its *possessing a language* as natural and essential to its biological mode of being; but he obscures the prejudice of so thinking (innocently enough) because he also admits that the specific paideutically acquired norms and powers of the self are among the possible variants of an underlying essential nature: he confuses, as I say, internal and external *Bildung*. So does very nearly the entire philosophical tradition from Parmenides to our own day. I realize how difficult that is to accept. And yet, if with Hume and Kant in the eighteenth century you already admit the empirically and transcendentally unanswerable (and unanswered) problem of locating the site of the self, you see at once how vulnerable all our speculations about science and morality are bound to be. Certainly, it's obvious that new-born infants, immensely gifted though they are, lack language and cannot function as selves at all. The mere fact that they spontaneously acquire a native language and a culture does not explain the depth of their achievement *if* there's a difference to be made out between internal and external *Bildung*.

All this explains why Taylor's treatment of modern analytic theories of language and meaning, running from Frege to Quine, to the Wittgenstein of the *Tractatus*, to Davidson, to McDowell, utterly misses the "externalist" connection with Hegel, Heidegger, Gadamer, and the whole of the hermeneutic vision. My own intuition has it that we cannot rightly understand the relationship between the natural and the human sciences, or the relationship between the arts and the sciences – essentially one and the same issue – if we do not address the externalist question in addition to its internalist mate. Thus, for instance, it's not the presence or absence of causality, or approximations to, or the failure to approximate, the true laws of nature that's decisive in answering Wittgenstein's question: it's the transformative import of our emergent competence to pursue any of the inquiries of the sciences and arts that threatens to disappear from view in the purely internalist accounts of the human.

I may as well add that we must also distinguish between what remains inchoate in Hegel and Gadamer: that's to say, what *can't* be found in either but which their own accounts presuppose, namely, the philosophical difference between the internalist and externalist forms of *Bildung*, the transformation of the human infant into a person *and* the evolutionary approach to the threshold of linguistically apt hominids or proto-linguistic societies of *Homo sapiens*. If we ignore or oppose this line of reasoning, we will never escape the crippling paradox of the social contract theory Rousseau so successfully dismantled: in effect, *man's constitution of himself*.[38] It was Darwin, of course, who supplied the *sine qua non* of the "invention" of the self. In the internalist sense, *Bildung* certainly accords with the artifactual entrenchment of our artifactual identity – our artifactual self-identity – by way of our linguistic scruple in the use of the "I": something much more convincing than, say, Kant's bafflement (in the first Critique) regarding the inexplicable ubiquity and experiential nullity of what Kant calls the "*Ich denke*."[39]

The decisive clue, I've been insisting, is that the human self or subject is an artifact of *cultural evolution*, the "metaphysical" transform of the members of *Homo sapiens* effected primarily by the mastery of a natural language, which makes the self-identity of the self possible, entrenched, as the artifact it is, among a society of similarly "second-natured" human beings, who, through their lifetime, construct and entrench their individual identities together by exercising their new-found powers. They remain individual agents but now share a "second nature" as the hybrid transforms that they become: their original biological gifts are "penetrated" by the collective powers of a shared language and cultural tradition they themselves internalize. This fixes the sense in which Darwinism has proved to be so immensely important for the redirection of philosophy and science in the interval spanning the pioneer work of Kant and Hegel and the publication and reception of *The Origin of Species* (1859). It also rounds out the sense in which the entire history of philosophy and science from its Greek beginnings to the late decades of the eighteenth century (or, perhaps, down to the second half of the nineteenth century) was unquestionably deprived of the conceptual resources afforded by the dawning of our modern notions of historicity and evolution.

Imagine! The entire achievement of the human world is the work of a hybrid being, a "natural artifact," whose original cognitive, affective, and effective talents are "penetrated" and transformed by the historied forces of its own ethos. You see at once how any such admission cannot fail to challenge all presumptions of strict universality and substantive necessity in every cognitive and rational inquiry. You see, for instance, how absurd it would be to suppose that language could possibly have been deliberately invented by a society of cooperating persons. Our second-natured nature is not a "natural-kind" nature at all but a shared collective history. It also signifies the importance of answering Wittgenstein's question in a way that collects these evolutionary complications.

In short, Taylor treats the "hermeneutic" evidence as sufficient by itself to stalemate or defeat reductionism ("radical naturalism"). Yet Taylor never confirms his claim, never (as far as I know) examines the deeper question of the difference between the cultural and the merely biological. The result is that we slip too easily into reading Taylor's objections to reductionism as if they had already earned the right to count as an analysis of the original emergence of the cultural world. But that cannot possibly be enough. Persons, languages, actions, artworks, technologies cannot but be metaphysically distinctive in the same *sui generis* way: that is, as culturally emergent; culturally penetrated, culturally formed and continually transformed; purposive, significative and significant; inherently interpretable; endlessly subject to historied (and interpretive) change. You may as well ask: What is left over from the concept of a person if you subtract whatever belongs to being a member of *Homo sapiens*? There's the question behind Wittgenstein's question at §621.

The weakness of reductive (and eliminativist) and/or dualistic rejoinders rests with their characteristic tendency to treat the most salient and ubiquitous anthropocentric features of human life as if *their* reality were more doubtful than that of the physical properties that also belong to the cultural world. Thus Sellars, after introducing what he terms "the scientific image" of the world, an unusually stern account of "the postulated objects of scientific theory" (which precludes the familiar physical things of the human world as readily as selves) concedes that "man is that being who conceives of itself in terms of the manifest image" – "a being [as Sellars says] that can almost be defined as a being that has intentions" – which serves here as a fair approximation to Taylor's "hermeneutic" option.[40] Sellars then considers what may be salvaged of "the synoptic view" – that is, of all that belongs to the "manifest image" within the space of the "scientific image." He answers candidly: "To the extent that the manifest [what belongs to the manifest image] does not survive in the synoptic view, to that extent man himself would not survive."[41] End of story. I hasten to add that Sellars does not explicitly support the eliminativist thesis here: he simply spells out what it requires. But, of course, it never surmounts its essential paradox.

The difficulties that confront the "scientific image" oblige us to consider whether, finally, the two images *could merge without clash in the synoptic view*." Sellars arrives at the following resolution: "The conceptual framework of persons is not something that needs to be reconciled with the scientific image, but rather something to be *joined* to it [in effect, adding "the language of community and individual intention" to the scientific image]." This, Sellars alleges, would permit us to "transcend the dualism of the manifest and scientific image of man-of-the-world" – but "only in imagination."[42] Elsewhere, pursuing the same argument, he says more bluntly: "the objects of the observational framework [in effect, the manifest image] do not really exist – there really are no such things."[43] The impasse is conceptually intolerable.

5.

I co-opt Wittgenstein's clever challenge therefore quite opportunistically, as a way of reviving the importance of the discovery that – after Darwin, after the failure of Kantian transcendentalism, after Hegel's decisive but unfinished reformulation of transcendent*al* inquiry as inherently *a posteriori*, historically horizoned, productively "negated" by any society's evolving experience of the world – the recovery of the externalist form of *Bildung* barely adumbrated in Vico, Herder, Humboldt, Hegel, Heidegger, Gadamer, Wittgenstein, McDowell (to name the figures Taylor chiefly consults) enables us to pose in a fresh way the question of the metaphysical distinction of human persons and human cultures.

I find here the dawning of a new phase of philosophical inquiry – a "new pragmatism" if I may name it that – which undertakes the historicized analysis of what it is to be a person or to belong to the encultured world that transforms new cohorts of *Homo sapiens* into hybrid artifacts. As a result, the argument prepares the ground for the continuous artifactual transformation of the cultural world itself. If you favor this line of argument, you realize that the unity of the natural and human sciences must be emergentist rather than reductionist: the sciences must be seen to be human sciences rather than disciplines that have (in Sellars's sense) successfully eliminated the fictitious reality of persons. Darwin's empirical account of the emergence of the human species lays the ground for the very different, subsequent evolution of the world of human culture – especially among the philosophical movements that count as Hegel's most promising progeny: the Marxists, the pragmatists, the existentialists, and the Hegelianized Marburg neo-Kantians.[44]

I leave for now the completion of a proper account of what a person, a cultural world, an action, an artwork, a run of speech, a human mind may be rightly said to be. To complete this part of the story would be to answer Wittgenstein's question in spades. But in closing this small part of a very large issue, we prepare the ground for the grander questions that begin to beckon, by tidying up a few strategic concerns. Those that command attention instantly and bid fair to set us on our way call for a more revealing sense of the failure of reductionist options and the heterodox complexities of the causal nexus encountered in cultural as opposed to merely physical contexts. As we may guess, these issues are very closely linked. Let me explain.

There's a fundamental challenge that must be aired regarding the supposed adequacy of applying to the human sciences the canonical views of causality developed for the physical sciences – in the light of the upstart requirements of the human sciences themselves: between what (for convenience) I shall call the "externalist" and "internalist" forms of causality. I mention the matter to alert you to what is potentially the single most important gain in any attempt to reconcile the physical and human sciences consistently with the argument that's now been sketched. If you take human *agency* to be the unique form of causality that it appears to be – well, the very point of Wittgenstein's question about distinguishing between "raising my arm" and "my arm's rising" – you will be led to concede that agency cannot be treated (as reductionists have always supposed it could) as straightforwardly open to causal explanation in accord with a "relational" or "externalist" model that holds cause and effect to be completely separable from one another in the way Hume originally supposed or indeed in any of the more complex versions of that intuition that might be put forward (as among the positivists, for instance).

This was, in fact, part of my motivation for pitting Taylor's "hermeneutic" views against Rosenberg's implicitly "reductionist" account. In effect, Rosenberg obligingly reads principle [L], which (as noted) he introduces as the main principle of "folk psychology" or "folk-theoretic science" in accord (precisely) with the externalist model of causality. The mistake is not merely his: it's inherent in the reductive treatment of the human sciences – even among those who yield along reductionist lines even where they insist they do not – for instance, Davidson among recent Anglo-American analysts, very possibly the inspiration for Rosenberg's own formula.[45] The telltale clue (apparent in Davidson) is obvious enough: wherever Davidson (following Aristotle's lead) speaks of beliefs and desires as the causes of actions – symptomatically, Davidson speaks in entirely abstract terms that never quite identify the material incarnation of what we mean – he deflects us from the analysis of "actions" to the analysis of "bodily movements" *and* from molar actions to functionally factored sub-molar physical movements and the like. (Think of the immensely diverse ways of making the same chess move.) The trick is to acknowledge all this *within* the analysis of [L] (or something close to it).

To provide such an account begins to reconcile the natural and human sciences. It also suggests two strategic truths that reductionists – even piecemeal and tentative reductionists – are bound to oppose: first, that the difference between the natural and the human sciences does not oblige us to refuse to construe the "mental" as falling within the purview of the "physical" non-reductively, it simply requires attention to the ineliminable presence (and meaning) of significative or semiotic complications; second, that the relevance of the physical realization of an action depends on the significative characterization of the molar action in question and thus confirms (against B. F. Skinner) the arbitrariness of behaviorism and the irrelevance (against Jaegwon Kim) of the supervenience doctrine. The particularities of material realization *have no pertinence at all* until they are *dependently (factorially) assigned within* the analysis of one or another action. The methodologies of the natural and the human sciences must, as a consequence, be seriously different.

I leave the implied lesson as a promissory note, though you may begin to guess how it affects the standard accounts of the philosophy of science. The heterodox correction – the only correction possible consistent with the idea that human persons are second-natured artifacts uniquely capable of the kind of causality that we call "agency" (involving freedom, choice, and deliberate and responsible action) – requires an internalist model of causality (as in my "raising my arm") capable of incorporating *whatever* externalist causal sequences enter, in some suitably *sub*functional or factorial way, *in* the analysis of molar actions.

This is a complex matter that requires a fresh beginning. But it needs to be mentioned in order to anticipate just how the theory being advanced might offer as its most important gain a reconciliation between the natural and the human sciences that eludes the usual deformation of the methodological distinctions between the two sorts of science. The fact is, we cannot guess at *any* consensually acceptable description of an otherwise unidentified molar action *from* the mere description of a bodily movement confined in purely physicalist terms; and we cannot guess that *any* action at all is embodied in a given bodily movement or kind of movement. (Think again of making a chess move.) Responsible analysis *goes entirely in the opposite direction*, if we have information only of the movement. We must first know what action is realized *in* what bodily movement *in* what context of discourse, if we are expected to be able to decide what other significant or significative descriptions may replace the molar description with which we first begin. We cannot say, for instance, that a finger's pressure on (what happens to be) a light switch constitutes "turning on the light." But then, *contra* Davidson and Rosenberg, we will be forced to admit the initial relevance of agency itself (hence, also, of the relevance of the self) – and then reductionism will be outflanked.

I have certainly not yet answered Wittgenstein's question, but the ground for an answer has now been laid. At the very least, we have a clearer sense of why we cannot say that "nothing need be added."

NOTES

1. Wilfrid Sellars, *Science, Perception, and Reality* (London: Routledge and Kegan Paul, 1963).

2. Charles Taylor, *A Secular Age* (Cambridge, MA: Harvard University Press, 2007), p. 2.

3. Taylor, *A Secular Age*, p. 100.

4. See Charles Taylor, *Hegel* (Cambridge, UK: Cambridge University Press, 1975); and *Hegel and Modern Society* (Cambridge, UK: Cambridge University Press, 1979).

5. Taylor, *Hegel*, p. 549. See Karl Marx, *Early Writings*, trans. and ed. T.B. Bottomore (London: C. A. Watts, 1963), p. 128.

6. Ernst Cassirer, *An Essay on Man* (New Haven, Conn.: Yale University Press, 1994), pp. 20–21. See Hippolyte Taine, *History of English Literature*, trans. H. van Laun (New York: Hold, 1872); cited by Cassirer.

7. See Marjorie Grene, "People and Other Animals," in *The Understanding of Nature: Essays in the Philosophy of Biology* (Dordrecht: D. Reidel, 1974), p. 458.

8. Ludwig Wittgenstein, *Philosophical Investigations*, trans. G. E. M. Anscombe (Oxford: Blackwell, 1953), §621.

9. See John McDowell, *Mind and World* (Cambridge, MA: Harvard University Press, 1994). For a sense of the analytic position both Taylor and McDowell oppose, see the influential paper by Richard Rorty, "Davidson, Truth and Pragmatism," in *Truth and Interpretation: Perspectives on the Philosophy of Donald Davidson*, ed. Ernest Lepore (Oxford: Blackwell, 1986). Rorty's piece, it should be said, is not entirely representative of the views he's defended in his "postmodernist" mode; but the paper does advance a strong version of late Anglo-American analytic philosophy.

10. See Noam Chomsky, *New Horizons in the Study of Language and Mind* (Cambridge, UK: Cambridge University Press, 2000).

11. For instance, in his "What is Human Agency?," "Self-interpreting Animals," "Language and Human Nature," "Interpretation and the Sciences of Man," "Rationality," in *Philosophical Papers*, 2 vols. (Cambridge, UK: Cambridge University Press, 1985).

12. Taylor, *Philosophical Papers*, vol. 1, "Introduction," p. 2.

13. See Noam Chomsky, "Review of B. F. Skinner's *Verbal Behavior*," *Language* 35.1 (1959), pp. 26–58.

14. See Charles Taylor, *The Explanation of Behaviour* (London: Routledge and Kegan Paul, 1964).

15. Taylor, *Philosophical Papers*, vol. 1, "Introduction," pp. 2–4.

16. The failure of the second theorem is, in fact, the fatal weakness of Jaegwon Kim's unyielding argument against all countermoves that are themselves opposed to reductionism's vindication applied to the so-called supervenience of the mental. See Jaegwon Kim, *Supervenience and Mind: Selected Philosophical Essays* (Cambridge, UK: Cambridge University Press, 1993), and *Physicalism, or Something Near Enough* (Princeton, N.J.: Princeton University Press, 2005).

17. Alexander Rosenberg, *Philosophy of Social Science*, 3rd edn. (Philadelphia: Westview, 2008), pp. 34, 36.

18. See, for instance, Alexander Rosenberg, *The Structure of Biological Science* (Cambridge, UK: Cambridge University Press, 1985).

19. Rosenberg, *Philosophy of Social Science*, pp. 16–17.

20. *Ibid.*, p. 17.

21. See, for instance, Nancy Cartwright, *How the Laws of Physics Lie* (Oxford: Clarendon Press, 1983), and Bas van Fraassen, *The Scientific Image* (Oxford: Clarendon Press, 1980).

22. See Hilary Putnam, *Ethics without Ontology* (Cambridge, MA: Harvard University Press, 2004).

23. Rosenberg, *Philosophy of Social Science*, p. 15.

24. *Ibid.*, p. 9.

25. See A. G. Cairns-Smith, *Genetic Takeover and the Mineral Origins of Life* (Cambridge, UK: Cambridge University Press, 1982)

26. Compare J. J. C. Smart, *Philosophy and Scientific Realism* (London: Routledge and Kegan Paul, 1963).

27. See Wittgenstein, *Philosophical Investigations*; and Arthur C. Danto, "The Artworld," *Journal of Philosophy* 61 (1964), pp. 571–584; and *The Transfiguration of the Commonplace* (Cambridge, MA: Harvard University Press, 1981).

28. See for a more sustained account of Danto's theories, my *Aesthetics: An Unforgiving Introduction* (Belmont: Wadsworth, forthcoming in 2009). There's reason to believe Danto has in recent years changed his theory in a drastic way.

29. See Richard Dawkins, *The Selfish Gene* (Oxford: Oxford University Press, 1989).

30. See, for instance, Donald Davidson, *Essays on Actions and Events* (Oxford: Clarendon Press, 1984); Alvin I. Goldman, *A Theory of Human Action* (Englewood Cliffs, N.J.: Prentice-Hall, 1970); and Arthur C. Danto, *Analytical Philosophy of Action* (Cambridge, UK: Cambridge University Press, 1973).

31. See Steven Weinberg, *Dreams of a Final Theory: The Scientist's Search for the Ultimate Laws of Nature* (New York: Vintage, 1994), chaps. 9, 12.

32. Compare Rosenberg, *Philosophy of Social Science*, pp. 17–19.

33. For a sense of the characteristic concerns of the unity of science movement, see Carl G. Hempel, *Aspects of Scientific Explanation* (New York: Free Press, 1965); and *Minnesota Studies in the Philosophy of Science*, vol. 1, ed. Herbert Feigl and Michael Scriven (Minneapolis: University of Minnesota Press, 1956).

34. See, particularly, "What is Human Agency," "Self-interpreting Animals," and "Theories of Meaning," in vol. 1 of Taylor's *Philosophical Papers*.

35. Taylor, *Philosophical Papers*, vol. 1, "Introduction," pp. 8, 10.

36. See Taylor, "Theories of Meaning," *Philosophical Papers*, vol. 2: for instance, pp. 256–263. Compare with McDowell's *Mind and Word*.

37. See John Tyler Bonner, *The Evolution of Culture in Animals* (Princeton, N.J.: Princeton University Press, 1980).

38. Versions of this paradox, apparently unnoticed, appear, for instance, in John R. Searle, *The Construction of Social Reality* (New York: Free Press, 1995); and Margaret Gilbert, *On Social Fact* (Princeton, N.J.: Princeton University Press, 1992).

39. See Immanuel Kant, *The Critique of Pure Reason*, trans. Paul Guyer and Allen W. Wood (Cambridge, UK: Cambridge University Press, 1998), particularly §§15–17.

40. Sellars, "Philosophy and the Scientific Image of Man," pp. 18, 40.

41. *Ibid.*, p. 18.

42. *Ibid.*, pp. 34, 40.

43. Wilfrid Sellars, "The Language of Theories," *Science, Perception, and Reality* (London: Routledge and Kegan Paul, 1963), p. 163.

44. See, for instance, Richard J. Bernstein, *Praxis and Action* (Philadelphia: University of Pennsylvania Press, 1975).

45. See, for instance, Donald Davidson "Actions, Reasons, and Causes," in *Essays on Actions and Events* (Oxford: Clarendon Press, 1982).

Joseph Margolis
Laura H. Carnell Professor of Philosophy
Philosophy Department
728 Anderson Hall
Temple University
Philadelphia, PA 19122
United States

Contemporary Pragmatism
Vol. 5, No. 1 (June 2008), 39–59

Editions Rodopi
© 2008

Cognitive Adaptation: Insights from a Pragmatist Perspective

Jay Schulkin

Classical pragmatism construed mind as an adaptive organ rooted in biology; biology was not one side and culture on the other. The cognitive systems underlie adaptation in response to the precarious and in the search for the stable and more secure that result in diverse forms of inquiry. Cognitive systems are rooted in action, and classical pragmatism knotted our sense of ourselves in response to nature and our cultural evolution. Cognitive systems should be demythologized away from Cartesian detachment, and towards transactions with others and with nature.

1. Introduction

In this essay I reiterate some key insights from the classical pragmatists (namely the sense of inquiry and naturalism, the search for stability) and place them in a contemporary context of cognitive neuroscience. Cognitive systems, as classical pragmatists understood, in the sense in which I suggest, is nothing like the old Cartesian, divorced, distant arbiter. They are linked to engage self-corrective inquiry (e.g. Dewey 1925, 1989; Meltzoff 2004). An adaptive mind was the very life-blood for Charles Darwin (1859, 1958) and William James (1890, 1952), and in what would later be important for characterizing cognitive systems forging coherence for action and underlies human experience. We come prepared with an evolved brain and set of cognitive predilections that are situated towards context, flexibility, and perceptual embodiment about objects that are conceptually rich and vital to behavioral adaptation.

Pragmatism emphasizes adaptation to the precarious. Inquiry is an outgrowth of *wanting to know*. Self-corrective inquiry needs to be harnessed to the felt insecurity and uncertainty that are not just remnants of our biological past; they are endless lively events in our present context that are not likely to be eradicated. As John Dewey (1925, 1989) would put it: we hunt for the stable amid the precarious (see also Godfrey-Smith 2002). Yet lurking within the mind-brain is unease about predators and concern about acquisition of food and shelter, along with unchecked levels of aspiration mixed with human gluttony. New identities are formed that, fashioned by diversity, generate novel expressions. Amusement and play are endemic to our condition in order to combat the insecurity and uncertainty of existence, but then so is our ability to eliminate thinking, to eschew it and to forge into endless authorities.

We do come into this world prepared to learn, inquire, and theorize. Whether this develops depends upon the culture to which one is exposed, as well as the temperamental properties and abilities one possesses. Self-corrective inquiry is the cornerstone of classical pragmatism (Smith 1985) and is reflected in some variants of modern cognitive science (Meltzoff 2004; Gopnik and Meltzoff 1999).

Common categories into which we can organize our responses are those that we inherit and those that we acquire (e.g. Carey and Smith 1993; Medin and Atran 1999; Gelman 2003). Evolution selected for a self-corrective capacity in our ability to get anchored to the world around us (Darwin 1859; Dewey 1910). Dewey, for example, understood that science, in part, is an extension of local adaptation, local problem solving.

The psychobiological propensities stem from the constraints of the human mind/brain and its computational abilities. Our hypothesis-generating abilities exist in the specific culture in which we are immersed and that shapes our thinking (Mill 1843, 1870; Peirce 1898, 1992). But some of the categories reflect the cognitive machinations of the mind/brain and how it innately operates in problem solving.

Abduction (hypothesis) is a term coined by Peirce (1878, 1899, 1992) for the genesis of a theory or idea that in turn guides the inference of conclusions, whether by induction or deduction (see also Dewey 1938; Hanson 1958; Heelan and Schulkin 1998). By providing the background against which observations are made (in addition to participating in a culture of inquiry), abduction (hypothesis formation) links ideas to reality, in addition to deduction and induction functions in human problem-solving. Peirce (1868, 1899, 1992) can be understood as generating cognitive models of human information processing and reasoning, representational models that underlie decision making and human action (Johnson-Laird 2001, 2002; Levi 2004; Weissman 2008).

The inductive mechanisms are not random, and the deductive mechanisms not so distant, because they are knotted to abduction. Our inferences are constrained by an orientation to events, the kinds of objects that are detected. Linking mammals and finding what seem like counter examples (such as the platypus, an egg laying mammal) first requires a broad way to link diverse kinds of events, which may (perceptual) or may not (conceptual) have clear common properties. The taxonomic and thematic conditions may be simple or complex, but there is always a background condition (e.g. Murphy 2002; Medlin and Atran 1999, 2004; Giere 2006). Moreover, the inductive devices are broadly conceived in a mind/brain ready to compute statistical probability, draw diverse inferences, and construct models (Johnson-Laird 2001) essential for information processing and coherent action.

Cognitive systems are tied to the broad-based objects that we encounter (e.g. Gallistel 1990; Lakoff and Johnson 1999). Cognitive systems reflect rough and ready heuristics that permeate problem solving (Simon 1962; Gigerenzer and Selton 2001), and not the mythology of perfection and detachment from seductive sensory pressures. We search for consistency and stability; we inquire and learn when our equilibrium is disrupted (Peirce 1878, 1992; Dewey 1925, 1989; Rescorla and Wagner 1972), but not only under those conditions.

Pragmatists such as Dewey emphasize plasticity, the many diverse forms of adaptation and human expression (Margolis 2002). Amidst this uncertainty is the use of instrumental reason – reason devoted to coping with the lack of certainty in the search for the stable and somewhat secure. Dewey (1925, 1989, p. 14) noted, perhaps somewhat hopefully, that "the natural and original bias of man is all toward the life objective." Problem-solving is rooted in the existential condition of coping with our surroundings. Knowing and acting are combined in action. Knowing is in the interactions with others, with the world. The knowing process takes place in the life world that we are adapting to, coping with, trying to make sense of (Dewey 1925, 1989; Godfrey-Smith 2002).

2. Cognitive Preconditions: Making sense of Living Things-Relations between Biology and Culture

As cognitive animals, humans look to understand and control. Nature and cultural categories of understanding converge at every step in our intellectual development (Cassirer 1946, 1953, 1957), and symbolic and computational systems permeate all levels of human understanding. Generic categories, of kinds both naturally and culturally derived, are operative early on in ontogeny (Carey and Gelman 1991; Keil 1979, 1983; Gelman 2003).

Consider the range of categories that we are prepared to generate quite early – animate and inanimate, animal and plant, objects in space, etc. (see Carey 1985, 2001; Keil 1983, 1992; Mandler 2004; Duchaine et al 2001; Pinker 1998; Dehaeane et al 2006). We are taxonomic animals; we categorize things (Carey and Gelman 1991; Keil and Wilson 2000). We also come prepared with a variety of useful heuristics for solving problems (Simon 1982; Barkow et al 1992; Gigerenzer and Selten 2001). Distinct ways of categorizing can include the following (adapted from Pinker 1994, 1998).

Ideas about living objects
Ideas about objects and mechanics
Ideas about language
Ideas about probability
Ideas about food sources (avoidance and approach)
Ideas about kinship relations
Ideas about fairness

There appear to be categories that we readily accept and objects that we look for in our surroundings (Barkow et al 1992; Medin and Atran 1999; Carey and Gelman 1991). This may reflect a form of folk biological discourse (e.g. avoiding foul meat, searching for warmth and security, connecting with others in common bonds, and expressing ourselves in symbolism rich in cognitive prowess). This sense of objects is rooted in bodily sensibility (Johnson 1987, 1990; Lakoff and Johnson 1999; Merleau Ponty 1942, 1967; Schulkin 2004). Objects are not detached, and knowing is accumulated via transactions with other things (Dewey 1925, 1989; Clark 1999; Thomas 2001). We come prepared to categorize things into living kinds of objects.

Distinctions between concepts in nature and culture blur as inquiry progresses (Dewey 1925, 1989; Clark 1999). Concepts of nature have roots in biology and concepts of culture derive from our cognitive capacity. We are as condemned by, or embedded in, the one as the other. The study of culture is the study of variation amidst some common themes (Atran et al 2005; Boyd and Richerson 1985).

Concepts of culture and nature are therefore intertwined. It is not simply from within culture that we evolved our categories and concepts. Categories of space, time, causation, the structure of syntax, and so forth, are conditions of the human mind that set the stage for the development of a culture (Sperber 1975; 1985; Atran 2002; Cassirer 1944, 1978; Pinker 1994, 1998; Reschler 2000). This is the functionalist position, envisioning mind as adaptive and problem-solving (Parrott and Schulkin 1993; Clark 1999). Such problem-solving, extended into social bonding – ways of conceiving social relationships, recognition of facial and bodily gestures – serves to guide us in the world.

Our cognitive abilities are both specific and general (Rozin 1976, 1998). Key to our evolution is our social nature. "Cognitive fluidity" (Mithen 1996) figures in our ability to do science and to study history. The cognitive revolution ushered in the notion that the mind matters. Biological categories are operative in the minds of children early on (Carey and Gelman 1991; Piaget 1954, 1971, 1975).

Evolutionary history reveals greater expression of, access to (Rozin 1976, 1998), and use of cognitive resources (Boyer 1990; Mithen 1996; Carey and Gelman 1991). Core features that go into self-corrective inquiry include an orientation to observation of objects, abduction or the genesis of ideas, tying ideas about the world to causation, and development of diverse tools that expands one's observations (e.g. Peirce 1892; Hansen 1958; Heelan and Schulkin 1998; Gigerenzer and Selten 2001).

That humans construct worlds of perception and experience does not mean that there is no "real" world. Within a biological context, problem solving is adaptive. If an animal cannot see an object, it compensates with another sense, such as hearing or smelling. The lenses from which the animal interprets the world are all theory-laden; nothing is given. But the theories that are part of the adaptive specializations of animals create a world for action. It is intelligent action that we witness in the natural world (Hauser 2000; Pinker 1998).

The evolution of our cognitive abilities, in other words, is fundamentally linked to the worlds we evolved from and are adapting to, and the worlds we extend by our inventions. The tools that help us see and hear become part of our evolutionary hardware; the apparently rigid separation between what we make to help us see and hear and what our brain provides is in fact permeable (e.g. Clark 1999, 2003; Wheeler 2005). The analysis of this niche is as important as the understanding of our mental abilities. The analysis of one without the other is at best banal, and at worst misleading.

3. Uncertainty, Discrepancy, Prediction, Inquiry

The familiar/unfamiliar cognitive distinction is as fundamental as the animate/ inanimate distinction (Rozin 1976; Keil 1979). These cognitive distinctions involve human expectations. They extend to the diverse ways in which we explore the world. They are fundamentally linked with how humans placate our fears of what we know and do not know.

Mythological discourse developed, in part, to quiet our fears and uncertainties. But myths and storytelling served to do more than help us to cope with uncertainty. They also served to teach, to deify, to ritualize, and to give "memory" a social embodiment. Visual representation provided a sense of control, of mastery over nature. Both tools and art were utilized for understanding. The brains of early humans evolved as they engaged the world around them. Today, if no problem is in sight, many humans create them. Humans conjure up new things about which to worry. We seem to need to struggle. Thus our nervous systems invent phantoms. But we do not have to create that many phantoms – for the world makes its presence known.

The most evolved parts of the central nervous system create ideational influences that construct arenas for fantasized action. The brain is a constructive organ. We create and model the environment to which we adapt. That does not entail that the representations are simple copies of the environment (e.g. Godfrey-Smith 1996). The brain evolved to create and organize action, but at times it runs rampant with aberrant results.

Perhaps the roots of the phantoms lie in our developmental past. Perhaps they are the legacy of the traumas of our early life in childhood, compounded with our biological inheritance. Early trauma, coupled with daily exposure to the ambiguities of everyday life, lead one to search for what might go wrong. The unease that is built into us has to do with the fact that, if we were wrong about a predator stalking the water hole life was over; there was no second chance. Bad events were dangerous – so much so that vigilance toward danger was perhaps more important than attention to good. This may suggest why there seem to be more negative emotions than positive ones. They have prominence and importance in our evolutionary past. Faster learning of what was bad or harmful was imperative (e.g. food sources, Rozin 1976; Rozin and Schulkin 1990).

It should not be surprising that a significant portion of our brains is oriented to detecting discrepancy, noticing uncertainty, capturing stability. After all, a common feature of our experience is pervaded by this sense of the world and the categories of thought that make coherent action possible (Dewey 1925, 1989; Kagan 2002).

The detection of a discrepancy of expected events results in greater behaviors that might reflect learning and inquiry (Rescorla and Wagner 1972). Informational control is a strong desire (Loewenstein 1994). Ambiguity is averse to a wide array of our decision-making behaviors (Baron 1988, 1994). Humans are prepared to recognize deviance from expectations (James 1890, 1952; Kagan 2002). We then search to fill in the information gaps (Rescorla and Wagner 1972; Loewenstein 1994). Diverse kinds of experiments in both animals and humans show that violation of expectations promotes learning. A broad array of learning occurs when expectations are thwarted through new problem solving search principles (Peirce 1870). Indeed, studies of decision-making suggest that humans search for ways to reduce informational uncertainty (Loewenstein 1994).

Although uncertainty and insecurity are found in the minds of many animals struggling to survive in nature, humans evolved intricate thoughts about this uncertainty. A core feature of our cognitive arsenal is knotted to the detection of danger. The same is true in many other species. But we are the ones who have a language (linguistic usage) to express our uncertainty and insecurity, and in an elaborate manner.

One might be prepared to accept that higher mammals, such as dolphins, apes, or monkeys, reflect on their experiences in some fashion. They certainly have evolved advanced conceptual frameworks for functioning in the world and communicating with one another (Hauser 2000). When considering animals and whether they experience "angst," one should look at their style of existence (e.g., whether they have other animals to fear), whether they have the limbic regions of the brain – the part of the brain that responds to the uncertainty as felt by the animals, – and their behavioral responses, sometimes similar to our own (Rosen and Schulkin 1998; LeDoux 1996).

4. Central Nervous System Response to the Uncertain and Precarious

Diverse regions of the brain are activated when an event becomes uncertain (Schultz 2002, 2004). This activity manifests itself across the neocortex, diverse limbic regions in the phylogenetically older cortex (amygdala, Rosen and Schulkin 1998), and brainstem sites. These neural sites detect and then help prepare the appropriate behavioral responses following the detection of uncertainty (Schultz 2002). For example, in macaques, there are two classes of neuronal populations; one is knotted to the prediction of reward and its reliability, and another is tied to failed expectations. Both figure in the organization of behavior. These neural sites are below the cortex. They are tied to the basal ganglia. However, different regions of the cortex, particularly frontal and cingulate cortices, are connected to the prediction of rewards (e.g. Schultz 2002).

A wide array of human brain imaging studies have documented that the regions of the frontal cortex are tied to uncertainty, to uncertain expectations. A number of studies have shown the greater the uncertainty, the greater the activation of the frontal and cingulate cortex (e.g. Critchley et al 2000). Uncertainty is often linked to risk and arousal. There are other measures linked to the activation of these cortical sites. Conversely, contexts that tend to decrease autonomic expression tend to decrease responses to uncertainty (Damasio 1996).

Humans are blessed with evolved brains that ponder the meaning of things, hypothesize and then generate explanations that are cumulative, elaborated, extended, and sometimes discarded. The uncertainty of life powerfully drives people to make sense of events, to understand, to conquer, or just to accept or deny them. The uncertainty of the present and the underlying insecurity that it generates pushes people to plan ahead, to prepare for what is to come, to want to control the course of events. But there is also joy in our advances as we labor away at our endeavors. The satisfaction in completion is consummatory and a source of pleasure (Dewey 1925, 1989).

5. Permanence and Change

Risk aversion is a common state for many people, for whom the safety of the herd takes precedence over the lonely stance of forging ahead into novel and uncharted terrain. One cognitive and practical way humans explore the new is by flavoring it with the old, the familiar. Humans often do this as we try new foods (Rozin 1976, 1998), and we do it by naming new places with old, street names, etc. (for example, New England, New Amsterdam). This is one form of cognitive adaptation.

The tension between the familiar and the unfamiliar underlies a basic psychobiological fact: one tends to stay with the familiar until one is forced into a new territory. One might sample what is new, but only from the purview of the familiar, the accustomed. The promise of permanence is more alluring than the risk of uncertainty.

Experience for classical pragmatists is not passive (Hendel 1959; Smith 1970; Godfrey-Smith 1996). The mind is construed in active terms, in terms in which cognitive adaptation, tracking events into coherence is a primary activity. Transactions with the world, the testing of ideas, self-corrective hypothesis testing, and a vulnerability in the pursuit of inquiry are what predominate – at least in the ideal, the normative goal. What packs experience with punch are the goals as they are being pursued; goals are endemic in action. Thought is embodied in action, not a spectator in the stands. Truth may be what is agreed upon, contingent by a community of inquirers, or what settles overtime, but in the give and take Dewey suggested that we live with "warranted assertions" (Dewey 1938). Reason is demythologized to adaptation and to shorter-term purposes (e.g. Simon 1962, 1982; Cherniak 1986; Kornblith 1993; Clark 2003).

But, as it is inevitable, change takes place, including scientific change from experiment and experience. These were basic to the new sciences that were evolving – the Romantic vision of science liberated from the scholasticism and rationalization of the past.

A philosophy of change became prominent in the 19th and 20th centuries (e.g. Whitehead 1929). The cultural air was rich in evolutionary theorizing (Eiseley 1959, 1961; Himmelfarb 1959/1962). Charles Darwin's own grandfather, Erasmus Darwin, (physician, poet, naturalist, evolutionist) wrote tomes in bequest to evolution, an appreciation of objects of nature (1789, 1991; 1794, 1801). Nature was alive (e.g. Coleridge 1840, 1956; see King-Hele 1986) and full of uncertainty and the precarious. Voyages to distant lands were idealized and realized – the voyage of the *Beagle*, namely Darwin's early exploits to South America, was just one of many such ventures sparking new ventures.

Other conceptions of change emerged through biology as the Aristotelian order of biological rigidity was replaced with biological fluidity. The static order of nature was undermined, by the developing intellectual arsenal or perspective that envisioned an evolving planet. This development first emerged in physics, with theories like the nebula hypothesis of the origins of the universe. Then, within biology, there developed an evolutionary sense. No longer was order rigidly ordained until eternity. Animal life evolved, competed, and survived or extinguished. Some species evolved but excelled in some functions and lost other functions.

Our sense of nature evolved as human intellectual organs and culture evolved, and as people realized that we were part of nature as well as of culture (Nash 1967; Oelscheager 1991; Schulkin 1996; Ruse 2006). Early in our evolutionary ascent, we were just part of nature. Initially, as we struggled to cope we sought to capture the shapes and sounds we were experiencing – they were sounds of nature.

The conception of nature, a real sense of reproductive and regenerative properties inherent in biological events is an important cognitive perspective on the world. What is apparent is a deep-seated sense of core cognitive orientation to biological events (Keil 1979, 1983, 1992; Wilson 2005). There is an autonomous set of predilections that humans come prepared to categorize biological kinds. They include: (1) reproductive faculties, (2) some form of internal structure, (3) developmental trajectory, (4) core and stable features over time, (5) essential features that are more than are captured by sensory properties, (6) trajectories that indicate purpose, or teleological expectations, and (7) properties that are inherent in the natural kind and that are linked to other objects.

As insecurity and uncertainty are basic to animal life, so too are risk and adventure. We evolved a set of cognitive predilections that focus on animate objects, on other possible experiences, on the sense of agency. We venture out toward new arenas of discourse. We enjoy novelty; we are attracted to and pursue new terrain. The lure of different lands pulls us to sojourn in new places. The roads are unfamiliar as are the faces and cultures. At times there is danger. Although in its extreme forms the pursuit of danger can be pathological, the acceptance of risk and the ensuing thrill are part of the travel. Risk must be not only accepted but also welcomed, for many worthy things necessitate risk as part of the adventure and the pursuit. Risk is felt. It is exciting. It is motivating. It is also aversive and frightening.

6. Taming Discomfort: Precommitments And Planning Ahead

The delight we feel in planning is considered a healthy psychological feature. Our planning is an attempt to stabilize the future as well as to control and predict it (Dewey 1925, 1989; Elster 1979, 1988). We accept the fact that our logic in thinking ahead is not pure. Our reason must be bounded by circumstance and good sense. We look to satisfy, not necessarily always to optimize, and our tools are instrumental and heuristic (Baron 1985, 1988, 1994; Simon 1982).

In a precarious world, little is safe and secure. Planning is, in part, a risk. If all planning were for the safe and the secure, then dead habit would be the result. Because we need to allow for both spontaneity and the forms of regularity that guide us, humans pursue an element of risk as we move ahead. Stability and adventure are intermingled. Risk remains a basic, even pleasurable, fact. Courage is required, but must be tempered with prudent good sense. Leaps of faith grounded in good sense should orient one, and courage bolsters the act of grounded faith – in the sense of living the good life, the life worth living, and many times by simply surviving (Neville 1974).

Expectations serve to ground and relieve the discomfort of uncertainty and risk, but sometimes also to exacerbate it. Humans stay attached to the familiar as we explore the unfamiliar. This is reflected in the kinds of objects that we eat, that nourish us (Rozin 1976). As we plan ahead the familiar guides us. More than this, however, expectations are the thread of planning ahead. Our expectations – our goals – guide us and are instrumental to how we envision our future.

Of necessity, we live with the fear and uncertainty that coexist with the acquired stability of laying plans. While continuing to act, we search for new reasons for action. It is imperative to avoid paralysis, lethargy, and negativism in response to the fear and uncertainty of the future. It is easy to declare futility, but fortune is one of the unexpected joys in life.

In planning, we must be responsive to the vector of possibilities and to the unexpected. Thus, if the plan is so rigid as to preclude novelty, life falters myopically. The sense of horizons opens fortune. It is hard and heartfelt, and not magic. There is also the luck of the muses as life turns in the direction that it does. Although there is no doubt an element of luck, fortune almost always is derived from labor. But at times "Fortuna" is just a great gift: a piece of grace, a surprise that resonates in an appreciative mind.

Keeping perspective is hard to do – impossible for some, difficult for almost all of us. All the while, the lure of the future helps to call us forward. Causation, in this regard, is not simply from the past; the future pulls seductively. The present is "spacious," as James suggested. It is extended as it receives the pushes of the past and the pulls of the future. But the past lingers powerfully. The backward pull of the familiar placates. The past comforts and ameliorates present fears; nostalgia calls us back.

Perhaps one of the key features as we plan ahead is the consideration of our commitments (Elster 1979, 1988). These represent the practices that guide us through life (Bourdieu 1980, 1990) and that represent our beliefs and desires. This future orientation reveals our intentional stances: the teleological. Our commitments organize what we do, what we strive for, what we allow as possible to pursue. To reduce conflict, perhaps, we limit our choices, but seemingly paradoxically, by this act we open up further possibilities. We reduce our options of what we envision as possible and impose upon ourselves rules of coherence. We remove ourselves, for example, from the people and places that may be deleterious, or we surround ourselves with those that are cheerful and positive. We commit ourselves and set a course of action by the decision to diet, to parent, to fulfill a job, to exercise, or to be faithful in marriage. Such commitments are at the basis of everyday action and organize a purposeful life.

Such commitments are the acts in social life serving as both the pushes and the pulls. They push us in a particular direction, and we are pulled toward the goal at the same time. There are times when we create our reality by opting for the forms of life that we do. Pre-commitments are essential to organizing what we do (Elster 1979, 1988). They provide order for our experience, even when what we are experiencing seems irrational, such as the hunger involved in losing weight. Commitments stabilize us. They establish the necessity of actions as we prepare for what is to come. Patterns of regularity are demonstrably present. Nature and culture, along with the mind, provide these patterns. The question is whether we deem them to be good. Although commitments bind us to pursue certain activities despite the inherent regularity that we encounter, insecurity and uncertainty linger.

The future is always unknown, and an element of uncertainty is pervasive. To lump all that matters into the present is to impoverish the present, to reduce it to a transient moment. An appreciation of the present is one thing; to make it all of life is quite another. At moments of extreme crisis, the present can seem overwhelming. Its scope is breadth-less and without dimensions. In normal life, the present is lived with the twin promises of planned goals and past experience. When one plans ahead, one seeks a balance of regularity and spontaneity. But when dead habits predominate, the habits surely deprive one of spontaneity, of creative novelty, of new goals. Rigidity is the primary mode, and life is lost to habit. Nevertheless, whole communities find refuge in habits, often when under stress, such as viewing cinema during the Depression, or praying during war. Such habits are not bad; they serve as pressure valves.

Past regularity is essential, the bedrock of order and coherent experience. Dewey described what he called "funded knowledge," in which truth is the cumulative wisdom of past experience. One does not discard this wisdom; one uses it for guidance as one engages the present and plans for the future. To eliminate the past to romantic oblivion or to overextend it into causal sterility is obviously too aberrant. A balanced vision prepares us for what is to come and stretches the past into the present amid the pulls of the future and the expressions of the present.

The vision of the present is one of actions, of events underway, a healthy actualization of human capabilities. We start from movement, engagement, and interaction. We do not start learning or preparing for the future from a fixed starting point. There are, perhaps, few a priori starting points, except for those that address with the structure of mind and culture. We are not static, but theory driven, centrifugal (in the vernacular of neuroscience), and anticipatory. Thinking and action are embodied, in preparation for the future. The connective nature of the activity is unique and refreshing.

Planning necessitates a flexibility of mind. It means that one changes one's views as new data become available. This is no easy task. We often look away and do not acknowledge what is contrary to our expectations. This is where a blend of balanced ontological insecurity with epistemological uncertainty can orient one to perceive the possible, perhaps not to look away from contrary data. How we use the resources of our environments is a consideration in planning ahead.

Planning ahead teaches us to distinguish between short and long-term agendas, because short-term modifications are inadequate for long-term issues. This is particularly true as one envisions one's life, what one would like to be, how one structures one's life, one's time frame, one's conceptions of future selves. Planning ahead is also essential to how one relates to others, including those about which one cares. It is also true of environmental and economic planning. Planning permeates human life.

As we plan ahead, we enlarge our notion of what it is to belong to a community. A future-oriented conception is one in which the vision of being in the world is not of an individual isolated from the environment, but of an individual within an environment and a community. In a community, national borders are transcended to some extent. The vision is one of nested and networked communities, individuals locating themselves in communities and building new ones.

We plan for what is to come, and we wait for the unexpected outpouring of what is out there to be encountered. The prudent recourse is to stretch the good as far as it can go and hope for the best. Good fortune might prevail for extended moments, stretching a life that has more good than bad. Good things emerge by fortune and labor, but labor mostly comes first. Fortune can rain on those who labor hard and with good sense.

7. Endless Bootstrapping: Inquiry without Frills

Because we are social animals, linked with others, our evolutionary history is lined with a propensity to achieve conflict resolution (de Waal 2000). Appraisal mechanisms of oneself and others are inherent, and expressed early (Kagan 1984, 2002) and in closely related species (Hauser 2000); cooperation is essential in primates. But deception and the evolution of the arms race are closely associated with our evolutionary past and our cultural/historical evolution.

It is the sense of the life world with others, our transactions, where theory and practice in everyday life in the sciences is to be to uncovered (e.g. Dewey 1928, 1989; Heelan and Schulkin 1998). These events are existential, historical, and should be knotted to self-corrective methods of inquiry and hypothesis testing broadly conceived across the spectrum of human experience (from art to religion). Central metaphors define our approaches to inquiry (Galison 1988); our cognitive arsenal provides the orientation and the set of skills (Carey 2004; Lakoff and Johnson 1999).

Epistemic diversity, like biological diversity, is the reality of the scientific enterprise and an adaptation. A combination of instruments, experiments and theory cut across the range of inquiry (Galison 1988). In this age of information, our dependence on and trust for one another as scientists is essential for meaningful inquiry. One of the reasons for this need is because scientists working on different aspects of the same project have a certain level of ignorance of one another's specialties.

The "Renaissance man" of earlier centuries, who could embody the knowledge of an era, is no longer with us. Today's scope of scientific knowledge is far too vast to be completely embraced by one person, hence the emergence of specialties and subspecialties in science and medicine. In our era of exponential leaps in scientific knowledge, the multiple levels of analysis required in the scientific enterprise necessitate that we work together, because the knowledge of each level is not – indeed, cannot possibly be – shared by all members of the group

A "laboratory frame of mind" is at the heart of this endeavor and Peirce (see Cadwallader 1974) established a philosophy of self-correction, set up the first experimental laboratory for psychophysics in America at Johns Hopkins University, understood nearly every facet of science as far as was possible in the 19th century, generated the syntax of expanded logic and the logic of relatives, and provided an understanding of the role of theory in scientific activity (Hanson 1958).

All experience of inquiry is embedded in practices that are rich with frames of reference (e.g. Hanson 1958; Heelan and Schulkin 1998); as we perceive the world around us, we presuppose background sets of inferences. These inferences are often not conscious or even necessarily accessible, but they pervade our biological adaptation and set the conditions for scientific reasoning (Rozin 1976).

Any form of inquiry needs to be self-corrective. Assumptions are questioned. Biases permeate any endeavor and their recognition is an important factor. Moreover, the recognition of biases in human decision-making functions by what social scientists call "sensitizing concepts," providing a context to understand how we decide. Some of these biases are simple rough heuristics that work well, have been selected by evolutionary factors and are part of our cognitive apparatus (Pinker 1998). Multiple cognitive systems operate across the many areas of inquiry that we pursue (see Simon 1962; Rozin 1976).

Research in the decision sciences reinforced a shift to the logic of heuristics in reasoning, or what Herb Simon (1962, 1982; Gigerenzer and Selten 2001) called "satisficing" – what has also been called "bounded rationality." All decision-making reflects the frameworks out of which one interprets one's world, amidst the life-world that one is participating in, breathing the air of. The mantle of perfect reason inherited from the Enlightenment is replaced with demythologized reason, problem solving rooted in human experience, existential and pragmatic (Cherniak 1986; Dayes 2001) – less than perfect decision-making – concerning the choices of everyday life.

The demythologizing of decision-making requires that one take hold of the fact that science works, there are advances to be proud of, but that human reasoning, scientific or otherwise, is replete with flaws. The realization that optimization is not a pedestal or Archimedean point, on which one can stand for all time, is not demoralizing; quite the contrary (e.g. Simon 1962, 1982; Baron 1985; Glovick, Griffin and Kahneman 2002; Gigerenzer and Selten 2001). Advances are made by self-correction; explanations evolve, get better, or are discarded. It is something John Dewey (1916) well appreciated. Dewey (1925, 1989), in fact, always appreciated that the experience of the knower was essentially embodied in information processing systems (Smith 1970; Godfrey-Smith 1996).

8. Conclusion

A rich evolutionary background sets the conditions for human cognition (Gardenfors 2003; Sterelny 2003) and shapes the science that takes place (Carruthers et al 2002).

Still, with an eye to the past and the organization of the mind/brain (Gazzaniga 1998) and our cultural expressions, these advances need to be linked to our existential fate; we are great information processing systems who have now uncovered great depths of scientific understanding. But we are obviously more than information processing systems; we are more than the methods of our age. There are a variety of forms of reasoning, but two stand out. One is the orientation towards method, the other is the orientation to synthesis and ideas – what Whitehead called the way of Ulysses vs. Plato (Whitehead 1929). Both are essential; one has been traditionally linked to the sciences, the other to the humanities. In fact, this is misleading, for both the sciences and the humanities individuals embody both of them. The distinction is real, but cuts across disciplines, just as perception, readiness, and traditions of practice are inherent in all disciplines of inquiry.

The issue is keeping inquiry open, people in all disciplines ready to appreciate the frail pursuit of truth. Truth is not easy even under the best of conditions. Reason, and its evolution as a normative goal, is to render life more meaningful; it is to live well, not as gluttons, but as humbled investigators and appreciators of this wondrous life. But within life are endless hardships. Some have greater access to Fortuna than others; stoic sensibility is a necessity for owning ones fate, demanding and inching out bit-by-bit morsels of worth (Spinoza 1668, 1955) Reason helps to imagine those great possibilities; the poet, the artist, the historian, the scientist, provide glimpses of wonder. They provide us with the teleological underpinnings of possibilities, our musement, and our abduction: moments set in the context of the meaning of life.

A self-corrective conception of investigation and invention cuts across the broad range of human inquiry that needs to be anchored in historical and existential recognition of the frail sense of our human achievements with regard to the treatment of one another. With an eye toward the anti-intellectual tendencies of the dominance of method at the expense of ideas, the abject denying of self-reflection, the discarding of the historical, demythologized reason reaches for the next glimmer of possibility in enriching human experience. As one noted scholar suggested, "pragmatism was designed to make it harder for people to be driven to violence by their beliefs" (Menand 2001). At least, that is the normative hope reflected by the first stanza of an Emily Dickinson poem: "Hope is the thing with feathers / That perches in the soul...."

REFERENCES

Atran, Scott. 2002. *In Gods We Trust*. Oxford: Oxford University Press.

Atran, Scott, Douglas Medin, and Norbert Ross. 2005. "The Cultural Mind," *Psychological Review* 112: 744–766.

Barkow, Jerome, Leda Cosmides, and John Tooby. 1992. *The Adapted Mind*. Oxford: Oxford University Press.

Baron, Jonathan. 1985. *Rationality and Intelligence*. Cambridge, UK: Cambridge University Press.

Baron, Jonathan. 1988, 1994. *Thinking and Deciding*. Cambridge, UK: Cambridge University Press.

Bourdieu, Pierre. 1980, 1990. *The Logic of Practice*. Palo Alto, Cal.: Stanford University Press.

Boyd, Robert, and Pierre Richerson. 1985. *Culture and Evolutionary Process*. Chicago: University of Chicago Press.

Boyer, Pascal. 1990. *Tradition as Truth and Communication*. Cambridge, UK: Cambridge University Press.

Cadwallader, T. C. 1974. "Charles S. Peirce (1839–1914) The First American Experimental Psychologist," *Journal of the History of the Behavioral Sciences* 10: 291–298.

Carey, Susan, and Rochel Gelman. 1991. *The Epigenesis of Mind: Essays on Biology and Cognition*. Hillsdale, N.J.: Erlbaum Press.

Carey, Susan. 1985, 1987. *Conceptual Change in Childhood*. Cambridge, MA: MIT Press.

Carey, Susan. 2001. "Cognitive Foundations of Artithmetic: Evolution and Ontogenesis," *Mind and Language* 16: 37–55.

Carey, Susan. 2004. "Bootstrapping and the Origins of Concepts" *Daedalus* 133 (Winter): 59–68.

Carey, Susan, and Carol Smith. 1993. "On Understanding the Nature of Scientific Knowledge," *Educational Psychologist* 28: 235–251.

Cassirer, Ernst. 1944, 1978. *An Essay on Man*. New Haven, Conn: Yale University Press.

Cassirer, Ernst. 1946. *Language and Myth*. New York: Harper & Row.

Cassirer, Ernst. 1953, 1957. *Philosophy of Symbolic Forms*. New Haven, Conn.: Yale University Press.

Cherniak, Christopher. 1986. *Minimal Rationality*. Cambridge, MA: MIT Press.

Clark, Andy. 1999. "An Embodied Cognitive Science?" *Trends in Cognitive Sciences* 3: 345–51.

Clark, Andy. 2003. *Natural-Born Cyborgs*. Oxford: Oxford University Press.

Coleridge, Samuel Taylor. 1840, 1956. *Confessions of an Inquiring Spirit*. Stanford, Cal.: Stanford University Press.

Critchley, H. D., E. M. Daly, E. T. Bullmore, S. C. R. Williams, T. Van Amelsvoort, D. M. Robertson, et al. 2000. "The Functional Neuroanatomy of Social Behaviour: Changes in Cerebral Blood Flow When People with Autistic Disorder Process Facial Expressions," *Brain* 123: 2203–2212.

Damasio, Antonio. 1996. "The Somatic Marker Hypothesis and the Possible Functions of the Prefrontal Cortex," *Philosophical Transactions of the Royal Society* 351: 1413–1420.

Darwin, Erasmus. 1789, 1991. *The Botanic Garden; A Poem in Two Parts: Part II, The Loves of Plants*. Oxford, UK: Woodstock Books.

Darwin, Charles. 1859, 1958. *The Origin of Species*. New York: Mentor Books.

Deheane, S., V. Izard, P. Pica, and E. Spelke. 2006. "Core Knowledge of Geometry in an Amazonian Indigene Group" *Science* 311: 381–384.

De Waal, Frans. 2000. "Primates – A Natural Heritage of Conflict Resolution," *Science* 289: 586–590.

Dewey, John. 1910, 1965. *The Influence of Darwin on Philosophy*. Bloomington, Ind.: Indiana University Press.

Dewey, John. 1925, 1989. *Experience and Nature*. La Salle, Ill.: Open Court.

Dewey, John. 1938. *Logic: The Theory of Inquiry*. New York: Holt, Rinehart.

Dickinson, Emily. 1891, 1955. "Hope Is the Thing with the Feathers," in *The Poems of Emily Dickinson, Variorum Edition*, ed. R. W. Franklin. Cambridge, MA: Harvard University Press.

Duchaine, Bradley, Leda Cosmides, and John Tooby. 2001. "Evolutionary Psychology and the Brain," *Current Opinion in Neurobiology* 11: 225–250.

Eiseley, Loren. 1959, 1961. *Darwin's Century*. New York: Anchor Books.

Elster, Jon. 1979, 1988. *Ulysses and the Sirens*. Cambridge, UK: Cambridge University Press.

Galison, Peter. 1988. "History, Philosophy and the Central Metaphor," *Science in Context* 3: 197–212.

Gallistel, Charles. 1990. *The Organization of Learning*. Cambridge, MA: MIT Press.

Gelman, Susan. 2003. *The Essential Child*. Oxford: Oxford University Press.

Giere, Ronald. 2006. *Scientific Perspectivism*. Chicago: University of Chicago Press.

Gilovich, Thomas, Dale Griffin, and Daniel Kahneman, eds. 2002. *Heuristics and Biases: The Psychology of Intuitive Judgment.* Cambridge, UK: Cambridge University Press.

Gigerenzer, Gerd, and Reinhard Selten. 2001. *Bounded Rationality.* Cambridge, MA: MIT Press.

Godfrey-Smith, Peter. 1996. *Complexity and the Function of Mind.* Cambridge, UK: Cambridge University Press.

Godfrey-Smith, Peter. 2002. "Dewey on Naturalism, Realism and Science," *Philosophy of Science* 69: S1–S11.

Gopnik, Alison, and Andrew Meltzoff. 1997. *Words, Thoughts and Theories.* Cambridge, MA: MIT Press.

Hanson, Norwood Russell. 1958, 1972. *Patterns of Discovery.* Cambridge, UK: Cambridge University Press.

Hauser, Marc. 2000. *Wild Minds.* New York: Henry Holt.

Heelan, Patrick, and Jay Schulkin. 1998. "Hermeneutical Philosophy and Pragmatism: A Philosophy of Science," *Synthese* 115: 269–302.

Hendel, Charles, ed. 1959. *John Dewey and the Experimental Spirit in Philosophy.* New Haven, Conn.: Yale University Press.

Himmelfarb, Gertrude. 1959, 1962. *Darwin and the Darwinian Revolution.* New York: Norton Press.

James, William. 1890, 1952. *The Principles of Psychology.* New York: Dover Press.

Johnson, Mark. 1987, 1990. *The Body in the Mind.* Chicago: University of Chicago Press.

Johnson-Laird, Philip Nicholas. 2001. "Mental Models and Deduction," *Trends in Cognitive Science* 5: 434–442.

Johnson-Laird, Philip Nicholas. 2002. "Peirce, Logic Diagrams, and the Elementary Operations of Reasoning," *Thinking and Reasoning* 8: 69–95.

Kagan, Jerome. 2002. *Surprise, Uncertainty and Mental Structure.* Cambridge, MA: Harvard University Press.

Keil, Frank. 1979. *Semantic and Conceptual Development: An Ontological Perspective.* Cambridge, MA: Harvard University Press.

Keil, Frank. 1983. "On the Emergence of Semantic and Conceptual Distinctions," *Journal of Experimental Psychology* 112: 357–385.

Keil, Frank. 1992. "The Origins of an Autonomous Biology," in *Minnesota Symposium in Child Psychology* 25: 103–138.

Keil, Frank, and Robert Wilson. 2000. *Explanation and Cognition*. Cambridge, MA: MIT Press.

King-Hele, D. G. 1986. *Erasmus Darwin and the Romantic Poets*. New York: Macmillan Press.

Kornblith, Hilary. 1993. *Inductive Inference and Its Natural Ground*. Cambridge, MA: MIT Press.

Lakoff, George, and Mark Johnson. 1999. *Philosophy in the Flesh: The Embodied Mind and Its Challenge to Western Thought*. New York: Basic Books.

LeDoux, Joseph. 1996. *The Emotional Brain*. New York: Simon and Schuster.

Levi, Isaac. 2004. "Beware of Syllogism: Reasoning and Conjecture According to Peirce," in *The Cambridge Companion to Peirce*, ed. Cheryl Misak. Cambridge, UK: Cambridge University Press.

Loewenstein, George. 1994. "The Psychology of Curiosity," *Psychological Bulletin* 116: 75–98.

Mandler, Jean Matter. 2004. *The Foundations of Mind*. Oxford: Oxford University Press.

Margolis, Joseph. 2002. *Reinventing Pragmatism: American Philosophy at the End of the Twentieth Century*. Ithaca, N.Y.: Cornell University Press.

Medin, Douglas, and Scott Atran. 1999. *Folkbiology*. Cambridge, MA: MIT Press.

Medin, Douglas, and Scott Atran. 2004. "The Naïve Mind: Biological Categorization and Reasoning in Development and Across Culture," *Psychological Reviews* 111: 960-983.

Meltzoff, Andrew. 2004. "The Case for Developmental Cognitive Science: Theories of People and Things," in *Theories of Infant Development*, ed. Gavin Bremmer and Alan Slater. Oxford: Blackwell.

Menand, Louis. 2001. *The Metaphysical Club*. New York: Farrar, Straus and Giroux.

Merleau-Ponty, Maurice. 1942, 1967. *The Structure of Behavior*. Boston: Beacon Press.

Mill, John Stuart. 1843, 1873. *A System of Logic*. London: Longmans, Green, Rader and Dyer.

Mithen, Steven. 1996. *The Prehistory of the Mind: The Cognitive Origins of Art and Science*. London: Thames and Hudson.

Murphy, Gregory. 2002. *The Big Book of Concepts*. Cambridge, MA: MIT Press.

Nash, Roderick. 1967. *Wilderness and the American Mind*. New Haven, Conn.: Yale University Press.

Neville, Robert Cummings. 1974. *The Cosmology of Freedom*. New Haven, Conn.: Yale University Press.

Oelschlaeger, Max. 1991. *The Idea of Wilderness*. New Haven, Conn.: Yale University Press.

Parrott, W. G., and J. Schulkin. 1993. "Neuropsychology and the Cognitive Nature of the Emotions," *Cognition and Emotion* 7: 43–59.

Peirce, Charles Sanders. 1868, 1992. "Questions Concerning Certain Faculties Claimed for Man," in *The Essential Peirce, Vol. 1*, ed. Nathan Houser and Christian Kloesel. Bloomington: Indiana University Press.

Peirce, Charles Sanders. 1878. "Deduction, Induction and Hypothesis," *Popular Science and Monthly* 13: 470–482.

Peirce, Charles Sanders. 1892. "The Architecture of Theories," *The Monist* 1: 61–76.

Peirce, Charles Sanders. 1899. *Reasoning and the Logic of Things*, ed. Kenneth Laine Ketner. Cambridge, MA: Harvard University Press, 1992.

Piaget, Jean. 1954. *The Construction of Reality in the Child*. New York: Basic Books.

Piaget, Jean. 1971, 1975. *Biology and Knowledge*. Chicago: University of Chicago.

Pinker, Steven. 1994. *The Language Instinct*. New York: William Morrow.

Pinker, Steven. 1998. *How the Mind Works*. New York: W. W. Norton.

Rescher, Nicholas. 2000. *Nature and Understanding*. Oxford: Clarendon Press.

Rescorla, R. A., and A. R. Wagner. 1972. "A Theory of Pavlovian Conditioning: Variations in the Effectiveness of Reinforcement Non-Reinforcement," in *Classical Conditioning: Current Research and Theory*, ed. W. J. Baker and W. Prokasy. New York: Appleton-Century-Crofts.

Rosen, J., and J. Schulkin. 1998. "From Normal Fear to Pathological Anxiety," *Psychological Review* 105: 325–350.

Rozin, P. 1976. "The Evolution of Intelligence and Access to the Cognitive Unconscious," *Progress in Psychobiology and Physiological Psychology* 6: 245-280.

Rozin, P. 1998. "Evolution and Development of Brains and Cultures," in *Brain and Mind: Evolutionary Perspectives*, ed. Michael Gazzaniga and Jennifer Altman. Strassbourg, France: Human Frontiers Sciences Program.

Rozin, P. and Schulkin, J. 1990. "Food Selection," in *Handbook of Food and Fluid Intake*, ed. E. M. Stricker. New York: Plenum Press.

Ruse, Michael. 2006. *Darwinism and its Discontents*. Cambridge, UK: Cambridge University Press.

Schulkin, Jay. 1996. *The Delicate Balance*. Lanham, Md.: University Press of America.

Schulkin, Jay. 2004. *Bodily Sensibility: Intelligent Action*. Oxford: Oxford University Press.

Schultz, W. 2002. "Getting Formal with Dopamine and Reward," *Neuron* 36: 241–263.

Schultz, W. 2004. "Neural Coding of Basic Reward Terms of Animal Learning, Game Theory, Microeconomics and Behavioral Ecology," *Current Opinion in Neurobiology* 14: 139–147.

Simon, Herbert. 1962. "The Architecture of Complexity." *Proceedings of the American Philosophical Society* 106: 470–73.

Simon, Herbert. 1982. *Models of Bounded Rationality*. Cambridge, MA: MIT Press.

Smith, J. E. 1985. "Experience in Pierce, James and Dewey," *Monist* 68: 538–554.

Sperber, Dan. 1975. *Rethinking Symbolism*. Cambridge, UK: Cambridge University Press.

Sperber, Dan. 1985. *On Anthropological Knowledge*. Cambridge, UK: Cambridge University Press.

Spinoza, Baruch. 1955. *On the Improvement of the Understanding*. New York: Dover.

Sterelny, Kim. 2003. *Thought in a Hostile World*. Malden, MA: Blackwell.

Thomas, E. 2001. "Empathy and Consciousness," *Journal of Consciousness Studies* 8: 1–35.

Wheeler, Michael. 2005. *Reconstructing the Cognitive World*. Cambridge, MA: MIT Press.

Weissman, David. 2008. *Styles of Thought*. Albany: State University of New York Press.

Whitehead, Alfred North. 1929. *The Function of Reason*. Princeton, N.J.: Princeton University Press.

Wilson, Robert. 2005. *Genes and the Agents of Life*. Cambridge, UK: Cambridge University Press.

Jay Schulkin
Departments of Physiology, Biophysics, and Neuroscience
Georgetown University
School of Medicine
Washington, DC 20007
United States

Contemporary Pragmatism
Vol. 5, No. 1 (June 2008), 61–77

Editions Rodopi
© 2008

Cephalic Organization: Animacy and Agency

Jay Schulkin

Humans come prepared to recognize two fundamental features of our surroundings: animate objects and agents. This recognition begins early in ontogeny and pervades our ecological and social space. This cognitive capacity reveals an important adaptation and sets the conditions for pervasive shared experiences. One feature of our species and our evolved cephalic substrates is that we are prepared to recognize self-propelled action in others. Our cultural evolution is knotted to an expanding sense of shared experiences.

1. Introduction

A key understanding of our species, something that the classical pragmatist understood, is our "lived experience" (Dewey 1925, 1989). In lived experience are the diverse often unspoken ways in which we share experiences and acknowledge each other's experiences. Underlying these events is a sense of agency and memory (James 1890, 1952). We come prepared to understand the world in terms of agents and action – human direction. We come prepared to share experiences and to exploit them, to form meaningful connections (Jaspers 1913, 1997).

At the heart of our evolution is a developed sense of agency knotted to diverse innate problem solving proclivities (Dewey 1925, 1989). Two concepts figure importantly in our understanding of each other – animacy and agency. These are two cardinal features in our cognitive lexicon that are replete with meaning. Animacy is tied in with agency; agency, in the sense in which I am using the term, is tied to our beliefs, desires, preferences and goals, our personal histories, our historical legacies. However, though linked, animacy is not the same as agency; something can obviously be alive without being an agent.

I suggest that an orientation toward understanding living objects and the cognitive/neural underpinnings of our understanding of the experiences of others is a fundamental adaptation. The argument here is that the cognitive achievement of first distinguishing animate from inanimate objects, followed by recognizing the beliefs and desires of others with regard to their personal histories, are two related, but distinct, cognitive adaptations that provide the basis of our ability to learn from the experiences of others.

2. Categories and Human Understanding

Inquiry takes place within a framework in which hitting on the right idea is embedded in a framework that has been successful and reveals something basic about a feature of cognitive capacities and about the objects of those categories (Kant 1787; Peirce 1878; Dewey 1896; Hansen 1958). Taxonomic and thematic conditions may be simple or complex, but there is always a background condition (e.g. Murphy 2002; Medin and Atran 1999, 2004; Giere 2006). Moreover, the inductive devices are broadly conceived in a mind/brain ready to compute statistical probability, draw diverse inferences, and construct models (e.g. Peirce 1983; Hacking 1965; Johnson-Johnson-Laird 2001, 2002) essential for information processing and coherent action.

There is a great range of categories that we are prepared to generate quite early – animate and inanimate, animal and plant, objects in space, etc. (see Carey 1985; 2001; Keil 1979; Mandler 2004; Duchain et al 2001; Pinker 1997; Dehaeane et al 2006). We also come prepared with a variety of useful heuristics for solving problems (Simon 1982; Barkow et al 1992; Gigerenzer and Selten 2001). Diverse taxonomic characterization is the staple of cognitive coherence. In other words, there appear to be categories that we readily accept and objects that we look for in our surroundings (Medin and Atran 1999; Carey and Gelman 1991).

Kinds of objects are understood relative to an orientation; for example, a characterization expressing how nature is understood by diverse groups. One such study is the management in the Mayan lowlands of Guatemala (Atran et al 1999). This is an area rich with diverse cultures, where three basic groups coincide: native Maya, immigrant Maya, and individuals of mixed European and Amerindian descent. They all live in the same habitat, yet they have different views and different responses to the care of nature. All three groups work from a theory of the objects in their natural environment. There is wide variation and diversity in our cognitive machinations and what we emphasize and what we overlook, and there is possibly a devolution of function about natural objects (Wolf and Medin, unpublished observations).

Interestingly, in this study the native Mayans do the most to help sustain the surrounding environment (Atran et al 1999; Medin and Atran 2004; Atran et al 2005). Not surprisingly, native Mayans also possess more expertise about natural objects in their terrain than the other two groups, but each has diverse categories and shared practices for understanding the plants and animals. The concept of an animate object is a basic one.

Core features that go into self-corrective inquiry include an orientation to observation of objects, abduction, or the genesis of ideas, tying ideas about the world to causation, and development of diverse tools that expands one's observations (e.g. Peirce 1892; Hanson 1958; Heelan and Schulkin 1998; Gigerenzer and Selten 2001).

Along with categorization, inductive mechanisms start early, and are grounded in diverse forms of orientation to events (e.g. Medin and Atran 2004). Induction is couched in an orientation; abductive mechanisms (the tendency to hit on the right idea, e.g. bats being mammals) are utilized because young children are grounded in both taxonomic and deductive mechanisms that ground for consistency.

Cognitive systems are means to engage the world, not something that cuts one off or separates mind from body; cephalic orientation in which continuity and unity of experience predominates the knowing process (Dewey 1925, 1989; Johnson 2007; Schulkin 2004).

3. Animate/Inanimate Distinction and Ontogeny

The distinction between what is animate and what is not occurs during early development (Keil 1979; Carey 1985). Such basic core conceptions reflect the development of a cognitive apparatus under the pressure of natural selection. Cognitive adaptation is rooted in evolution, a world of problem-solving and local adaptation (e.g. Rozin 1976). The predominance of problem-solving abilities is strongly linked to the machinery of adaptation and is oriented to coping, striving, and understanding.

Cognitive systems are rooted in the worlds that humans inhabit (Clark 1999). The evolution of our cognitive abilities is fundamentally linked to the worlds we evolved from and are adapting to, and the extensions of our world we create by our inventions. The tools that help us see and hear become part of our evolutionary hardware; the apparently rigid separation between what we make to help us see and hear and what our brain provides is in fact permeable (e.g. Clark 2003).

Research in developmental psychology has expanded on the work of Piaget, suggesting that the child imposes order early on, much earlier than Piaget postulated (see Carey 1985; Mandler 2004). Children track objects, generate inferences to background orientations that provide perspective, and use time, probability of events, familiar/unfamiliar comparisons and other cognitive devices early on in ontogeny.

Piaget (1954, 1972) argued that young children are animistic (see also Frazer 1921, 2000; Malinowski 1948, as the concept was applied to primitive thinking). Piaget stated that young children over-attribute the concept of animacy to more objects than they should. But one study by Dolgin and Behrend (1984) found that animism is not an all-pervasive phenomenon in young children, not an unconstrained cognitive attribution. Young children rarely made mistakes distinguishing between prototypical animate and inanimate objects (see also Gelman et al 1995); they are not necessarily prone to the over-attribution of animacy to inappropriate objects. While our species may be over-prepared to attribute the concept of animacy and infuse objects with rich symbolic expression, we also learn to limit the attribution. The attribution of a category, such as agency or animacy, is not all or none, and expands as theorizing is deepened by greater accuracy and the expression of knowledge (Gelman 2003).

Diverse evidence suggests that young children recognize that natural events can exist independent of human action (e.g. Gelman et al 1995). Moreover, there is evidence that children believe that animals and inanimate objects are expressions of different kinds of motion. Evidence suggests that children may appreciate that an animal or thing can cause its own movement before understanding how that can occur; the storehouse of knowledge grows amidst a basic framework.

With regard to children's understanding of animacy and agency, it is much debated how early and how deep the orientation is. We do know that the concept of animacy is not as pervasive (i.e. unrestrained) in young children's thinking as Piaget suggested. Piaget was right to highlight its importance in understanding the world around us, as there is substantial evidence that children are equipped with such orientations early in life, and that the animate/inanimate categorization is one of them.

Amidst the development of perceptual competence, cognitive events occur that are rich in information processing. These include the creation of conceptual categories (Mandler 2004; Keil 1979; Keil and Wilson 2000) and the imposition of diverse categories against background theory (Hanson 1958; Murphy 2002; Medin and Atran 2004; Lakoff and Johnson 1999). Such cognitive events, whether implicit or explicit, provide coherence and underlie the organization of action. They are used to pick out kinds of objects and to track events. Keeping track of objects (Sterelny 2003), looking to determine essential features (if there are any) both apparent and not, are fundamental cognitive events (e.g. Kripke 1980) and figure importantly in the development and expression of thought (Gelman 2003). Young children fix reference to objects, even though the original features may not determine how that object is understood. An orientation to core features, essential features which may or may not be manifest, is an organizing principle.

4. Knowing Animate Agents

In a world in which our transactions with one another are the fabric of our social life, a sense of a living agent that is rich with plans and projects is a running theme for the classical pragmatists (James 1892, 1907; Dewey 1925). Core cognitive orientations tied to social practice is how we are oriented to the world. Core concepts, such as animacy and agency in addition to senses of space, time, probability, and language, figure in the rich symbols that permeate our world (e.g. Pinker 1994, 1998). These abilities are intertwined and are reflected in everyday activities (Neville 1974; Weissman 2000).

Like the concept of animacy, our notion of agency is semantically rich (e.g. Gallagher 2005). At the heart of it is an ownership of one's actions, or the devolution of ownership that can occur through pathology (Jaspers 1913, 1997).

Recognizing others as agents is an essential adaptation for learning. At the heart of learning is something social: learning from other people's experiences. Importantly, we come prepared to understand the beliefs and desires of others. It is a core feature of humans as a species (e.g. Dennett 1987; Premack and Premack 1983; Leslie 1987).

Little children go from broad imitative representations to discerning and then using to their own advantage the beliefs and desires of others in orchestrating behavioral responses (Tomasello and Call 1997; Tomasello et al 2005).

The following table displays major steps in human cognitive development, with specific focus on social-cultural dimensions and their effects (from Tomasello and Call 1997).

Infancy: Understanding others as intentional

1. Following attention and behavior of others: Social referencing, attention following, imitation of acts on objects
2. Directing attention and behavior of others: Imperative gestures, declarative gestures
3. Symbolic play with objects: Playing with "intentionality" of object

Early childhood: Language

1. Linguistic symbols and predication: Inter-subjective representations
2. Event categories: Events and participants in one schema
3. Narratives: Series of interrelated events with some constant participants

Childhood: Multiple perspectives and representational re-descriptions

1. Theory of mind: Seeing situation both as it is and as other believes it to be
2. Concrete operations: Seeing events or object in two ways simultaneously
3. Representational re-description: Seeing own behavior/cognition from "outside" perspective

What is distinctive about our species is the degree to which we share and participate toward common ends; shared intention linked to the considerations of others is one of our most important cognitive adaptations (Tomasello et al 1993; Tomasello et al 2005; Baron-Cohen 1995). Before two years of age the rudiments of this ability are expressed (Kagan 1984). Shared space (see e.g. Mead 1932, 1934) is bound to shared representations of others – of their experiences, beliefs, desires, and goals. Three factors are critical: the recognition of animation, awareness of the goals and pursuits of other individuals, and the recognition of their beliefs, desires, future plans (Tomasello et al 1993). Each of these cognitive events is critical for our cultural evolution and a shared sense of inquiry (Mead 1932, 1934).

As we are social animals, our intentions link us to others, and our recognition of others' intentions, and our shared intentions provide common currency, shared experiences (e.g. Schutz 1932, 1967; Mead 1932, 1934). Shared intentions are the lifeblood of human meaning and human connectedness (Jaspers 1913, 1997). There is nothing abstract about this. It is indeed an important cognitive adaptation, a fundamental way in which we also share vulnerabilities (Nussbaum 2004). Diverse forms of perception, including joint attention tasks to objects, demonstrate how early this appears. As Tomasello et al (2005) recognized, the key feature in collaborative endeavors is the ability to share intentions, to recognize agency amidst animacy, something with goals or plans.

Before two years of age these cognitive abilities are pervasive. The "social act" (Mead 1932, 1934) – my consideration of you, and your consideration of me (whether good or bad) – is an inter-subjective event. Learning from others is embodied in the engagement of others, learning from their experiences. It requires my purview of others; it is the fall away from idiocy and the loss of the world of others. Collaborative endeavors are not an aberration, but an essential feature of our species.

5. Cognitive/Neural Predilection to Detect Self-Propelled Movement

One feature that the neonate distinguishes is self-propelled motion, whether something is self-generated (e.g. Premack 1990; Mandler 2004). Infants are quite capable of determining something about object direction and object motion (Spelke et al 1995). Children's orientation to others reflects fundamental recognition of animate self-propelled objects (Carey 1985).

Data suggesting that the recognition of an object's motion is a primary perceptual event, rich in semantic possibilities. We come prepared to reason about the trajectory of objects (motion and trajectory of motivational states) and their being part of biological kinds, the attribution of animacy and agency; the sense of embodied cognitive systems requires one to see (at least one another) as revealing these two properties (Leslie 1987; Premack 1990). What is not resolved, particularly with regard to the central nervous system, is how specific the brain codes are for these categorical differences (e.g. Warrington and Shallice 1984; Caramazza and Shelton 1998; Martin and Caramazza 2003; Martin 2007); perhaps the human nervous system is prepared to detect movement based on animate objects and those based on inanimate objects (Premack 1990).

The nervous system is oriented to recognize the detection of agency on the basis of features of movement; this is knotted to our ability to infer other people's self-propelled sense of movement (Premack 1990). There is evidence that the perception of self-propelled action, as opposed to action forced on one, may be modulated by different and overlapping regions of the brain. Diverse brain imaging studies have shown (e.g. Blakemore et al 2003; Castelli et al

2000; Ferrer et al 2003) that whether something is perceived as intentional and self-propelled is an important variable in activating a number of regions of the brain (e.g. right middle frontal gyrus, left superior temporal sulcus).

Interestingly, in experiments using fMRI, vignettes of social action were demarcated from mechanical action, and a different neural pattern of neural activity was clearly noted (Martin and Weisberg 2003). The vignettes were not human or animal figures, only the configuration of shapes. Regions of the temporal lobe and amygdala linked to face recognition and more generally to animated or living objects (see also Martin et al 2000; Martin 2007) were more active in the vignettes that depicted agency and social context than a non-social context.

We can conclude that our brains are prepared to recognize animated objects, motion and action (Blakemore and Decety 2001). The detection of motion and our sense of being a causal agent are embedded in the concept of agency (e.g. Whitehead 1927, 1953; Premack 1990). The detection of movement knotted to intentionality is an important discrimination in understanding others (Jacob and Jeannerod 2003). The brain comes prepared to discern, or at least try to discern, such relationships and regions of the brain are prepared to understand something about animate agents (Wheatley et al 2007).

The ability of "perspective taking," the detection of the self-propelled actions of others, is an evolved central state. It is an active state in the consideration of the experiences of others, and is tied to communicative competence and essential human bonds and well-being (e.g. Jaspers 1913, 1997; Nussbaum 2004). The information processing that entails this ability is a cognitive and behavioral achievement. While perception and action are represented in similar regions of the brain (Jeannerod 1999), these events are linked to broad-based cognitive semantic processing in the organization of action (Nelissen et al 2005). An interesting fact here is that neurons in the brain that are active when I do something are the same as those activated when I watch you do the same thing. The important finding is that these neurons coordinate observation and orchestration of goal-directed action patterns, and perhaps underlie the perception of intentional action.

6. Devolution of Function: Autism and The Understanding of Other Human Beings: Decreased Interest in Animate Agents

Two key cognitive features stand out in individuals with autism; they are less comfortable with human contact, and in some instances (when controlling for IQ) are better able to solve problems that reflect mechanical (as compared to social) issues than normal individuals (Leslie 1987; Baron-Cohen 1995, 2000). While the ability to discriminate between animate and inanimate objects is present in autism, it is compromised (Baron-Cohen 1995, 2000). There is an association between autistic symptoms and a preference for inanimate objects, and decreased human animate contact. Autism is marked by a specific lack of interest in people and interpersonal interactions. This is a fundamental impairment in gaining a foothold in the "life world" (Schutz 1932, 1967), the world of acknowledged human experiences and gaining fundamental human meaning through significant connections with others (Jaspers 1913, 1997).

Autism, a developmental disability, impairs the ability to form social bonds, to parse the social space of another human being, through the attribution of beliefs and desires (Baron-Cohen 1995, 2000). They are impaired in a basic human contact of meaning (Jaspers 1913, 1997). Animate agents, object contact, a recognition of something as animate or inanimate (expressing intentional direction or not) is a fundamental cognitive tracking event of objects (Premack and Premack 1995) and is one way in which we are rooted in our understanding of each other. Facial expressions, eye contact, and shared attention (e.g. shared mutual awareness of common focus) on someone's face are obviously important sources of information (Darwin 1872, 1965; Ekman 1972). Young children and adults use this information in forming attachments. An appreciation of these events is compromised in autism (Baron-Cohen 1995, 2000; Dalton et al 2005) that is more pronounced in boys (Baron-Cohen et al 2005). An understanding of animacy is importantly knotted to a social semantic network in the brain (Legerstee 1992; Martin 2007).

7. Watching and Learning from Others: Cognitive/Neural Systems, Language, and Action

Diverse senses of embodied cognitive systems are inherent in the organization of action (Barsalou 2003; Wilson 2002). Our cognitive evolution, with its extra premium on memory and language, implodes our cognitive capabilities; our cultural evolution draws on all resources as our memory and communicative systems are both internal and external to us (Donald 1991; Clark 1997).

Moreover, common regions of the brain that underlie the syntactical features of language production and comprehension (frontal cortex and basal ganglia, Ullman 2001, 2004) also underlie diverse forms of cognitive events, including statistical reasoning and various forms of emotional informational processing. These areas are linked to action, but there is no separation between action and cognitive systems (Schulkin 2004; Jackson and Decety 2004; Barton 2006). While diverse regions of the brain underlie the animate/inanimate distinction, a word's depiction of an action (viewing a hammer) is more likely to activate motor and pre-motor areas of the cortex (see e.g. Martin and Caramazza 2003; Caramazza and Mahon 2005). Importantly, looking at action words (Hauk et al 2004; Pulvermuller et al 2005), and the performance of an action activate many of the same regions of the brain (e.g. Perani et al 1995; Martin et al 2000). The coherence in the organization of the brain is the tight link between cognitive systems and action and function.

One's sense of agency and the attribution of agency to others is something that our brain comes prepared to do (Ferrer and Frith 2002). It underlies one of our senses of "causal efficacy" (Whitehead 1927, 1953) that is replete with the feeling of causation, of generating and moving something (James 1890, 1952). In part, this sense of causation is passive. Imitating others is represented in many different regions of the brain that reflect representations of action, of motion, of agency (Chaminade et al 2005). Representations of action words and regions of the brain that underlie action, and category-specific prepared knowledge about objects linked to action, show that cognitive systems traverse most, if not all, regions of the brain (Schulkin 2004; Jackson and Decety 2004). Importantly, these areas of the brain underlie the important adaptation of shared experience, a sense of community (Dewey 1934) and meaning (Jaspers 1913, 1997).

Learning from others necessitates the unfolding of the lived experiences (Dewey 1938, 1979) of those cumulative moments that have been instructive, that have taught us something that is important for us to know.

8. Conclusion: Animacy and Agency Demythologized in Prepared Cognitive Systems

We are prepared to see the world using animacy and agency as dominant categories, just as we come prepared to associate tastes of foods and gastrointestinal distress. Prepared kinds of learning set the background in which education and learning from others take place (Rozin 1976). The conception of nature demythologized allows us to recognize our roots in evolution in the natural world; that does not denigrate the all-pervasive cultural features that permeate our existence.

Nature alive is a full-fledged ideal of Wordsworth and Whitehead, nature coming into being and perishing; in Thoreau and Darwin, nature is realized as part of the human spirit and evolutionary legacy. Nature demythologized is the full recognition of the omnipresent dangers of our creations, the Frankensteins that linger, neutral with regard to their being, but not with regard to their use. The concept of agency is put in perspective where it finds expression in everyday considerations, in our activities, in learning, in history, in religious quests.

The origins of our psychological explanations are perhaps found in the fundamental distinction between animate and inanimate objects. Core knowledge, such as these two categories, permeate the cognitive architecture that includes concepts about physical objects, both living and non-biological, causation, as well as an orientation towards others – their experiences, expectations and intentions. The classificatory distinction of the living from non-living is a fundamental cognitive adaptation and expanded and developed. Categorical attributions of animacy and agency are dominant early, but not totally unconstrained (Gelman 2003), and they are intertwined. Both categories matter in determining the world around us (e.g. Atran 1990; Boyer 2002).

REFERENCES

Adolphs, R., N. L. Denburg, and D. Tranel. 2001. "The Amygdala's Role in Long Term Declarative Memory for Gist and Detail," *Behavioral Neuroscience* 112: 983–992.

Altman, J. 1966. "Autoradiographic and Histological Studies of Postnatal Neurogenesis," *J. Comp. Neurology* 124: 431–474.

Atran, Scott. 1990. *Cognitive Foundations of Natural History*. Cambridge, UK: Cambridge University Press.

Atran, Scott, Douglas Medin, and Norbert Ross. 2005. "The Cultural Mind," *Psychological Review* 112: 744–766.

Atran, Scott, Douglas Medin, Norbert Ross, E. Lynch, J. Coley, E. Ucan-Ek, and V. Vapnarsky. 1999. "Folkecology and Commons Management in the Maya Lowlands," *Proceedings of the National Academy of Sciences* 96: 7598–7603.

Bandura, A. 2006 "Toward a Psychology of Human Agency," *Perspectives on Psychological Science* 1: 164–180.

Barkow, Jerome, Leda Cosmides, and John Tooby. 1992. *The Adapted Mind*. Oxford: Oxford University Press.

Baron-Cohen, Simon. 1995, 2000. *Mindblindness*. Cambridge, MA: MIT Press.

Baron-Cohen, S., H. A. Ring, S. Wheelwright, E. T. Bullmore, M. J. Brammer, A. Simmons, and S. C. R. Williams. 1999. "Social Intelligence in the Normal and Autistic Brain: An fMRI study," *European Journal of Neuroscience* 11: 1–8.

Bird-David, N. 1999 "Animism Revisited," *Current Anthropology* 40: 567–591.

Blakemore, S. J., and J. Decety. 2001. "From the Perception of Action to the Understanding of Intention," *Nature Reviews* 2: 561–567.

Blakemore, S. J., P. Boyer, M. Pachot-Louard, A. Meltzoff, C. Segebarth, and J. Decety. 2003. "The Detection of Contingency and Animacy from Simple Animations in the Brain," *Cerebral Cortex* 13: 837–844.

Boyer, Pascal. 2002. "Religious Thought and Behavior as By-products of Brain Function," *Trends in Cognitive Science* 7: 119–124.

Brook, Andrew, and Kathleen. Akins, ed. 2005. *Cognition and the Brain*. Cambridge, UK: Cambridge University Press.

Caramazza, A., and J. R. Shelton. 1998. "Domain Specific Knowledge Systems in the Brain," *Journal of Cognitive Science* 10: 1–34.

Carey, Susan. 1985, 1987. *Conceptual Change in Childhood.* Cambridge, MA: MIT Press.

Carey, Susan. 2001. "Cognitive Foundations of Artithmetic: Evolution and Ontogenesis," *Mind and Language* 16: 37–55.

Carey, Susan, and Rochel Gelman. 1991. *The Epigenesis of Mind: Essays on Biology and Cognition.* Hillsdale, NJ: Erlbaum Press.

Carter, Sue, Izja Lederhendler, and Brian Kirkpatrick. 1997, 1999. *The Integrative Neurobiology of Affiliation.* Cambridge, MA: MIT Press.

Cassirer, Ernst. 1944, 1978. *An Essay on Man.* New Haven: Yale University Press.

Cassirer, Ernst. 1946. *Language and Myth.* New York: Harper and Row.

Castelli, F; F. Happe, U. Frith, and C. Frith. 2000. "Movement and Mind: A Functional Imaging Study of Perception and Interpretation of Complex Intentional Movement Patterns," *NeuroImage* 12, 314–325.

Chaminade, T., A. Meltzoff, and J. Decety. 2005. "An fMRI Study of Imitation: Action Representation and Body Schema," *Neuropsychologia* 43(1): 115–127.

Clark, Andy. 1999. "An Embodied Cognitive Science?" *Trends in Cognitive Sciences* 3: 345–51.

Clark, Andy. 2003. *Natural-Born Cyborgs.* Oxford: Oxford University Press.

Dalton, K. M., B. M. Nacewicz, T. Johnstone, H. S. Schaefer, M. A. Gernsbacher, H. H. Goldsmith, A. L. Alexander, et al. 2005. "Gaze Fixation and the Neural Circuitry of Face Processing in Autism," *Nature Neuroscience* 8: 519–526.

Darwin, Charles. 1872, 1965. *The Expression of Emotions in Man and Animals.* Chicago: University of Chicago Press.

Deheane, S., V. Izard, P. Pica, and E. Spelke. 2006. "Core Knowledge of Geometry in an Amazonian Indigene Group," *Science* 311: 381–384.

Dennett, Daniel. 1987. *The Intentional Stance.* Cambridge, MA: MIT Press.

Dewey, John. 1896. "The Reflex Arc Concept in Psychology," *Psychological Review* 3: 357–370.

Dewey, John. 1910, 1965. *The Influence of Darwin on Philosophy.* Bloomington: Indiana University Press.

Dewey, John. 1929, 1960. *The Quest for Certainty.* New York: Capricorn Books.

Dewey, John. 1925, 1989. *Experience and Nature.* La Salle, Ill.: Open Court.

Dewey, John. 1938. *Logic: The Theory of Inquiry*. New York: Holt, Rinehart.

Dolgin, K. G., and D. A. Behrend. 1984. "Children's Knowledge about Animates and Inanimates," *Child Development* 35: 1645–1650.

Duchaine, Bradley, Leda Cosmides, and John Tooby. 2001. "Evolutionary Psychology and the Brain," *Current Opinion in Neurobiology* 11: 225–250.

Ekman, P. 1972. Universals and Cultural Differences in Facial Expressions of Emotion," in *Nebraska Symposium on Motivation, 1971*, ed. J. Cole. Lincoln: University of Nebraska Press.

Ferrer L., H. Bratt, V. R. Gadde, S. Kajarekar, E. Shriberg, K. Sonmez, A. Stolcke, and A. Venkataraman. 2003. "Modeling Duration Patterns for Speaker Recognition," Eurospeech 2003 *Proceedings:8th European Conference on Speech Communication and Technology*. Bonn, Germany: ISCA.

Frazer, James George. 1921, 2000. *The New Golden Bough*. New York: Bartleby.com.

Freud, Sigmund. 1924, 1960. *A General Introduction to Psychoanalysis*. New York: Washington Square Press.

Gallagher, Shaun. 2005. *How the Body Shapes the Mind*. Oxford: Oxford University Press.

Gallagher, Shaun, and Andrew Meltzoff. 1996. "The Earliest Sense of Self and Others: Merleau-Ponty and Recent Developmental Studies," *Philosophical Psychology* 9: 213–236.

Gallistel, Charles. 1990. *The Organization of Learning*. Cambridge, MA: MIT Press.

Gelman, R., F. Durgin, and L. Kaufman. 1995. "Distinguishing Between Animates and Innanimates: Not by Motion Alone," in *Causal Cognition*, ed. Dan Sperber, David Premack and Ann James Premack. Oxford: Clarendon Press.

Gelman, Susan. 2003. *The Essential Child*. Oxford: Oxford University Press.

Gibbs, Raymond. 2006. *Embodiment and Cognitive Science*. Cambridge, UK: Cambridge University Press.

Giere, Ronald. 2006. *Scientific Perspectivism*. Chicago: University of Chicago Press.

Gigerenzer, Gerd, and Reinhard Selten. 2001. *Bounded Rationality*. Cambridge, MA: MIT Press.

Gould, E., and B. McEwen. 1993. "Neuronal Birth and Death," *Current Opinion in Neurobiology* 3: 676–682.

Greene, J. D., R. B. Sommerville, L. E. Nystrom, J. M. Darley, and J. D. Cohen. 2001. "An fMRI Investigation of Emotional Engagement in Moral Judgment," *Science* 293: 2105–2108.

Hacking, Ian. 1965. *The Logic of Statistical Inference*. Cambridge, UK: Cambridge University Press.

Hanson, Norwood Russell. 1958, 1972. *Patterns of Discovery*. Cambridge, UK Cambridge University Press.

Heelan, Patrick and Jay Schulkin. 1998. "Hermeneutical Philosophy and Pragmatism: A Philosophy of the Science," *Synthese* 115: 269–302.

Iacoboni, M. 1999. "Cortical Mechanisms of Human Imitation," *Science* 286: 2526–2528.

Jackson, P. L., and Jean Decety. 2004. "Motor Cognition," *Current Opinion in Neurobiology* 14: 259–263.

Jacob, Pierre, and Marc Jeannerod. 2003. *Ways of Seeing*. Oxford: Oxford University Press.

James, William. 1890, 1917. *The Principles of Psychology*. New York: Henry Holt.

James, William. 1907, 1969. *Pragmatism*. Cleveland: Meridian Books.

Jaspers, Karl. 1913, 1997. *General Psychopathology*. Baltimore, Md.: Johns Hopkins University Press.

Jeannerod, Marc. 1999. "To Act or Not to Act: Perspectives on the Representation of Action," *Quarterly Journal of Experimental Psychology* 52: 1–29.

Johnson, Mark. 2007. *The Meaning of the Body: Aesthetics of Human Understanding*. Chicago: University of Chicago Press.

Johnson-Laird, Philip Nicholas. 2001. "Mental Models and Deduction," *Trends in Cognitive Science* 5: 434–442.

Johnson-Laird, Philip Nicholas. 2002. "Peirce, Logic Diagrams, and the Elementary Operations of Reasoning," *Thinking and Reasoning* 8: 69–95.

Kagan, Jerome. 1984. *The Nature of the Child*. New York: Basic Books.

Kant, Immanuel. 1787, 1985. *Critique of Pure Reason*. New York: St. Martins Press.

Keil, Frank. 1979. *Semantic and Conceptual Development: An Ontological Perspective*. Cambridge, MA: Harvard University Press.

Keil, Frank, and Robert Wilson. 2000. *Explanation and Cognition*. Cambridge, MA: MIT Press.

Kripke, Saul. 1980. *Naming and Necessity*. Cambridge, MA: Harvard Universsity Press.

Lakoff, George, and Mark Johnson. 1999. *Philosophy in the Flesh: the Embodied Mind and Its Challenge to Western Thought*. New York: Basic Books.

Langer, Susanne. 1937. *Philosophy in a New Key*. Cambridge, MA: Harvard University Press.

Legerstee, M. 1992. "A Review of the Animate-Inanimate Distinction in Infancy: Implications for Models of Social and Cognitive Knowing," *Early Development and Parenting* 1: 57–67.

Lennox, James. 2001. *Aristotle's Philosophy of Biology*. Cambridge, UK: Cambridge University Press.

Leslie, Alan. 1987. "Pretense and Representation: the Origins of 'Theory of Mind'," *Psychological Review* 94: 412–426.

Malinowski, Bronislaw. 1948. *Magic, Science and Religion*. New York: Doubleday.

Mandler, Jean Matter. 2004. *The Foundations of Mind*. Oxford: Oxford University Press.

Martin, A. 2007. "The Representation of Object Concepts in the Brain," *Annual Review of Psychology* 58: 25–45.

Martin, A., and A. Caramazza. 2003. "Neuropsychological and Neuroimaging Perspectives on Conceptual Knowledge," *Cognitive Neuroscience* 30: 195–212.

Martin A., L. G. Ungerleider, and J. V. Haxby. 2000. "Category Specificity and the Brain," in *The New Cognitive Neurosciences*, ed. M. S. Gazzaniga. Cambridge, MA: MIT Press.

McGinn, Colin. 1997, 1999. *Ethics, Evil, and Fiction*. Oxford: Oxford University Press.

Mead, George Herbert. 1932, 1980. *The Philosophy of the Present*. Chicago: University of Chicago Press.

Mead, George Herbert. 1934, 1972. *Mind, Self and Society*. Chicago: University of Chicago Press.

Medin, Douglas, and Scott Atran. 1999. *Folkbiology*. Cambridge, MA: MIT Press.

Medin, Douglas, and Scott Atran. 2004. "The Native Mind: Biological Categorization and Reasoning in Development and Across Culture," *Psychological Review* 111: 960–983.

Meltzoff, Andrew. 2004. "The Case for Developmental Cognitive Science: Theories of People and Things," in *Theories of Infant Development*, ed. Gavin Bremmer and Alan Slater. Oxford: Blackwell.

Merleau-Ponty, Maurice. 1962, 1970. *The Phenomenology of Perception*. London: Routledge and Kegan Paul.

Mithen, Steven. 1996. *The Prehistory of the Mind: The Cognitive Origins of Art and Science*. London: Thames and Hudson.

Murphy, Gregory. 2002. *The Big Book of Concepts*. Cambridge, MA: MIT Press.

Neville, Robert Cummings. 1974. *The Cosmology of Freedom*. New Haven, Conn.: Yale University Press.

Nelissen, K., G. Luppino, W. Vanduffel, G. Rizzolatti, and G. A. Orban. 2005. "Observing Others: Multiple Action Representation in the Frontal Lobe," *Science* 310: 332–336.

Nussbaum, Martha. 2004. *Hiding from Humanity*. Princeton, N.J.: Princeton University Press.

Peirce, Charles Sanders. 1868, 1992. "Questions Concerning Certain Faculties Claimed for Man," in *The Essential Peirce, Vol. 1*. ed. Nathan Houser and Christian Kloesel. Bloomington: Indiana University Press.

Peirce, Charles Sanders. 1878. "Deduction, Induction and Hypothesis," *Popular Science and Monthly* 13: 470–482.

Peirce, Charles Sanders. 1883. *Studies in Logic by Members of the Johns Hopkins University*. Boston: Little Brown.

Peirce, Charles Sanders. 1892. "The Architecture of Theories," *The Monist* 1: 61–76.

Piaget, Jean. 1954. *The Construction of Reality in the Child*. New York: Basic Books.

Piaget, Jean. 1972. *The Child and Reality* trans. A. Rosin. New York: Penguin Books.

Piaget, Jean. 1971, 1975. *Biology and Knowledge*. Chicago: University of Chicago.

Pinker, Steven. 1994. *The Language Instinct*. New York: William Morrow.

Pinker, Steven. 1998. *How the Mind Works*. New York: W. W. Norton.

Premack. David. 1990. "The Infant's Theory of Self-Propelled Objects," *Cognition* 36: 1–16.

Premack, David, and Ann James Premack. 1983. *The Mind of the Ape*. New York: Norton Press.

Prinz, Jesse. 2004. *Gut Reactions*. Oxford: Oxford University Press.

Rozin, P. 1976. "The Evolution of Intelligence and Access to the Cognitive Unconscious," in *Progress in Psychobiology and Physiological Psychology*, ed. James Sprague and Alan Epstein. New York: Academic Press.

Rozin, P. 1998. "Evolution and Development of Brains and Cultures," in *Brain and Mind: Evolutionary Perspectives,* ed. Michael Gazzaniga and Jennifer Altman. Strassbourg, France: Human Frontiers Sciences Program.

Sabini, John, and Maury Silver. 1982. *Moralities of Everyday Life*. Oxford: Oxford University Press.

Sabini, John, and Jay Schulkin. 1994. "Biological Realism and Social Constructivism," *Journal for the Theory of Social Behavior* 224: 207–217.

Schulkin, Jay. 2004. *Bodily Sensibility: Intelligent Action*. Oxford: Oxford University Press.

Schutz, Alfred. 1932, 1967. *The Phenomenology of the Social World*, trans. George Walsh and Fredrick Lehnert. Evanston, Ill.: Northwestern University Press.

Simon, Herbert. 1982. *Models of Bounded Rationality*. Cambridge, MA: MIT Press.

Skrbina, David. 2005. *Panpsychism in the West*. Cambridge, MA: MIT Press.

Spelke, E. S., A. Phillips, and A. L. Woodward. 1995. "Infants' Knowledge of Object Motion and Human Action," in *Causal Cognition*, ed. Dan Sperber, David Premack, Ann James Premack. Oxford: Clarendon Press.

Sperber, Dan. 1975. *Rethinking Symbolism*. Cambridge, UK: Cambridge University Press.

Sperber, Dan. 1985. *On Anthropological Knowledge*. Cambridge, UK: Cambridge University Press.

Sterelny, Kim. 2003. *Thought in a Hostile World*. Oxford: Blackwell.

Tomasello, M., M. Carpenter, J. Call, T. Behne, and H. Moll. 2005. "Understanding and Sharing Intentions: The Origins of Cultural Cognition," *Behavioral and Brain Sciences* 28: 675-691.

Varela, Francisco, Evan Thompson, and Eleanor Rosch. 1991. *The Embodied Mind*. Cambridge, MA: MIT Press.

Warrington, E. K., and T. Shallice. 1984. "Category-Specific Semantic Impairment," *Brain* 107: 829–854.

Weissman, David. 2000. *A Social Ontology*. New Haven, Conn.: Yale University Press.

Wells, Gordon. 1999. *Dialogic Inquiry*. Cambridge, UK: Cambridge University Press.

Whitehead, Alfred North. 1927, 1953. *Symbolism*. New York: Macmillan Company.

Jay Schulkin
Departments of Physiology, Biophysics, and Neuroscience
Georgetown University
School of Medicine
Washington, DC 20007
United States

Contemporary Pragmatism
Vol. 5, No. 1 (June 2008), 79–108

Editions Rodopi
© 2008

C. S. Peirce, Antonio Damasio, and Embodied Cognition: A Contemporary Post-Darwinian Account of Feeling and Emotion in the 'Cognition Series'

Lara M. Trout

A post-Darwinian conception of feeling and emotion is necessary in order to better appreciate the embodied, personalized, and socialized nature of cognition in Peirce's late 1860's *Journal of Speculative Philosophy* "cognition series." Peirce *both* distinguishes between *and* renders synonymous the terms "feeling" and "emotion," a fruitful ambiguity that underscores how easily one's process of thinking can be influenced by idiosyncratic concerns. My reading of this series is a proactive one in which I employ the work of Antonio Damasio to highlight the implicit post-Darwinian embodiment themes in this series.

What might be called the affective themes of Charles Sanders Peirce's work are, taken collectively, a consistently neglected area of Peircean scholarship. This is despite the fact that feeling, emotion, sentiment, interest, agapic love, and sympathy all play significant roles throughout Peirce's corpus. Scholars who *do* undertake an investigation of affective themes, tend to do so from a perspective that overlooks the context of the human organism contending for survival against an external physical environment. In other words, there is often a neglect of the post-Darwinian evolutionary and embodiment themes that inform Peirce's writings.[1]

This neglect is understandable to the extent that Peirce himself often leaves these themes implicit, hence making them easy to overlook. Nonetheless, Peirce was a self-consciously post-Darwinian thinker who, while he preferred a Lamarckian evolutionary model, took seriously the embodied nature of human cognition. Drawing a connection between Peirce's ideas and the work of contemporary neuroscientist Antonio Damasio facilitates a proactively interpretive reading of the latent post-Darwinian thematic in Peirce's work. What follows is part of the larger project that thematizes Peircean affectivity, a term I give the following working definition, which is influenced by Damasio's work: *The on-*

going body-minded communication between the human organism and its individual, social, and external environments, for the promotion of survival and growth. This communication is shaped by biological, individual, semiotic, social, and other factors.[2] The examples of Peircean affectivity I focus on here are feeling, emotion, association, and habit.

A post-Darwinian conception of feeling and emotion is necessary in order to better appreciate the embodied, personalized, and socialized nature of cognition in Peirce's late 1860s *Journal of Speculative Philosophy* "cognition series." In this series, Peirce *both* distinguishes between *and* renders synonymous the terms "feeling" and "emotion," a fruitful ambiguity that underscores how easily one's process of thinking can be influenced by idiosyncratic concerns. My reading of this series is a proactive one in which I employ the work of Antonio Damasio to highlight the implicit post-Darwinian embodiment themes in this series. My aim is to reinforce Peirce's conviction that "to make single individuals absolute judges of truth is most pernicious," since an individual's flow of cognition is inescapably influenced by personalized and socialized interests (W2:212).[3]

I begin by showing how Peirce's account of feeling can be linked with Damasio's account of homeodynamics, that is, the on-going bodily motion that promotes an organism's survival through on-going environmental assessment. I then turn to Peirce's "cognition series," first highlighting his insight that we can *feel* that certain beliefs are indubitably certain, when they, in fact, reflect deep-seated personal and socialized beliefs/associations/habits. I highlight the fact that, for Peirce, beliefs are habits that, in turn, are associations of nerves. I thus use the terms "habit" and "association" synonymously. When I think it is contextually helpful to remind the reader that beliefs are habits (i.e. belief-habits), and habits are associations, I do so.

Next, I focus on Peirce's discussion of cognition, feeling, and emotion, in order to highlight post-Darwinian survival themes. These themes underscore the on-going assessment that humans make regarding the survival value of objects in their environment. I focus here on how Peirce *distinguishes between* feeling (as always accompanying the flow of thought, without necessarily disturbing thought's flow) and emotion (as not always present in the flow of thought, but disruptive to thought's flow when it is present). I also examine Peirce's statements about the "uselessness" of emotions and the affective nature of all human cognition. Finally, I explore the *blurring* between feeling and emotion, which occurs in "Some Consequences of Four Incapacities" in the context of Peirce's discussion of attention and habit-formation. He uses the term "emotion" to refer to the subtle affective coloring he also attributes to feeling. This blurring underscores the inescapability of personalized affectivity in human cognition and the fact that the thinking process can encounter subtle emotional disturbance at any time. This disturbance is due to the personalized and socialized semiotic nature of the associations (and thus habits) we each form based on our interactions with the external world. To highlight this point, I use examples of racist associations/habits that target people of color. Clearly our habits are not only *personally* shaped, based on our survival-interests as unique organisms. They are also shaped *socially*. Among the contributing factors to social-shaping are one's experiences of the socio-political aspects of reality, such as discrimination and privilege.

I conclude by underscoring the necessity of a communal pursuit of knowledge on Peirce's scheme, a pursuit that is informed by the Critical Common-sensist spirit, which acknowledges how easily our thoughts can be shaped by background beliefs that undermine reasonableness.

1. Peircean Feeling and the work of Antonio Damasio

In his 1866 Lowell Lectures Peirce says, "Feelings, we all know, depend upon the bodily organism. The blind man from birth has no such feelings as red, blue, or any other colour; and without any body at all, it is probable we should have no feelings at all...." (W1:495). Feelings are also *mind*-derived for Peirce. They are the felt dimension of cognition and the portal through which objects *outside* the human organism are rendered as cognitions or ideas *within* the organism (W2:227).[4] For Peirce, the basic point of contact between the human organism and the external world is "feeling" or "sensation," terms he uses synonymously in the "cognition series." In "Questions Concerning," for example, Peirce's notes,

> The pitch of a tone depends upon the rapidity of the succession of the vibrations which reach the ear. ... These impressions must exist previously to any tone; hence, the *sensation* of pitch is determined by previous cognitions. Nevertheless, this would never have been discovered by the mere contemplation of that *feeling*. (W2:197, emphasis mine)

This synonymous usage signals the inseparability of qualitative immediacy and environmental confrontation.[5] Feelings/sensations are continuously triggered by objects external to the human body, which stimulate nerve-firings in the sense organs. Feeling or sensation involves the grouping of nervous impulses (by means of hypothetic synthesis) such that a rudimentary sorting of things can occur – e.g. these red objects are different from those blue ones – or these are "pleasurable circumstances" and those are "painful" (W1:472, 495–496; W2:197ff). To have feelings requires *both* body and mind. An important point on this front is that Peirce attributes *bodily motion* to feelings. In "Some Consequences," he says, "There is some reason to think that, corresponding to every feeling within us, some motion takes place in our bodies" (W2:230). As I argue below, a post-Darwinian interpretation of this bodily motion clarifies the embodied, personalized, and socialized dimensions of Peircean cognition. Contemporary neuroscientist Antonio Damasio is a resource for rendering these post-Darwinian themes more explicit.

Damasio's work involves the scientific investigation of emotion and feeling in their relationship to the body and mind of the human organism. He operates from an evolutionary perspective that is sensitive to the embodied, instinctive, semiotic, and social dimensions of the human experience, which are inseparable from concerns for promoting the survival and flourishing of self and species. In what follows, I draw from his three books: *Descartes' Error: Emotion, Reason, and the Human Brain* (Damasio 1994), and *The Feeling of What Happens: Body and Emotion in the Making of Consciousness* (Damasio 1999), and *Looking for Spinoza: Joy, Sorrow, and the Feeling Brain* (Damasio 2003).[6] While Damasio does not specifically highlight and define the term "affectivity," he uses the phrase "process of affect" to refer to "the complex chain of events" that are involved in emotion and feeling (Damasio 2003, 27; cf. Damasio 1999, p. 342n10). He also applauds Spinoza's use of the Latin *affectus* as "'the modifications of the body, whereby the active power of the said body is increased or diminished, aided or constrained, and also the ideas of such modifications' (Spinoza, *The Ethics,* Part III)" (Damasio 2003, 301n3). I thus use the term "theory of affectivity" as a working description of Damasio's work in this context, with the proviso that his work is on-going and grows from book to book. Damasio himself notes, in fallibilist fashion, "I have a difficult time seeing scientific results, especially in neurobiology, as anything but provisional approximations, to be enjoyed for awhile and discarded as soon as better accounts become available" (Damasio 1994, xviii). Damasio's research is, nonetheless, aimed at formulating and testing his hypotheses scientifically, as he documents in each of his books.

The compatibilities between Damasio's work and Peirce's thought are striking.[7] While we should not force a point for point match between the two, Damasio's theory of affectivity sheds considerable light on affective themes in Peirce's thought, especially the implicit ones. My efforts in this article involve a selective treatment of Damasio's work as it pertains to my project.

1.1. Homeodynamics and survival

Damasio pairs human affectivity with homeostasis. The human organism is a "homeostasis machine" in constant body-mind interaction with its environment. Homeostasis refers to the *on-going* environmental assessment an organism undertakes to promote its own survival and well-being (Damasio 2003, 30–35). Damasio describes homeostasis in the following way:

> All living organisms from the humble amoeba to the human are born with devices designed to solve *automatically*, no proper reasoning required, the basic problems of life. Those problems are: finding sources of energy; incorporating and transforming energy; maintaining a chemical balance of the interior compatible with the life process; maintaining the organism's structure by repairing its wear and tear; and fending off

external agents of disease and physical injury. The single word homeostasis is convenient shorthand for the ensemble of regulations and the resulting state of regulated life. (Damasio 2003, 30, Damasio's emphasis)

Damasio suggests that homeo*dynamics* is a more apt term since it better suggests the constant activity of the body.[8] I agree with this suggestion and will, from this point forward, be using the term "homeodynamics" to convey the processes outlined in the above passage.

An organism depends, then, upon the homeodynamic regulation of its internal life-processes. Damasio's theory of affectivity starts with this biological truism. Human affect involves the on-going appraisal of internal and external environments, whereby changes in environment are detected. Any given change signals either a potential threat or boon to the organism's survival/flourishing. The organism then addresses "the problem" of either protecting itself from or capitalizing upon the situation at hand (Damasio 2003, 35–36). The changes and responses involved range from the subtle to obvious, and from microscopic to macroscopic, all part and parcel of the human organism's on-going homeo-dynamic assessment of the environment (ibid., 55–56).

Affective behaviors involve an evolutionary continuum which spans from the behavior of single-celled organisms[9] to the self-controlled behaviors of human organisms (ibid., 40ff, 51ff). They also involve stimuli occurring both outside the organism and within the organism. Internal stimuli, such as cues arising from hunger or hormones, contribute to the highly individualized interest(s) which characterize a human organism's intentionality towards the world (Damasio 2003, 39).[10] External stimuli, that is, the wide range of physical things and events that we encounter outside of our physical bodies, are filtered through personalized interest(s) as well. These dimensions of individuality will be discussed more fully below, where they are paired with human embodiment and uniqueness in the context of Peirce's discussions of cognition.

The lowest levels of homeodynamic/affective behaviors include the operation of the immune system, metabolism maintenance, and "basic reflexes" (Damasio 2003, 37). The next levels include "pleasure and pain behaviors," as well as drives (Damasio 2003, 32–34). These lower levels shade into the next higher level, which Damasio calls the "emotions-proper" (Damasio 2003, 38ff). Emotions-proper include what are conventionally considered emotions, like fear and sadness. Damasio notes that "emotions *in the broad sense*" is an appropriate classification of all homeodynamic activity up to and including emotions-proper (ibid., 35, my emphasis). If continued to its furthest human potential, affective behavior is accompanied by *feelings*, whereby the human is aware of the affect being experienced.[11] This awareness, in turn, allows for the planning of future actions, so that opportunities and obstacles can be anticipated (Damasio 2003, 51ff, 176ff; Damasio 1999, 284–285). The complexity of affective appraisal and response increases with the increasing complexity of the environment (ibid.).

The human brain and mind[12] are, from an evolutionary perspective, adaptations for survival and flourishing (Damasio 1994, 89–90).[13]

1.2. Feelings and representation

Damasio argues that feelings depend upon having a brain with the capacity to represent to itself what is going on in the body (Damasio 2003, 109). *Human* feelings involve a sophistication of representation whereby the brain is able to represent to itself *both* the body and the self (Damasio 1999, 279ff).[14] For the sake of clarity, henceforth I will use "feeling" to convey "human feeling." Feelings are signs, then, and they require a brain with semiotic capacity, to use Peircean vocabulary, and self-awareness. They allow us to feel our emotions (in the broad sense) – like thirst or sadness – and to be aware of these feelings.[15]

Given any affect, feelings occur based on the mapping (or representation) of the resultant bodily response in the somatosensory regions of the brain, namely the insula, SII, SI, and the cingulate cortex (Damasio 2003, 105ff). Damasio offers the following "hypothesis...in the form of a provisional definition": "a feeling is *the perception of a certain state of the body* along with the perception of a certain mode of thinking and of thoughts with certain themes" (Damasio 2003, 86, my emphasis).[16] The primary source of feelings is "the brain's body maps" (ibid., 85). The nature of feelings as *perceptions* is similar to Peirce's equation of feeling and sensation in his early writings, including the "cognition series." Note that Damasio highlights the reliance of feelings upon information about the body.

Feelings allow humans to register, for future reference, the survival value of objects in their environment. In fact, Damasio considers virtually all objects to be affectively salient for the human organism. This should come as no surprise, given that our homeodynamic balance requires our constant appraisal of objects in our environment for signs of benefit or danger. Thanks to human memory, the affective salience of encountered objects is recalled, becoming part of the information we 'take in' from the world regarding the objects we perceive, whether we are conscious of it or not (Damasio 1999, 47, 57–58):

> As far as I can fathom, few if any perceptions of any object or event, actually present or recalled from memory, are ever neutral in emotional terms. Through either innate design or by learning, we react to most, perhaps all, objects with emotions, however weak, and subsequent feelings, however feeble. (Damasio 2003, 93; cf. ibid. 309n3)

This feltness of objects resonates strongly with Peirce's work on the felt dimension of cognition and association in the "cognition series." Damasio helps to articulate the interweaving dimensions involved in the feltness of a sign, noting as he does that innate, individual, and social influences play crucial roles in an object's affective coloring (cf. Damasio 2003, 48–49). In what follows, for the sake of simplicity, I construe "object" broadly to refer to events, as well as "entities as diverse as a person, a place, a melody, a toothache, a state of bliss" (Damasio 1999, 9).

It should be noted that there is a subtle difference in the timing Peirce and Damasio each attributes to feeling and emotion. For Damasio, feelings follow immediately after emotions; feelings are neural representations of the bodily motions that occur in emotions (Damasio 2003, 28ff, 49ff, 64–65, 80, and Chapter Three, esp. 85–88 and 96–106). For Peirce, emotions in their paradigmatic form – where they "produc[e] large movements in the body" – occur immediately after feelings (W2:230). This is because they are based upon information conveyed by feelings, which will be discussed below. This difference between Damasio and Peirce does not diminish the parallels I draw in this article. For both Damasio and Peirce, a feeling and its corresponding emotion involve human homeodynamics.

2. Peirce's "Cognition Series"

2.1. Seeds of Critical Common-sensism

Peirce's mature doctrine of Critical Common-sensism (CCS), articulated in the 1900s, is foreshadowed in the late 1860s "cognition series." Peirce's "triangle dipped in water" metaphor, in "Questions Concerning Certain Faculties Claimed for Man," illustrates that there is no ultimate beginning to any of our cognitions (W2:210–211). Rather there is always-already a fund of previous cognitions (i.e. beliefs) that underlies any of our reasoning processes. Critical Common-sensism involves taking a critical attitude towards these grounding beliefs, to determine whether any of them can be doubted. The "cognition series" gives clues as to how personalized and socialized dimensions of experience can result in deep-seated belief-habits that reside in the fund of common-sense beliefs from which a person or community reasons. Such common-sense beliefs can function so automatically that we are not aware of them, that is, they can function *non-consciously*.

In "Questions Concerning," Peirce denies that humans have a Cartesian-style "intuition detector" faculty with which they can determine whether a given cognition is mediated or not (W2:193ff). He says,

> There is no evidence that we have this faculty, except that we seem to *feel* that we have it. But the weight of that testimony depends entirely on our being supposed to have the power of distinguishing in this feeling whether the feeling be *the result of education, old associations, etc.*, or whether it is an intuitive cognition.... (W2:194, emphasis mine)

The ability to make such a distinction, of course, assumes we have the very intuitive faculty in question (ibid). The remainder of discussion on this issue focuses on examples of cognitions that seem to be intuitive premises from which cognition may proceed but which, in fact, are themselves conclusions, or syntheses, which have brought about unity to a manifold in sensation or in thought (W2:195ff).

Of particular interest for my project is Peirce's point that our feelings may be "the result of education, old associations, etc." (W2:194). With this comment he makes room for both social influence (via education) and individual idiosyncrasy (via old associations) to influence our feelings. Moreover, since "old associations" are strongly influenced by social as well as individual factors, Peirce also sets the stage for personal uniqueness to arise within a social context.[17] In addition, he also notes that these modes of influence can be virtually undetectable, because the felt sense of indubitability corresponding to each is so strong. What seem to be unmediated intuitions are, in fact, the result of unnoticed processes:

> [J]ust as we are able to recognize our friends by certain appearances, although we cannot possibly say what those appearances are and are quite unconscious of any process of reasoning, so in any case when the reasoning is easy and natural to us, however complex may be the premises, they sink into insignificance and oblivion proportionately to the satisfactoriness of the theory based upon them. (W2:199)

Peirce has planted seeds of social critique here. The "indubitable" quality of some feelings can promote oppression by cultivating prejudice about oppressed groups in a society. For example, the following is taken from the personal correspondence of Louis Agassiz, the famous nineteenth century naturalist and proponent of polygenesis, the theory that human races are different species, each with its own origin (Gould 1981, 39):

> It was in Philadelphia that I first found myself in prolonged contact with negroes; all the domestics in my hotel were men of color. I can scarcely express to you the painful impression that I received, especially since *the feeling that they inspired in me* is contrary to all our ideas about the confraternity of the human type [*genre*] and the unique origin of our species. *But truth before all.* Nevertheless, I experienced pity at the sight of this degraded and degenerate race, and their lot inspired compassion in me in thinking that they are really men. Nonetheless, *it is impossible for me to repress the feeling that they are not of the same blood as us.* (quoted in Gould 1981, 44–45, emphasis mine)

In this passage, Agassiz appeals to the "truth" of "the feeling that [the 'negroes'] inspired in" him (ibid). The strength of his feeling is used to ground the "indubitability" of his prejudice. It also holds in place a personally idiosyncratic view of the world that is *at the same time* socio-politically informed. Agassiz's reaction to "negroes" reflects the personal idiosyncrasy of a man who had never before seen someone whose phenotype reflected African descent (ibid). A native of Switzerland, he had only just taken up residence in the United States. His reaction also illustrates the socio-political influence of the discussions of polygeny in nineteenth century United States, where the doctrine took root as a primarily American scientific theory (ibid., 42). Stephen Jay Gould notes that polygeny occurred within a Euro American scientific mainstream that took for granted the superiority of Caucasians (ibid., 30–42). In addition, Agassiz was more specifically influenced by the work of Samuel Morton, whose skull-measuring experiments (which are now considered unsound) supported Caucasian superiority and the inferiority of non-Caucasian races (Menand 2001, 103–105).[18] Thus Agassiz's exclusionary thinking is informed by *both* idiosyncratic and socio-political factors.

Let us now examine the personalized embodiment issues that shape the idiosyncrasy of one's associations, or habits. As socialized as one's encounters with the external world are, he or she can only encounter this world from the perspective of his or her body, so it makes sense to start there.

2.2. The Unique Human Body

Using our not-so-indubitable feelings as a starting point, recall that Peirce's references to feelings takes for granted that they occur in a body. Damasio provides a contemporary scientific validation of the linkage between feelings and the body by highlighting the connection between mind and nerve cells, a connection that Peirce made himself:

> [T]he mind arises from or in a brain situated within a body-proper with which it interacts; ... due to the mediation of the brain, the mind is grounded in the body-proper; ... the mind has prevailed in evolution because it helps maintain the body-proper; and...*the mind arises from or in biological tissue – nerve cells – that share the same characteristics that define other living tissues in the body-proper.* (Damasio 2003, 191, emphasis mine)[19]

If we are to appreciate fully the individualized dimension of associations/ habits, however, we cannot stop with the insight that mind implies body. We must emphasize that *my* mind implies *my* body. This point is implicit in Damasio's comment that an organism's body provides a boundary between it and the world outside:

> Life is carried out inside a boundary that defines a body. Life and the life urge exist inside a boundary, the selectively permeable wall that separates the internal environment from the external environment. The idea of organism revolves around the existence of that boundary. ... If there is no

boundary, there is no body, and if there is no body, there is no organism. Life needs a boundary. (Damasio 1999, 137)

My body encloses and includes the personal boundaries through which I interact with the external world. To simply discuss the body-*in-general* can eclipse the deeply individualized nature and perspective of human embodiment.[20] For all the shared types of homeodynamic functioning among humans, the bodily functions that promote life also take on individualized permutations. Regarding nutrition alone, food allergies, metabolic rate, and bodily chemicals (such as adrenaline and hormones) are some of the factors that individualize a person's nutritional needs and schedule. These factors are, in turn, influenced by external environmental factors such as the availability of food, difficulties in avoiding genetically and chemically treated foods, pressures to conform to a feminine or masculine body type, etc. In addition, men and women have different bodily experiences that are, in turn, individualized for each person: "Sexually differential biological processes – menstruation, pregnancy, child-birth, lactation, and sexual maturation in women and phallic maturation, paternity, emissions, and so on in men..." (Grosz 1993, 202).[21]

Another passage from Damasio puts a crowning touch on this personalized embodiment of mind. This is especially pertinent given Peirce's stress, in the present essay series, on cognition as an on-going semiotic process (W2:209ff, 223ff). Damasio says,

> I believe that the foundational images in the stream of mind are images of some kind of body event, whether the event happens in the depth of the body or in some specialized sensory device near its periphery. The basis for those foundational images is a collection of brain maps, that is, a collection of patterns of neuron activity and inactivity...in a variety of sensory regions. Those brain maps represent, comprehensively, the structure and state of the body at any given time. Some maps relate to the world within, the organism's interior. Other maps relate to the world outside, the physical world of objects that interact with the organism at specific regions of its shell. (Damasio 2003, 197)[22]

This passage illustrates the highly individualized nature of the ideas that flow through each human's mind. It also highlights the semiotic nature of the mind's relation to external objects. In order to survive, a human organism must be aware of the potential threat or benefit represented by objects in its vicinity. This awareness varies in its level of consciousness, but is ever-present. Recall the above discussion of the affective salience of virtually all objects. The external objects surrounding the individual are signs to the individual, and they affect her associations by virtue of the information they carry regarding her individualized experience with them. Colapietro addresses this point from a Peircean perspective: "we are in continuous dialogue with the natural world," so that we may effectively "*read* our potentially hazardous environment" (Colapietro 1989, 21, emphasis in original).

For Peirce this personalized information, that is, the affective salience of objects, is relayed through feelings and associations, which are part of the cognition process itself. His discussions in "Some Consequences" – of feeling, emotion, interest, and association – are particularly revelatory regarding homeo-dynamic-semiotic themes.

2.3. Peircean Homeodynamics

2.3.1. Cognition

Peirce describes cognition as an on-going semiotic process. It reflects the categories of experience, exhibiting three dimensions: material ("how it feels"), denotation (how it is connected to external objects and/or internal associations), and representation of an object (W2:227). "Thought" is used in two senses, first, as a synonym for cognition, and secondly as a cognition whose representative dimension is most prominent. In what follows, I will (for clarity) refer to thought only in this second sense, not as a synonym for cognition in general. Thought in this latter sense, of having a prominent representative dimension, designates a cognition that is connected to preceding cognitions by "a relation of reason," such that it has a "rational character" (W2:230–231).

Before discussing the other two dimensions of cognition, I want to place this description of thought firmly within a Peircean context, so as to more easily trace its trajectories. For Peirce, a "rational" or "reasoned" connection between cognitions draws on generalization(s) or aim(s) regarding human conduct and/or the other habits of the natural world. In the "cognition series," Peirce's focus is on grasping generalizations of nature that offer *explanations*. He describes this by contrast, "By there being no relation of reason to the determining thoughts, I mean that there is nothing in the content of the thought which explains why it should arise only on occasion of these determining thoughts" (W2:230). Humans' rationality is demonstrated in their grasp of the generalizations/habits of nature, which account for why things occur as they do (cf. W2:226, 229, 263–264, 272). For example, if one has the cognition, "That is thunder," it would be rational to have the subsequent cognition, "Maybe it will rain." The linkage of thunder and rain reflects generalizations about the natural world, namely the meteorological patterns that explain why thunder and rain are connected. It would probably *not* be rational to have the cognition, "That is thunder," followed by the subsequent cognition, "Rocks fall," because this connection does not reflect a generalization about the natural world that explains why "Rocks fall" is connected to a cognition about thunder.

Often connections that are rational are shared by others in one's community, but with a significant qualification. Others in one's community are likely to agree that thunder could lead to rain. In fact, when it comes to scientific inquiry into the workings of the natural and social world, communal verification of the regularities / generalizations / habits of nature is *required*, characterizing Peircean objectivity itself[23] (W2:270–271). Reality, on Peirce's scheme, exists outside of humans but cannot be described without human communities giving it voice. The linkage between "rational" and "communal agreement," however, needs to be temporarily suspended in contexts of creative insight. This qualification reflects Peirce's fallibilism, the view that knowledge is always open to future revision. The community that describes reality and often underwrites the rationality of cognition is, ultimately, "without definite limits, and capable of an indefinite increase of knowledge" (W2:239). It is an *ideal* community, which is "indefinitely" subject to future epistemological growth (ibid). An important source for this growth is the individual community member who has insight into generalities not (yet) grasped by the rest of the community. In this case, the individual is a source of creative hypotheses that can be tested scientifically and embraced to the extent they are verified. In these creative scenarios, the insightful individual her/himself is *rational* even though in disagreement with her/his community. Peirce himself models this maverick rationality in his *Monist* "cosmology series" of the 1890s, where he presents innovative scientific views that challenge the mechanistic cosmological models popular among his scientific peers.

In the present "cognition series," Peirce's focus is on rationality that *does* reflect communal agreement, with only subtle hints towards the maverick rationality that pushes a community towards epistemological growth.[24] Here his concern with the rational flow of thought implies a community that agrees on how reality works. Disturbances to the rational flow of cognition, i.e. disturbances to *thought's* flow, are rooted in the feelings that underwrite each cognition. These feelings, fueled by one's associations, can be the home of non-conscious prejudice.

Returning to the other two dimensions of cognition, denotation or "attention" refers to "the power by which [cognition] at one time is connected with and made to relate to [cognition] at another time" (W2:232). It is the dimension of cognition whereby old associations, which are habits, are brought to bear on the current flow of one's cognitions. For our cognitions not only relate to external objects, but also to our past experience with external objects. This will be discussed more fully below.

For Peirce associations/habits occur in one's nervous tissue and thus are embodied (ibid.). The actual *feel* of the nerve firings specific to each association/habit are what give cognition its felt aspect. The ideas in our respective minds literally have a feel to them. Often it is so subtle as to escape notice, but not always. For example, think about the police. This idea probably has a discernible feltness to you based on encounters you, or people you care about, have had with the police.[25] Let us examine more closely the role of feeling in cognition.

2.3.2. Feeling

In a passage leading up to a description of *emotions* as producing "large movements in the body," Peirce makes three important comments about *feeling*. Each of these comments supports a homeodynamic account of the human organism:

> There is some reason to think that, [1] corresponding to every feeling within us, some motion takes place in our bodies. [2] This property of the thought-sign, since it has no rational dependence upon the meaning of the sign, may be compared with what I have called the material quality of the sign; [3] but it differs from that latter inasmuch as it is not essentially necessary that it should be felt in order that there should be any thought-sign. (W2:230)

First, Peirce proposes that feelings involve bodily motion, i.e. "corresponding to every feeling within us, *some motion takes place in our bodies*" (ibid., my emphasis). Since feeling is one of the elements of cognition itself, and cognition is an ongoing process, this means that our bodies are always in motion and this motion corresponds, to some degree, to our cognition (W2:211, 223–224, 227). Second, Peirce notes that the feltness of a sign has "no rational dependence upon the meaning of the sign" (W2:230). This is compatible with the individualized, embodied reaction to an object, which serves as a sign to *my own* body-minded organism of its unique value to me, but not necessarily to anyone else. Think, for example, of your favorite childhood food. There is a *feel* to this object that is unique to you. My favorite food, for example, was macaroni and cheese. Some may argue that the feel of "macaroni and cheese" would be the same for anyone who also had this food as her or his childhood favorite. Feelings, for Peirce, are not that simple, however. The feel of macaroni and cheese *to me* involves my personal associations such as the kitchen of my childhood house, the plastic bowl with my favorite cartoon character on it, and my stirring in extra milk into my helping to achieve that "just right" texture. This combination of associations informing my feeling is mine alone, involving the uniqueness of my embodied experience of the world. As I will continue to demonstrate below, the felt dimension of cognition lends uniqueness to *all* cognitions, even those that seem to evoke no bodily response. This brings us to the next point regarding the above passage.

Third, Peirce says that "it is not essentially necessary that [the bodily motion] should be *felt* in order that there should be any thought-sign" (ibid., my emphasis). What Peirce seems to suggest here is that it is not necessary that the bodily-motion aspect of a thought-sign be *noticed* in order that there should be any thought-sign. For example, "The sky is blue," is unlikely to trigger a noticeable bodily response for most adults. Peirce notes that this felt dimension is less "prominent" compared to the felt-ness of other types of cognitions, such as emotions and "sensations proper"[26] (ibid.). This is because the "relation of reason" between the thought and other cognitions "detracts from the attention given to the mere feeling" (ibid). This supports my interpretation of the third point highlighted in the above passage. Our thoughts have a felt dimension, but it is inconspicuous, so as to easily escape notice.

Damasio notes that the work done by the body to maintain its homeodynamic balance is often unnoticed by the human organism. He notes, "The background state of the body is monitored continuously" (Damasio 1994, 153). This is the quiet humming of homeodynamics, and it results in "background feelings," (ibid., 150–153). Background feelings are so named, because the organism's focus at any given time is usually turned outward:

> But the fact that our focus of attention is usually elsewhere, where it is most needed for adaptive behavior, does not mean the body representation [i.e. feeling] is absent, as you can easily confirm when the sudden onset of pain or minor discomfort shifts the focus back to it. The background body sense is continuous, although one may hardly notice it, since it represents not a specific part of anything in the body but rather an overall state of most everything in it. (Damasio 1994, 152)

In the same passage we are examining, Peirce describes feeling/sensation in a manner compatible with Damasio's background feeling, despite Peirce's antiquated physiological account:

> In the case of a [feeling or] sensation, the manifold of impressions which precede and determine it are not of a kind, the bodily motion corresponding to which comes from any large ganglion or from the brain, and probably for this reason the [feeling or] sensation produces *no great commotion in the bodily organism*; and the [feeling or] sensation itself is not a thought [i.e. cognition in general sense] which has a very strong influence upon the current of thought [i.e. cognition whose representative dimension is prominent] except by virtue of the information it may serve to afford. (W2:230, emphasis mine)

Note that Peirce says, "the [feeling or] sensation itself is not a thought which has a very strong influence upon the current of thought *except by virtue of the information it may serve to afford*" (ibid., my emphasis). This is a significant qualification, as it bookmarks (with little elaboration) the possible influence of feeling on thought. I will demonstrate below that this influence is broader than it seems at first blush, since Peirce does not maintain the sharp distinction between feeling and emotion outlined at this point in "Some Consequences." For now, however, let us examine how Peirce *does* distinguish between feeling and emotion.

Peirce says that the process of cognition has an embodied element of feeling or sensation. This element usually stays in the background, but may impact the flow of cognition if the information it carries requires a disruption. If Peirce wanted to be more reader-friendly at this point, he might have reminded us that, for all our powers of cognition, humans are still animal organisms whose survival is not guaranteed. Humans need food, shelter, etc., and live in a complex environment that must be successfully navigated in order to secure individual and species survival. However sophisticated self-control becomes, it is still rooted in the physical survival of the human organism. When the information conveyed by feelings is of a disruptive nature, the affective state of *emotion* is triggered.

2.3.3. Emotion

Contrasting emotion to feeling/sensation, Peirce says,

> An emotion, on the other hand, comes much later in the development of thought – I mean, further from the first beginning of the cognition of its object – and the thoughts which determine it already have motions corresponding to them in the brain, or the chief ganglion; consequently, it produces large movements in the body, and independently of its representative value, strongly affects the current of thought. (W2:230)

Peirce links emotion and instinct by specifically attributing animality and lack of self-control to the emotions. As he puts it,

> The animal motions to which I allude, are, in the first place and obviously, blushing, blenching, staring, smiling, scowling, pouting, laughing, weeping, sobbing, wriggling, flinching, trembling, being petrified, sighing, sniffing, shrugging, groaning, heartsinking, trepidation, swelling of the heart, etc., etc. To these may, perhaps, be added, in the second place, other more complicated actions, which nevertheless *spring from a direct impulse and not from deliberation*. (ibid., my emphasis)

Emotion is not an episode that "happens" to an otherwise static body. Rather, in its paradigmatic occurrences, such as someone flinching in fear, emotion arises in an organism whose homeodynamics require a more pronounced bodily response than usual, due to environmental conditions. Moreover, Peirce links emotion to *instinctive* survival mechanisms, which makes sense. Disruptions in homeodynamics significant enough to disturb the flow of thought (as emotions do) *should*, in some contexts, be accompanied by an uncontrolled instinctive response. In his later work Peirce readily admits that we should not trust "vitally important" matters to reason, due to its fallibility. The instinctive automatic response triggered by an emotion, then, need not be problematic. But it *can* be, which is Peirce's concern in the "cognition series."[27]

As survival-rich as emotions can be, in some contexts they can – to give additional socio-political examples – contribute to social injustice. Fear and anger can result in discrimination ranging from dirty looks, to hate crimes, to the courtroom. Legal scholar Patricia Williams notes, "[A]s long as they are not unlearned, the exclusionary power of free-floating emotions make their way into the gestalt of prosecutorial and jury disposition and into what the law sees as a crime, sees as relevant, justified, provoked, or excusable" (Williams 1991, 67).

Peirce's description of the bodily commotion involved in emotion goes beyond the above list of specific "animal motions," to include "other more complicated actions, which nevertheless *spring from a direct impulse and not from deliberation*" (W2:230, emphasis mine). These other actions, I would argue, include socially-derived prejudices, such as racism, that can manifest through an emotional response to an object or a person, a response that could be either conscious or non-conscious. For an example of a conscious racist response, Williams had the following experience in 1986, after buzzer systems had been installed in many New York City stores, as a crime prevention measure. (The basic idea was to deny entry to suspicious looking people during business hours, without denying access to upstanding customers.) Williams writes,

> I was shopping in Soho and saw in a store window a sweater that I wanted to buy for my mother. I pressed my round brown face to the window and my finger to the buzzer, seeking admittance. A narrow-eyed, white teenager wearing running shoes and feasting on bubble gum glared out, evaluating me for signs that would pit me against the limits of his social understanding. After about five seconds, he mouthed 'We're closed,' and blew pink rubber at me. It was two Saturdays before Christmas, at one o'clock in the afternoon; there were several white people in the store who appeared to be shopping for things for *their* mothers. (Williams 1991, 44–45, his emphasis)

While we cannot know with certainty the white store clerk's emotional state when denying Williams' entry into the store, arguably he was acting on an exclusionary emotional reaction to the color of her skin. Given the time of day (1:00pm) and the fact that white people were shopping in the store when Williams pressed the buzzer to seek entrance, the store was clearly open, thus his telling Williams, "We're closed," was not a rational response (ibid.). This response did seem to be *conscious*, however, given these contextual details.

On the non-conscious front, neural scientist Joseph LeDoux notes,

> [E]motions, attitudes, goals, and intentions can be activated *without awareness*, and ... these can influence the way people think about and act

in social situations. For example, physical features (like skin color or hair length) are enough to activate racial or gender stereotypes, regardless of whether the person possessing the feature expresses any of the behavioral characteristics of the stereotype. This kind of *automatic activation of attitudes* occurs in a variety of different situations and appears to constitute *our first reaction to a person.* And once activated, these attitudes can influence the way we then treat the person, and can even have influences over our behavior in other situations. (LeDoux 1996, 61–2, emphasis mine)[28]

These examples indicate that emotional responses can be both complex and impulsive, overtaking the inclusiveness of reasonable behavior. Peirce's attunement to the subtlety with which this emotional take-over can occur is reflected in his ultimate blurring between emotion and feeling, which he introduces later in "Some Consequences."

2.4. Contextualizing the "uselessness" of emotions

In "Questions Concerning," Peirce asserts the idiosyncratic dimension of emotions:

> [A]ny emotion is a predication concerning some object, and the chief difference between this and an objective intellectual judgment is that while the latter is relative to human nature or to mind in general, the former is relative to the particular circumstances and disposition of a particular man at a particular time. (W2:206)

Recall the above description of thought, as a cognition that is connected to preceding cognitions rationally or reasonably. Peirce's reference to an "objective intellectual judgment" is based on the same idea, such that "intellectual" is synonymous with "rational" and "reasonable" in this context. An "intellectual" judgment draws on generalizations/habits of the natural world or human conduct and thus offers explanation regarding the object (cf. W2:226–227, 229). And others would agree with this judgment, such that it is "objective." An emotion is *not* focused on generalizations that others would agree with, but is uniquely individual, "relative to the particular circumstances and disposition of a particular man at a particular time" (W2:206).

The apparent worthlessness of an emotion's idiosyncratic connection to the cognitions that precede it is asserted in the next essay, "Some Consequences,"

> That which makes us look upon the emotions more as affections of self than other cognitions, is that we have found them more dependent upon our accidental situation at the moment than other cognitions; but that is

only to say that *they are cognitions too narrow to be useful.* The emotions, as a little observation will show, arise when our attention is strongly drawn to complex and inconceivable circumstances. (W2:229, my emphasis)

Peirce, I would argue, is not trying to deny the usefulness of the emotions in so far as they promote the human organism's survival in the present. The two passages just quoted imply that emotions are compatible with the homeodynamics of the human organism. Peirce says that emotions are "relative to the particular circumstances and disposition of a particular man at a particular time" and are "more dependent upon our accidental situation at the moment than other cognitions" (W2:206, 229). I think Peirce is aware that we need, at times, privately tailored emotions to protect the well-being of our bodies. "Complex and inconceivable circumstances" can be dangerous and thus may call for tailored emotional responses, to ensure survival, even and especially if an intellectual judgment is not ready to hand (W2:229).

His exaggerated wording in this context (namely that emotions "are cognitions too narrow to be useful") stresses a *logical* point, which is made in the third and final essay, "Grounds of Validity of the Laws of Logic." In "Grounds," Peirce argues for taking a socialized stance in our reasonings, when we *do* have time to deliberate. Ever the logician of science, he aspires after a communal pursuit of truth and reality. From the standpoint of science, he cannot abide the self-centered immaturity of emotions or any other type of cognition that excludes the perspectives of others. This brings us to another important affectivity issue.

2.5. *All* cognitions are affections of the self

Peirce explicitly acknowledges the affectivity characterizing *all* cognitions, including thoughts. This should not come as a surprise, since feeling is the material dimension of any thought. It is still a point worth highlighting, in order to more easily trace its implications in conjunction with the semiotic nature of human experience, and Peirce's theory of association. The following passage from "Some Consequences," was cited above. I include it again with different emphases:

That which makes us look upon the emotions more as affections of self *than other cognitions*, is that we have found them more dependent upon our accidental situation at the moment *than other cognitions*; but that is only to say that they are cognitions too narrow to be useful. (W2:229, emphasis mine)

This passage implies that thoughts are "affections of the self" (although less so than emotions are), and that thoughts are "dependent upon our accidental situation at the moment" (although less so than emotions are) (ibid.). Peirce says, as noted above, that a thought differs from an emotion because its material quality, or feltness, falls into the background, because attention is focused on the rational relation between the present thought and the cognitions which determine it (W2:230). Nonetheless, our thoughts *are* personalized, reflecting the idiosyncracies of our embodiment at the moment, our surrounding environments, and our unique associations.

Peirce's eventual blurring of the distinction between feeling and emotion underscores the affective dimension of all cognition, such that emotions are not the only cognitions that are too idiosyncratic to be of use logically. This blurring occurs in the context of Peirce's examination of the denotative aspect of cognition, where the affective-semiotic character of human experience comes more clearly into focus.

2.6. Affective-Semiotic Experience: Attention, Association, Habit

Attention, or the denotative aspect of cognition, is affective, reflecting on-going communication between the human organism and the external world. All thoughts are affections of the self due to the personalized associations that each person has with the objects in her world. We do not simply represent external objects to ourselves; we also represent our *experience* with these objects. Thus, objects are signs for us *privately* in addition to being signs in public senses, that is, regarding meanings shared with others in our community. Red licorice, for example, is a sign for me of my brother (because it is his favorite candy), in addition to its other more public meanings (as, say, a type of candy of a particular color).

The formation of "nervous associations" ("associations" for short) is made possible by *attention*, which Peirce describes as "the power by which thought at one time is connected with and made to relate to thought at another time" (W2:232). Attention allows us to focus on particular objects in our world and to "produc[e] an effect upon memory," which is a habit or association (ibid.). Attention not only creates new associations/habits to guide our future behavior, it also draws on past associations/habits to guide our present behavior. Peirce gives the following description of habit-formation:

> A habit arises, when, having had the sensation [or feeling] of performing a certain act, *m*, on several occasions *a, b, c,* we come to do it upon every occurrence of the general event, *l*, of which *a, b,* and *c* are special cases. That is to say, by the cognition that
> Every case of *a, b,* or *c,* is a case of *m*,
> is determined the cognition that
> Every case of *l* is a case of *m*. (W2:232)

Peirce is talking about the felt regularity, the "groove," that we fall into when we perform or avoid a particular action on numerous occasions. When I was a teenager, for example, I took up all-season, long-distance running. I learned that if I ran in cold weather, I would develop severe chills shortly after finishing. I also learned – the hard way – that I was very susceptible to illness, if I did not take a hot shower immediately after these runs. Mapping this onto Peirce's formula, the "sensation of performing a certain act, *m*, on several occasions *a, b, c*" involved the feltness of how effective the hot showers were after a few particular runs on particular occasions (ibid.). This feltness/sensation went significantly beyond the feel of hot water. It was the gestalt feeling/sensation that included the felt effectiveness of the shower for preventing illness.[29] This feltness/sensation led me to *generalize* that "running in the cold" – in other words, "the general event, *l*" – is a case of (and also a *sign* of) "needing to take a hot shower afterward" (ibid.). As a result, running in the cold has an affective-semiotic charge for me in this respect.

Attention allows us to track the regularities of our world, as I did regarding my bodily responses to weather conditions, so we can adjust our behavior accordingly. It shapes our memory, via habit-formation, regarding future behaviors (W2:232). Attention accomplishes its tracking by means of the information provided by feelings, which detail the success, or lack thereof, of our interactions with the external world.

Attention also guides present activity by *drawing upon* one's pre-existing habits, such as those that, to this day, help keep me healthy after I run in the cold. Thus attention allows us to continually form new habits, while also drawing upon old ones. My running example hints at the survival value of both paying attention and attention's relationship, via feelings, to habit/association and memory.

The running example, premised on *my own* body-temperature issues, also hints at the *personalized* associations/habits that attention produces, in addition to more conventional ones. Peirce focuses on these towards the end of "Some Consequences," and in the process, introduces a fruitful terminological ambiguity between feeling and emotion.[30] Recall that in "Questions Concerning," Peirce says that "old associations" may be factors which shape our *feelings* (W2:194). Here in "Some Consequences," Peirce briefly elaborates upon this issue, highlighting the semiotic dimension of human affectivity. Note the change from the term "feeling" to the term "emotion":

> Everything in which we take the least interest creates in us *its own particular emotion*, however slight this may be. This emotion is a sign and a predicate of the thing. Now, when a thing resembling this thing is presented to us, a similar *emotion* arises; hence, we immediately infer that the latter is like the former. (W2: 237, emphasis mine)

And,

All association is by signs. Everything has its subjective or emotional qualities... (W2:238).

Recall the red licorice-brother example. Also, I take "slight interest" in Kelly green Volkswagon "bugs," because they remind me of my childhood, as this was the kind of car my mother drove. This kind of car is a *sign* to me, representing not only rational ideas like, "these cars were popular in the United States in the 1970s." It is also a sign of mother-child love, thus having its own particular emotion *for me*. If my mother had only driven this car for one day during my childhood, I probably would not have a memory of it. The repeated exposure to my mother driving me around in this car, however, led to an association or habit, by which I learned to connect this type of car with my mother and the related feeling/emotion.

Peirce's change in terminology from feeling to emotion, I would argue, reflects his insight into the unique affectivity that characterizes the associations each person makes. He uses "emotion" in the above passages to convey a subtle affective resonance he earlier ascribed to "feeling." This blurring underscores the fact that objects have differing affective, that is, felt/emotional, resonances depending on one's personal and socially-mediated experience. Since my embodiment and homeodynamics are highly individualized, so are the affective semiotics that inform my associations. For example, some people associate airplanes with the pleasant, subtle feeling of convenient travel. Others associate airplanes with the unpleasant, not-so-subtle emotion of fear, say, of crashing or of a claustrophobia attack. We are, once again, reminded of Damasio's account of affectivity and homeodynamics, discussed above. All objects have a personalized affective salience for the human organism, who is constantly monitoring her environment to promote the survival of her unique body. Our survival is promoted through attention to external objects, in order to pursue those that promote our survival and to avoid those that threaten it. This, in turn, promotes planning for the future and optimizes creative decision-making.

2.7. Disturbances of Thought's Rational Flow

Now that Peirce's blurring between feeling and emotion has been addressed, we can explain how affective-semiotics can influence the flow of thought. Recall Peirce's comment that the information carried by feelings can influence the (rationally connected) flow of thought (W2:230). His discussion of attention and personalized association/habit are revelatory in this respect. As we have just seen, feeling and emotion can shade into one another, converging into a personalized affective salience that applies to the objects in our environment. Thus, the information conveyed by the (often backgrounded) felt dimension of cognition can trigger a personalized affective response that disturbs thought's rational flow. For example, I used to do grief counseling for college students who had had a family member die. Many of them reported that, in the months following their loss, they had trouble focusing consistently during lectures. Everything would be going fine during, say, a history lecture: note-taking, understanding, etc. Then the professor would refer to something associated with the loved one who had died – for example, she might mention France. As a result, the rational connectedness of the student's thought would be interrupted. France is associated with the loved one, and the felt dimension of "loved one" – the "information" conveyed by the feeling – would be intense grief. Students in scenarios like this would often experience a debilitating surge of emotion that would derail their formerly rational thought-flow.

This is not to imply that this affective response is *purely* personal; it reflects numerous social factors including the cultural norms shaping the relationship with the family member, as well as norms dictating the appropriate expression of grief for men and for women. In cases like the store clerk's prejudice against Williams, this point is especially clear. We cannot simply refer to "personalized" affectivity overriding rational thought flow. "Socialized" affectivity needs to be invoked as well. Racism against people of color in the United States is a bigger affective issue than merely the exclusionary habits of an individual here or there. Thus we need to invoke *"personalized/socialized* affectivity," regarding the unique affective-semiotic salience of the objects in our respective experiences. This is ultimately a Peircean reminder that the personal is inescapably socially-shaped.

The implications of Peirce's blurring of feeling and emotion are significant when juxtaposed with the rationality of thought. Let us re-examine the following points. (1) Peirce says that the felt dimension of cognition is always present, and it can disturb thought's rational flow depending on the information the feeling conveys (W2:230). (2) Emotion involves idiosyncratic responses to circumstances, as well as reactions that "spring from a direct impulse and not from deliberation" (W2:230). (3) Peirce does not maintain the sharp distinction between feeling and emotion that he establishes earlier in "Some Consequences." (4) Instead, he renders the terms synonymous, to an extent, by noting that the personalized associations we have with objects give subtle *emotional* coloring to these objects. (5) Peirce attributes to emotions idiosyncratic, as distinct from rational, connections between thoughts.

Therefore, blurring the distinction between feeling and emotion, introduces into the flow of cognition an ever-present idiosyncratic dimension, whereby the rational flow of thought can easily be disturbed by one's personalized and socially-shaped associations. Again, consider Agassiz's exclusionary reaction to African-Americans working in his hotel. His thinking process is clearly influenced by a personal, and socially-shaped, feeling that he found "impossible ... to repress" (quoted in Gould 1981, 45). This feeling resonates with Peirce's observation that anything that interests us "creates in us its own particular emotion" (W2:237). Agassiz's personalized/socialized affectivity disturbed the rational flow of his thinking process.

3. Conclusion

A post-Darwinian interpretation of feeling and emotion in the "cognition series," helps us see just how necessary, for Peirce, a communal approach to epistemology is. Individual thinkers, left to their own devices, can easily be influenced by prejudiced feelings that seem clear and distinct, but are really rooted in personalized/socialized exclusionary influences. Recall, in "Questions Concerning," Peirce's denial that humans have a faculty by which they can determine whether a particular cognition is or is not an intuition: "There is no evidence that we have this faculty, except that we seem to *feel* that we have it. But the weight of that testimony depends entirely on our being supposed to have the power of distinguishing in this feeling whether the feeling be *the result of education, old associations, etc.*, or whether it is an intuitive cognition..." (W2:194, emphasis mine). That we cannot make this distinction points to our need for *communal* inquiry into truth and knowledge. It also points to our need to be ever-vigilant Critical Common-sensists who are aware of how easily prejudices can impact the cognition process. If we are to successfully cultivate feeling and emotion through aesthetics and through the experimental practice of science, we must humbly acknowledge how easily growth-inhibiting interests can undermine these efforts.

ACKNOWLEDGEMENTS

I would like to thank Doug Anderson and Marcia Moen for comments on earlier drafts of this piece.

NOTES

1. See, for example, "Mimicking Foundationalism: on Sentiment and Self-Control" (Hookway 1993); *Truth, Rationality, and Pragmatism* (ibid. 2000); "Peirce on Philosophical Hope and Logical Sentiment" (Kemp-Pritchard 1981); "Peirce's Semiotic Theory of Emotion" (Savan 1981); "Cognition and Emotion in Peirce's Theory of Mental Activity" (Stephens 1981); "Noumenal Qualia: C.S. Peirce on Our Epistemic Access to Feelings" (ibid. 1985). Even studies of Peirce's account of the agapastic evolution of the universe (that is, evolution by means of agapic love) neglect post-Darwinian and embodiment themes. See, for example, "Eros and Agape in Creative Evolution: A Peircean Insight" (Hausman 1974), "Philosophy and Tragedy: The Flaw of Eros and the Triumph of Agape" (Hausman 1993), and "'Evolutionary Love' In Theory and Practice" (Ventimiglia 2001). Two notable exceptions regarding the embodiment theme in Peirce: Vincent Colapietro's *Peirce's Approach to the Self* (Colapietro 1989, 69ff), and Marcia Moen's "Peirce's Pragmatism as a Resource for Feminism," (Moen 1991, 438–443).
2. My use of the term resonates with the *Oxford English Dictionary* (OED) definition of "affectivity," as "emotional susceptibility," while it also specifies an on-going body-mind-environmental interaction that informs this "emotional susceptibility" (Oxford 2004, "affectivity, *psychol.*" p. 1). According to the OED, "affectivity" is

derived from "affective," an adjective strongly associated with the emotions (ibid.). Definitions of "affective" include "[o]f or pertaining to the affections or emotions; emotional" and "[o]f, pertaining to, or characterized by feelings or affects" (ibid., "affectivity" p. 1, and "affective, *a.*" p. 2). The term "affect," is derived from the Latin *afficĕre* which means "to act upon, dispose, constitute" (ibid., "affect, n." p. 1).

3. *Writings of Charles S. Peirce, Volume 2*, page 212 (Peirce 1984–86). A note on subsequent citations of Peirce's work is in order. Hereafter references to the *Writings of Charles S. Peirce* conform to the standard notation "W," followed by the volume and page numbers. "W4:134" for example, signifies volume four of the *Writings*, page 134. References to the *Collected Papers* will use "CP" followed by the volume number, then paragraph number. For example, "CP 5.441" signifies volume 5 of the *Collected Papers*, paragraph 441 (Peirce, 1958–65). References to *The Essential Peirce, Volume One* will be referred to by EP1, followed by the page number (Peirce 1992a). Finally, references to *Reasoning and the Logic of Things* will be abbreviated RLT followed by the page number (Peirce 1992b).

4. The ideational dimension of feelings – by which a physical object can be made into a corresponding idea in my mind – is not fully present in Peirce's earlier writings, like the "cognition series." Its emergence can be seen in his 1890s *Monist* "cosmology series," where Peirce uses the terms "feeling" and "idea" synonymously. A passage from "The Architecture of Theories": "The one primary and fundamental law of mental action consists in a tendency to generalisation. *Feeling tends to spread*; connections between *feelings* awaken *feelings*; neighboring *feelings* become assimilated; *ideas* are apt to reproduce themselves. These are so many formulations of the one law of the growth of mind" (EP1 291, my emphasis). A passage from "The Law of Mind": "[T]here is but one law of mind, namely, that *ideas tend to spread* continuously and to affect certain others which stand to them in a peculiar relation of affectibility. In this spreading they lose intensity, and especially the power of affecting others, but gain generality and become welded with other *ideas*" (EP1 313, emphasis mine).

5. Viewed through the lens of Peirce's phenomenological categories, qualitative immediacy and environmental confrontation reflect firstness and secondness, respectively. Thirdness is present to the extent that feeling/sensation involves synthesis, which is reflected in the passage just quoted (W2:197). The presence of all three categories in this context reflects what, for Peirce, is the "phenomenological richness" of human experience (Moen 1991, 435).

6. I do not draw directly on Damasio's many research publications. Readers interested in citations for these articles will find them in the endnotes for each of his books.

7. Damasio does not seem to be familiar with Peirce's work. The only reference to Peirce I found in the three above books is a footnote citing, without elaboration on Peirce's ideas, the latter's "Spinoza's Ethic," from *The Nation* 59 (1894): 344–345, in which Peirce makes the point that "Spinoza's ideas are eminently ideas to affect human conduct...." (ibid.) (cited in *Looking for Spinoza*, 333–334n5). Damasio is, however, familiar with William James' work in psychology. He is also well-versed in philosophy and is deeply appreciative of the impact philosophy has on our worldviews. In *Descartes' Error* he offers an insightful and detailed critique of the Cartesian mind/body dualism, including its effect on the practice of medicine in the West (Damasio 1994, 247–252, 254–258). Peirce would approve of the spirit of this critique.

8. "The word homeodynamics is even more appropriate than homeostasis because it suggests the process of seeking an adjustment rather than a fixed point of balance" (Damasio 2003, 302n5). Damasio credits Steven Rose for coining this term (ibid).

9. "There is abundant evidence of 'emotional' reactions in simple organisms. Think of a lone paramecium, a simple unicellular organism, all body, no brain, no mind, swimming speedily away from a possible danger in a certain sector of its bath – maybe a poking needle, or too many vibrations.... Or the paramecium may be swimming speedily along a chemical gradient of nutrients toward the sector of the bath where it can have lunch. ... *The events I am describing in a brainless creature already contain the essence of the process of emotion that we humans have – detection of the presence of an object or event that recommends avoidance and evasion or endorsement and approach*" (Damasio 2003, 40–41, emphasis mine).

10. Damasio notes external vs. internal stimuli is a common way of distinguishing typical examples of emotion (e.g. happiness, sadness, anger, etc.) from, say, hunger or thirst (Damasio 2003, 35, 302n7).

11. This awareness characterizes *human* feelings, but not the feelings of all non-human animals. Technically speaking, following Damasio's account, there are two basic levels of feelings. First, there is the feltness of the bodily commotion itself. These types of feelings occur in many non-human animals. A scared squirrel, say, has feelings which correspond to its emotion. Second, there is the *awareness* of this feltness, or the *feeling* of a feeling. This awareness is found in humans, but is not likely to be found in all non-human animals. The scared squirrel is not likely to *know* it feels scared. To have this kind of feeling – that is, the feltness of "I am feeling scared" – there needs to be a "second-order" representation which brings together the first-order feelings (of the bodily commotion) and a sense of self (Damasio 1999, chap. 9: "Feeling Feelings," 279–285). Damasio explains this issue fully in his book *Feeling What Happens* (1999), but in his more recent *Looking for Spinoza* (2003) he leaves the issue to the side. It should be noted here that Peirce seems to use feeling in a sense that captures *both* of the level of feelings that Damasio distinguishes (feltness and awareness).

12. Damasio's conception of "mind" is narrower than Peirce's. For Damasio, it is due to the sophistication of their brains that humans have "mind," mind being a *process* by which they can "[form] neural representations which can become images, be manipulated in a process called thought, and eventually influence behavior by helping predict the future, plan accordingly, and choose the next action" (Damasio 1994, 90; cf. Damasio 1999, 337n7). For more on Damasio's treatment of "images" see Damasio 1999, 9, 317–323. Neural representations of objects and events in their environments allow humans to creatively adapt to environmental changes. Human behavior is thus shaped not only by the immediate presence of concrete objects and circumstances, such as experiencing a storm as it seriously damages one's shelter. Human behavior is also shaped by *representations*, which make thinking possible, whereby we can plan behavior without the concrete presence of the objects/circumstances in question, such as building more adequate shelter once the storm is over (cf. Damasio 1994, 89–91). For Peirce, on the other hand, "mind" is inclusive of Damasio's conception, but is much broader, referring to the characteristics of an organic system as contrasted with a purely mechanical one: feelings, reactions, and habit-taking (EP1 290–293). Mind is thus found everywhere in the organic Peircean cosmos (EP1 293, 297). As for what makes humans unique in contrast to other animals, it is the higher degrees of self-control they can achieve (CP 5.533–534).

13. The more basic affective/homeodynamic behaviors are nested within the higher forms (Damasio 2003, 37–38). Damasio stresses that evolution does not throw away the old as it brings in the new (Damasio 1994, xiii–xiv). The complexity of human feelings is not free-standing, but has roots in the most basic bodily processes. Moreover, homeodynamics does not consist of a "tidy" set of relations, such that a "simple linear hierarchy" could be established (Damasio 2003, 38). Damasio uses the metaphor of "a tall, messy tree with progressively higher and more elaborate branches coming off the main trunks and thus maintaining a two-way communication with their roots. The history of evolution is written all over that tree" (ibid.).

14. Ultimately for Damasio, representing the self to the brain in this context also involves signals from the body (Damasio 1999 154, 168–194).

15. Two counter examples: (1) Feeling without awareness: The squirrel cannot have awareness of its feeling, as noted above. (2) Awareness without feeling (inspired by Descartes' Sixth Meditation): If we related to our bodies merely as a captain does to her ship, we would have consciousness (i.e. awareness) of the workings of our ship, but we would not *feel* them. Human feelings as the final stage of Damasio's affective process include *both* awareness/consciousness *and* feltness of the homeodynamic processes occurring in our bodies.

16. Damasio's feeling-hypothesis has considerable experimental support (Damasio 2003, 86, 96–104, 106, 123). While evidence is strong that feelings are fundamentally based upon body maps originating in the brain's somatosensory regions, it is still not clear (as of 2003) just *how* these maps are translated into feelings (Damasio 2003, 88, 198).

17. Vincent Colapietro notes that in Peirce's scheme, "The self is distinguishable but not separable from others; *indeed, the identity of the self is constituted by its relations to others*" (Colapietro 1989, 73, emphasis mine).

18. Gould discusses Samuel Morton's work in *The Mismeasure of Man* (Gould 1981, 50–69). Morton hypothesized that racial superiority and inferiority could be determined by the size of human skulls. Gould argues that an assumption of the superiority of the Caucasian race non-consciously informed Morton's infamous skull-measuring experiments. Morton's work, the records of which Gould studied closely, was riddled with bad methodology that unduly favored Caucasian "superiority," yet this same work shows no intentional fraud. There was no evidence of cover up, despite the egregiously biased and ad hoc efforts to skew the results towards white superiority (Gould 1981, 54–69). Thus Morton himself provides an example of thinking that is shaped by exclusionary, and arguably non-conscious, socio-political associations.

19. With these remarks, Damasio explicitly pits himself against the modern conception of mind / body dualism (Damasio 2003, 187ff). The emergence of mind, Damasio argues, is grounded in representations made possible by different regions of the brain. In *The Feeling of What Happens*, Damasio suggests that human consciousness is the result of a triad of representations: organism, object, and their relationship (Damasio 1999). This presents a striking parallel to Peirce's conviction that the human is a (triadic) sign. It is beyond the scope of this project to pursue comparisons and contrasts between the two on this point.

20. Amélie Rorty reflects this sensitivity to individualized embodiment when she argues that the causes of a person's experience of an emotion should include personal genetic factors, that is, "a person's constitutional inheritance, the set of genetically fixed threshold sensitivities and patterns of response" (Rorty 1980, 105). Focusing too generally on human embodiment can also eclipse shared, socio-politically-informed

embodied experiences, such as discrimination and privilege, among individuals of the same race, sex, etc.

21. Grosz's list occurs in the context of a broader point than mine, as she highlights the socio-cultural meanings attached to these bodily functions for women and men (ibid.). Our projects are compatible, as the individualized bodily functions I detail here occur unavoidably within social meanings. See Grosz's "Bodies and Knowledges: Feminism and the Crisis of Reason" for an exploration of how the body matters epistemologically, as well as a detailed critique of Western canonical portrayals of reason as transcending bodily particularities to achieve neutral objectivity (ibid., 187–215).

22. Damasio references several of his own scientific publications on this front (Damasio 2003, n10; cf. A. Damasio and H. Damasio, 1994; Damasio, 1989a; Damasio 1989b). He is, however, careful to qualify that he is *not* claiming to know exactly how the images in question are made: "There is a major gap in our current understanding of how neural patterns become mental images. The presence in the brain of dynamic neural patterns (or maps) related to an object or event is a *necessary* but not sufficient basis to explain the mental images of the said object or event. We can describe neural patterns – with the tools of neuroanatomy, neurophysiology, and neurochemistry – and we can describe images with the tools of introspection. How we get from the former to the latter is known only in part" (Damasio 2003, 198, Damasio's emphasis).

23. Cf. CP 7.259, c.1900; CP 7.266, c.1900.

24. One such hint is his dismal-sounding parenthetical observation (in "Questions Concerning,") which concludes a description of the power of testimony on the individual. He notes that as a small child, one "begins to find that what these people about him say is the very best evidence of fact. So much so, that testimony is even a stronger mark of fact than *the facts themselves*, or rather than what must now be thought of as the *appearances* themselves. (I may remark, by the way, that this remains so through life; testimony will convince a man that he himself is mad.)" (W2:202, Peirce's emphasis). The danger of being convinced of one's madness hints at the possibility for the individual to be at odds with her community. This possibility grows, in the 1877 Logic of Science essay, "Fixation of Belief," into a celebration of the power of individuals to challenge their community: "[I]n the most priestridden states some individuals will be found who are raised above that condition. These men possess a wider sort of social feeling; they see that men in other countries and in other ages have held to very different doctrines from those which they themselves have been brought up to believe; and they cannot help seeing that it is the mere accident of their having been taught as they have, and of their having been surrounded with the manners and associations they have, that has caused them to believe as they do and not far differently" (W3: 251–252).

25. Donna Beegle, who writes on how to effectively advocate for those born into generational poverty, describes the feelings that those in poverty commonly have with concepts like "police" and "teachers": "Police – Often hurt the people we love. Act/feel like the 'enemy.' Unfriendly, out to get us, and should be avoided"; "Teachers – Feel/look like the 'enemy'..." (Beegle 2006, 37). Beegle's research begins from her own experience as someone born into generational poverty, who made her way from a GED, to an AA, to a BA, an MA, and finally a doctoral degree in Educational Leadership (ibid., 3–10).

26. Peirce does not clarify what he means by "sensations proper" in this context (W2:230). Presumably he is referring to sights, sounds, smells, tastes, and textures as cognitions in which the sense data itself is the prominent feature. These sensory cognitions are different than the feelings/sensations constituting the material dimension

of thought, since the bodily information of the feelings/sensation in this latter case is of a more general nature (that is, the body in general vs. a specific sense organ) and is much more subtle (ibid.).

27. In his later writings, Peirce explains that "instinct" can be broadly construed to reflect both in-born habits, as well as socialized ones. In a 1902 discussion of logic, he notes, "If I may be allowed to use the word 'habit,' without any implication as to the time or manner in which it took birth, so as to be equivalent to the corrected phrase 'habit or disposition,' that is, as some general principle working in a man's nature to determine how he will act, then an instinct, in the proper sense of the word, is an inherited habit, or in more accurate language, an inherited disposition. *But since it is difficult to make sure whether a habit is inherited or is due to infantile training and tradition, I shall ask leave to employ the word "instinct" to cover both cases*" (CP 2.170, my emphasis). Thus for Peirce, "instinct" can refer to both natural habits that have been determined from birth, like breathing, *and* socialized belief-habits, like belief-habits about race and sex. This broad construal of instinct is reflected in his synonymous uses of "instinct" and "sentiment," in contexts where he conveys the social-shaping of sentiment that occurs in society, such as his 1898 essay "Philosophy and the Conduct of Life" (RLT 110–111).

28. LeDoux cites studies done by social psychologist John Bargh (Bargh 1992, 1990).

29. It should not come as a surprise that the feeling/sensation in this case involves the synthesis of multiple factors, as one of the primary themes in "Questions Concerning," is the synthesis that informs our cognition, even though we are often unaware of this synthesis (W2:195ff, 199). Regarding feeling/sensation, Peirce gives the following example, which was quoted earlier, "The pitch of a tone depends upon the rapidity of the succession of the vibrations which reach the ear. ... These impressions must exist previously to any tone; hence, the *sensation* of pitch is determined by previous cognitions. Nevertheless, this would never have been discovered by the mere contemplation of that *feeling*" (W2:197, emphasis mine). The feeling itself, in other words, involves synthesis of a multiplicity, in this case, of "the succession of the vibrations" (ibid.).

30. Peirce makes a brief reference to these individualized connections as "association by resemblance," but does not elaborate on his use of this term in this context (W2:238). In his later writings, he describes associations by resemblance as those involving creative connections between ideas, in contrast to the connections merely provided by experience (cf. CP 7.392, 7.437 (c.1893); CP 4.157 (c.1897); CP 7.498 (c.1898)).

REFERENCES

Bargh, John. 1990. "Auto-motives: Preconscious Determinants of Social Interaction," in *Handbook of Motivation and Cognition*, ed. T. Higgins and R.M. Sorrentino (New York: Guilford), pp. 93–130.

Bargh, John. 1992. "Being Unaware of the Stimulus vs. Unaware of Its Interpretation: Why Subliminality Per Se Does Matter to Social Psychology," in *Perception Without Awareness*, ed. R. Bornstein and T. Pittman (New York: Guilford).

Beegle, Donna. 2006. *See Poverty ... Be the Difference!* Working Draft. Communication Across Barriers.

Colapietro, Vincent. 1989. *Peirce's Approach to the Self: A Semiotic Perspective on Human Subjectivity*. Albany: State University of New York Press.

Damasio, Antonio. 1989a. "Time-locked Multiregional Retroactivation: A Systems Level Proposal for the Neural Substrates of Recall and Recognition," *Cognition* 33: 25–62.

Damasio, Antonio. 1989b. "The Brain Binds Entities and Events by Multiregional Activation from Convergence Zones," *Neural Computation* 1: 123–132.

Damasio, Antonio. 1994. *Descartes Error: Emotion, Reason, and the Human Brain*. New York: Avon Books.

Damasio, Antonio. 1999. *The Feeling of What Happens: Body and Emotion in the Making of Consciousness*. New York: Harcourt.

Damasio, Antonio. 2003. *Looking for Spinoza: Joy, Sorrow, and the Feeling Brain*. New York: Harcourt.

Damasio, Antonio, and Hanna Damasio, 1994. "Cortical Systems for Retrieval of Concrete Knowledge: The Convergence Zone Framework," in *Large-Scale Neuronal Theories of the Brain*, ed. Christof Koch (Cambridge, MA: MIT Press), pp. 61–74.

Gould, Stephen Jay. 1981. "American Polygeny and Craniometry Before Darwin," in *The Mismeasure of Man* (New York: W.W. Norton), pp. 62–104.

Grosz, Elizabeth. 1993. "Bodies and Knowledges: Feminism and the Crisis of Reason," in *Feminist Epistemologies*, ed. Linda Alcoff and Elizabeth Potter (New York: Routledge), pp. 187–215.

Hausman, Carl. 1974. "Eros and Agape in Creative Evolution: A Peircean Insight." *Process Studies* 4: 11–25.

Hausman, Carl. 1993. "Philosophy and Tragedy: The Flaw of Eros and the Triumph of Agape," in *Tragedy and Philosophy*, ed. N. Georgopoulos (New York: St. Martin's Press), pp. 139–153.

Hookway, Christopher. 1993. "Mimicking Foundationalism: on Sentiment and Self-control," *European Journal of Philosophy* 1(2): 156–174.

Hookway, Christopher. 2000. *Truth, Rationality, and Pragmatism*. Oxford: Oxford University Press.

Kemp-Pritchard, Ilona. 1981. "Peirce on Philosophical Hope and Logical Sentiment," *Philosophy and Phenomenological Research* 42: 75–90.

LeDoux, Joseph. 1996. *The Emotional Brain*. New York: Simon and Schuster.

Moen, Marcia. 1991. "Peirce's Pragmatism as Resource for Feminism," *Transactions of the C.S. Peirce Society* 27: 435–450.

Oxford English Dictionary Online. 2004. Oxford University Press.

Peirce, Charles S. 1992a. *The Essential Peirce: Selected Philosophical Writings: Volume One (1867–1893)*, ed. N. Houser and C. Kloesel (Bloomington: Indiana University Press).

Peirce, Charles S. 1992b. *Reasoning and the Logic of Things*, ed. Kenneth Laine Ketner (Cambridge, MA: Harvard University Press).

Peirce, Charles S. 1984–86. *Writings of Charles S. Peirce: A Chronological Edition: Volumes 2–3*, ed. E. Moore, M. Fisch, C.W.J. Kloesel, et al. (Bloomington: Indiana University Press).

Peirce, Charles S. 1958–65. *Collected Papers of Charles Sanders Peirce*, ed. C. Hartshorne, P. Weiss, and A. Burks (Cambridge, MA: Harvard University Press).

Savan, David. 1981. "Peirce's Semiotic Theory of Emotion," *Graduate Studies at Texas Tech* 23: 319–334.

Stephens, G. Lynn. 1981. "Cognition and Emotion in Peirce's Theory of Mental Activity," *Transactions of the C. S. Peirce Society* 17: 131–140.

Stephens, G. Lynn. 1985. "Noumenal Qualia: C. S. Peirce on Our Epistemic Access to Feelings," *Transactions of the C.S. Peirce Society* 21: 95–108.

Ventimiglia, Michael. 2001. "'Evolutionary Love' in Theory and Practice." PhD dissertation (University Park: Pennsylvania State University).

Williams, Patricia J. 1991. *The Alchemy of Race and Rights.* Cambridge, MA: Harvard University Press.

Lara M. Trout
Assistant Professor of Philosophy
Philosophy Department
University of Portland
Buckley Center 135
5000 N Willamette Blvd.
Portland, OR 97203
United States

Contemporary Pragmatism
Vol. 5, No. 1 (June 2008), 109–119

Editions Rodopi
© 2008

Industry and Quiescence in the Aesthetic Appreciation of Nature

Rita Risser

Allen Carlson has argued that a science-based model of appreciation is most appropriate in the aesthetic appreciation of nature. While I find his model of appreciation coherent and valuable, I reject his argument that this model ought to be preferred to others, such as an emotion-based or a formalist model of appreciation. Carlson's rejection of these other models is exclusionary and runs counter to pragmatist ideals. I argue for an alternative model, one which accommodates both cognitive (e.g., science-based) and noncognitive (e.g., emotion-based and formalist) models of appreciation, which I call the aesthetic-attention model of appreciation.

1. Introduction

In the aesthetic appreciation of nature, one may take either a cognitive or a noncognitive approach. A cognitive approach is knowledge-based and emphasizes deliberate and considered appreciative responses. A noncognitive approach is not knowledge-based and emphasizes responses which simply arise as an awareness in the appreciator. Often it is assumed that the noncognitive model holds in the appreciation of nature. A flower just is, without much thought, found beautiful.

Allen Carlson has challenged this assumption.[1] He does not deny that one might have noncognitive, quiescent experiences of nature, but he thinks there is a better way to appreciate nature, one which is knowledge-based. In what follows I take issue with Carlson's argument. While I find his model of aesthetic appreciation coherent and valuable, I reject the claim that this model ought to be preferred to other, noncognitive, models.

I then argue for an alternative model, one which accommodates both cognitive and noncognitive bases for appreciation which I call the aesthetic-attention model of appreciation. I begin by showing how Carlson's model draws on John Dewey's aesthetics. I conclude by showing how Carlson's exclusionary position runs counter to broader pragmatist ideals.

2. Dewey's Aesthetics

In *Art as Experience* Dewey opens with a picture of human existence as a matter of thriving and flourishing within given environments.[2] The way in which humans go about such thriving and flourishing is by deliberately transforming these environments into progressively more satisfactory arrangements. Furthermore, this activity, when it is effective, is deeply satisfying. Human thriving, then, is a deliberate and creative undertaking which Dewey considered 'artistic'. The overall satisfaction one feels with the resolution of artistic activity, he called aesthetic experience. In short, Dewey's claim is that human thriving is *artistic* (deliberate and creative), and that there are moments of heightened *aesthetic* awareness of such activity.

In a mid-twentieth century commentary on Dewey, Milton Mayeroff argues that Dewey's picture of human thriving as fundamentally an affair of doing and making, where thinking is employed primarily to resolve problems, depicts humans as nothing more than problem-solving creatures.[3] This picture, Mayeroff thinks, neglects the "quiet dimension" of human existence.[4] Humans also have experiences which are not so frankly ends-oriented or cases of problem solving (even broadly construed). For example, humans have experiences which are simply a "... responsive passivity in allowing life to reveal itself and bring about a deepened awareness".[5] For Mayeroff, then, humans have distinct sorts of experiences, not all of them having to do with "... resolving practical difficulties ... [hence] surely it is unduly narrow to think of man primarily in terms of problem-solving activity".[6] Mayeroff thinks that a complete picture of human thriving and flourishing must also represent quiet experiences.

In a riposte to Mayeroff, Beatrice Zedler argues that Mayeroff has overlooked Dewey's proposal that there are moments in human thriving which involve a heightened (quiescent-like) awareness of one's achievements.[7] Human thriving is not aimless. It is ordered, cumulative, and directed toward a satisfying conclusion. This, Dewey referred to as an experience's consummate end – perhaps best understood as its just end. While consummate experience is organically connected to 'regular' experience, it is qualitatively distinct. It involves a heightened awareness of and pleasure in a problem well-solved. It is what counts, on Dewey's view, as an aesthetic experience. Moreover, Zedler thinks, consummate experience, wherein one grasps something in its "absorbing finality" and basks in the satisfaction of an effective solution, is very much like what Mayeroff calls a quiescent experience.[8]

Still, Mayeroff's concern remains: not *all* experiences are occasioned by active, deliberate problem-solving, since there are experiences which are wholly quiet. Finding quiescence only at the peaks of the problem-solving process is to miss his point that there may be experiences which are from beginning to end quiet experiences, such as a heightened awareness of something as its own end, and not as a consummate end to a problem well-solved. Moreover, these are genuine experiences, not just nascent or undeveloped experiences.

Mayeroff is correct that these sorts of experiences are not forefront in Dewey's picture of human thriving and flourishing. Perhaps this is because, at least in *Art as Experience*, Dewey was centrally concerned to show how *artistic* experience, i.e., deliberate and creative experience, is a model for human thriving. Dewey does, also, recognize the experience of delighting in the "qualitative immediacy" of an object or environment – this is the basic structure for what he considers aesthetic experience.[9] Still, Dewey focuses on showing how artistic experiences occasion such aesthetic experience, and not on how quiet experiences might be aesthetic experiences in themselves. Mayeroff maintains that Dewey's picture of human flourishing is incomplete as it does not sufficiently represent these sorts of experiences.

This debate between Dewey/Zedler and Mayeroff is an early form of a current debate in aesthetics between cognitivists and non-cognitivists about the aesthetic appreciation of nature. Problem-solving is knowledge-based, and, in contrast to quiescent experience it is deliberately and intently developed. In short, it is an industrious experience. Quiescent experience is not knowledge-based, it simply comes about as an awareness. Applying these models of experience to aesthetic appreciation there are: cognitive (knowledge-based, industrious) models of appreciation, and, noncognitive (quiescent) models of appreciation. A problem arises, however, in applying these models to the aesthetic appreciation of nature. It is hard to see how cognitive models are applicable in the appreciation of nature. What sort of problem is there to be unraveled or resolved in nature in order to aesthetically appreciate it? Indeed, is this the route to finding beauty in the natural world at all?

Allen Carlson thinks that it is and argues for a (Dewey-inspired) cognitive model of appreciation. Furthermore, he argues against noncognitive models as inappropriate. Carlson's cognitive model is coherent and valuable, however, echoing Mayeroff's concern regarding neglected aspects of experience, I reject Carlson's arguments against noncognitive models of appreciation. I will turn now to Carlson's model. I follow with two noncognitive models before proposing the aesthetic-attention model of appreciation which, I argue, accommodates both cognitive and noncognitive bases for appreciation.

3. Cognitive Models of Appreciation

Most basically, cognitive models of appreciation entail that knowledge and evaluation go hand in hand. More precisely, knowledge about *the kind* of thing being appreciated and its evaluation go hand in hand. It is easy to see how this is the case for artworks. If one reads a biography and then later learns that the work is actually a hoax, this will likely change one's evaluation of the work simply because it is now understood to be a different kind of work. Cognitive models of appreciation may also entail, more strongly, that a knowledge of the norms for the kind of object being appreciated and *proper* evaluation go hand in hand. For example, one must have some idea that a well researched biography is a good biography whereas a very poorly researched one is not, in order to arrive at an evaluation appropriate for biographies. Cognitivism, then, has two requirements. The basic requirement is that one must have some idea about the kind of object one is appreciating, for example, whether it is a biography or a hoax, in order for appreciation to be cogent. A stronger requirement is that one must also have knowledge of the norms for the kind of thing one is appreciating in order to arrive at its proper evaluation.

Applying cognitivism to the aesthetic appreciation of nature requires first that one have some idea about the kind of thing nature is. Carlson's view, roughly, is that nature is the pristine material world, and, this kind of thing is ordered and systematic.[10] Moreover, he argues, there is a proper and improper way to appreciate nature. Since science reveals the order and systems of nature to us, it also provides the norms for its appreciation. For example, scientific knowledge about semi-arid deserts supplies the norms for the correct appreciation of this sort of environment. Science tells us that this sort of environment ought to have ground-hugging, relatively sparse vegetation. It would be inappropriate, therefore, to wander through a semi-arid desert lamenting the lack of lush vegetation. Scientific cognitivism, then, is the view that the scientific knowledge (e.g., the geology, ecology, and so forth) of a given natural environment is the proper basis both for how it is understood and how it is evaluated.

It is possible to be a cognitivist about the aesthetic appreciation of nature without being a *scientific* cognitivist. Such a view is developed by Malcolm Budd.[11] He agrees with Carlson that nature must be appreciated for the kind of thing it is, or, as he puts it, nature must be appreciated *as* nature. However, he has a completely different view about the kind of thing nature is. Whereas Carlson advances a positive conception of nature (it is the ordered and systematic pristine material world), Budd advances a negative conception of nature: it is the opposite of art. For Budd, then, nature is simply 'not art'.

> ... the aesthetic appreciation of nature as nature, if it is to be true to what nature actually is, must be the aesthetic appreciation of nature *not* as an intentionally produced object (and so not as art).[12]

While Budd's view is cognitivist in that it entails nature be appreciated as the kind of thing it is (i.e., as not-art), he does not think that there are, furthermore, norms for the appropriate appreciation of this kind of thing. It is difficult to imagine what the norms could be for appreciating not-art. Indeed, if to appreciate art is, essentially, to appreciate it according to norms (e.g., biographies are well-researched things), then to appreciate something as not-art is to reject norms on principle. The upshot for Budd's view is that one is free to bring, or not, any knowledge and experience to bear on the aesthetic appreciation of nature, as long, that is, as one appreciates nature *as* nature, and not as art.

Nick Zangwill has pointed out that Carlson and Budd's cognitivist views are on a continuum.[13] Both are versions of what he calls the Qua thesis. They both claim that nature must be appreciated *as* nature but they differ about what this amounts to.

> According to the strong version [Carlson], we must subsume things under either the correct scientific or the correct common sense natural categories. We must appreciate a natural thing as the *particular kind of thing* it is. But all the weak Qua thesis [Budd] holds is that one need only appreciate a natural thing as *a* natural thing.[14]

Zangwill, however, questions if one really needs to always knowingly appreciate nature *as* nature. For example, he asks whether his appreciative response to the 'daintiness' of a polar bear swimming under water requires him to,

> ... consider the underwater-swimming polar bear as a beautiful living thing [Carlson's view] or a beautiful natural thing [Budd's view] or just a beautiful thing [Zangwill's view]. I think the last will do. It is a formally extraordinary phenomenon. ... It is ... a beautiful spectacle. It has a free, formal beauty.[15]

Certainly it is possible to appreciate nature as nature, but, noncognitive appreciation, wherein cognizance about the nature of nature is absent, is also possible.

4. Noncognitive Models of Appreciation

Characteristic of noncognitive models of appreciation is that they are not knowledge-based. Nor do they entail normative judging. An example of a noncognitive model of aesthetic appreciation, argued for by Noël Carroll, is the emotion-based model.[16] He argues that a basic way to appreciate nature, one which is not founded on specific knowledge or proper understanding, is to simply appreciate the natural world by being emotionally moved or aroused by it. As, for example, when one is moved by the grandeur of a water fall. For this, specific knowledge of the water fall is not required. Of course, emotional arousal has a cognitive dimension (using Dewey's lexicon, all experience is to some degree funded by other experiences, both perceptual and conceptual), but emotion-based appreciation is noncognitive in the sense that it does not flow from a knowledge of the kind of thing nature is, nor is it calculated according to scientific norms for that kind of thing.

Carroll does not claim that non-cognitivism is to be preferred to cognitivism in the appreciation of nature, rather, along the lines of Mayeroff, he simply argues for the possibility of distinctively noncognitive experiences of nature within the entirety of experience. Cognitivism does not cover every possible or valueable approach to appreciation. Whereas cognitive appreciation is arguably something like problem-solving, for example, requiring the un-covering of the order and systems of nature and calculating its value according to the norms for these systems; non-cognitivists do not try to understand or resolve anything. For example, on the emotion-based model one merely opens oneself to an environment and becomes immersed in "... a certain emotional state by attending to its aspects".[17] Or, as Mayeroff puts it, in quiescent experience there is "... not so much a question to be answered as an awareness to be felt."[18]

Formalism is another notable noncognitive model of appreciation. Formalists about the aesthetic appreciation of nature restrict appreciation to its directly perceptible or empirical properties. These will include very basic properties such as shape, color, or, sound. As well, depending upon how these basic properties are organized, they will serve as the basis for more complex formal properties such as verve or delicacy. However, even these more complex formal properties do not require knowledge of matters external to the object or environment. For example, they do not require a scientific understanding of the order and systems of a natural environment, one need only directly experience the environment in question.

Carlson rejects the notion that directly perceptible or empirical properties are a sufficient basis for the aesthetic appreciation of nature. For him, appreciation minimally requires a knowledge of the kind of thing being appreciated, and this is not gained by simply looking at the object or environment in question. Furthermore, following strong cognitivism, he thinks that proper appreciation proceeds according to norms. But, it is very difficult to establish norms for formal appreciation. One either delights in the delicacy of a polar bear swimming under water or one does not. For the cognitivist, the subjective freedom of both emotion-based and formal appreciation is not conducive to *proper* appreciation. If one wants more than subjective preference in the aesthetic appreciation of nature, if one wants objectively valid judgments, then, one is better off applying a norm-based model of appreciation such as the science-based model.

5. The Triviality of Quiescence

Not only are noncognitive responses irremediably subjective, Carlson continues, they are superficial.[19] They are not responses to nature as what it essentially is. Recall that for Carlson nature is the ordered and systematic pristine material world. He has a hard time seeing how emotional responses to, or a formal delight with, the pristine material world are responses to nature for the kind of thing that it is, namely, ordered and systematic. Since noncognitive responses are not directed toward nature's identifying aspects they fail to be deep or serious. Consider an example provided by cognitivist Glenn Parsons: while one might formally appreciate a bat's

... glittering or textured [skin] ... such properties are somewhat superficial ones, given that their appreciation involves no understanding of the sort of creatures that bats are.[20]

Carlson would agree, the appreciation of a non-specific display of texture does not go deep because it does not involve a knowledge or understanding of the underlying order and systems of the creature. Carlson sums up,

[a]ccording to scientific cognitivism, aesthetic appreciation of nature is possible without scientific knowledge, but it will not be fully appropriate – it will be superficial, mistaken or defective in some way.[21]

It is questionable, however, if only science gets at the deep and serious aspects of nature, that is, if only science can reveal the nature of nature.[22] For example, Carroll thinks that emotional responses get at a deep, primitive aspect of nature. He argues that emotions which are "bred in the bone" are as effective as science in revealing what is "naturally salient" in pristine nature.[23] Such evolutionary shaped dispositions to be emotionally aroused by pristine nature seem to be, if anything, a response to nature for what it is – just not knowingly so. Budd also observes, there is no reason to think that such responses are not deep, "... if depth of response is a matter of intensity and 'thoroughgoingness' of involvement."[24]

Formalism also gets at deep aspects of the natural world. In one sense, it gets at its interior or intrinsic aspects. In another sense, it gets at its nature as something which exists apart from the domain of art. This is Budd's argument. Formal appreciation gets at the nature of nature insofar as it entails the appreciation of nature as not-art. This is to appreciate nature with subjective freedom, and without norms for correctness. Even if formal appreciation is transferable to art appreciation, all this means is that at times artworks can be appreciated *as if* they were natural objects, which they are not, hence they require in addition to formal appreciation their own (norm-based) mode of appreciation *as art*. Formalism, like emotion-based responses to nature, are a response to nature for what it is – just not knowingly so.

My position is that all these bases, including, scientifically revealed order and systems, primitive emotions, and formal properties, get at germane aspects of nature. What is more important is that any given basis be taken up in the distinctively aesthetic appreciation of nature. I elaborate this point in the following section. In other words, no particular basis for appreciation is more or less appropriate in the appreciation of nature. As long as one is engaged in a genuine aesthetic response to nature, then, one is engaged in its 'proper' aesthetic appreciation. To exclude or marginalize certain bases for appreciation, as Carlson does, leaves the aesthetic appreciation of nature overall diminished.

Carlson would object, here, that a science-based model of appreciation also contributes to human flourishing by being in line with environmentalist goals.[25] A science-based model of appreciation provides a way to find value in un-scenic nature, that is, in nature which arouses no emotions and is formally unremarkable, but which might have environmental value. However, it must be possible to advance environmentalism on ethical and political grounds. That is, if we adopt a science-based aesthetics because we ought to value un-scenic nature, what is the argument for this 'ought'? If there is an argument for why we ought to value un-scenic nature (for example, because it has intrinsic or inherent value as pristine nature), then this is the better argument for advancing environmentalism. Carlson's model of appreciation provides a valuable alternative to traditional models of appreciation, especially those which are typically directed toward scenic nature. But, it does not trump these other models.

6. The Aesthetic-Attention Model of Appreciation

A question which can be put to both the non-cognitivist and the cognitivist is to ask how their respective models are specifically models of *aesthetic* appreciation. For example, how is an emotion-based response to nature a distinctively aesthetic response? Merely responding emotionally to the natural world, say with fright, is not necessarily to aesthetically appreciate it. As Budd points out,

> ... not every emotional response to nature ... [is] an aesthetic response, let alone an aesthetic response to nature as nature; and not only does he [Carroll] not provide an account of what makes a response an aesthetic response, some of his examples of emotional responses to nature are definitely not aesthetic responses.[26]

Carlson is equally doubtful that all noncognitive responses to nature are necessarily aesthetic responses. He thinks that some emotional responses to nature, as well as most responses of wonder, "... move beyond the realm of aesthetic appreciation altogether and into that of what might be termed the religious veneration of nature."[27]

Similarly, one might ask how a science-based appreciation of an environment is an aesthetic one. Merely evaluating natural environments according to scientific norms, for example, finding an environment to be an exemplary semi-arid desert, is not necessarily to aesthetically appreciate the desert. In both noncognitive and cognitive models of aesthetic appreciation what makes appreciation distinctively aesthetic is the heightened awareness of, and pleasure in, the object of appreciation – whether revealed by science, emotions, formal properties, and so forth. Consider again Parson's example of appreciating a bat. Science reveals bats to be fashioned or ordered, ingeniously, for "... the task of sonar emission and detection".[28] And, (he paraphrases Richard Dawkins) one may find this fashioning "exquisite".[29] Scientific knowledge is a necessary part of this response, but it is finding the fashioning of bats 'exquisite' which makes it an aesthetic response.

By heightened awareness I mean a disinterested awareness.[30] This is an awareness of the object of appreciation *itself*, or, *as such*. For example, if one appreciates a desert as a good site for a building project, this is not appreciating the natural environment as such, hence it does not count as the aesthetic appreciation of this environment. However, while a heightened or disinterested awareness must be of the object or environment itself, this awareness need not be directed by knowledge of the kind of object or environment in question. Awareness may be directed by other aspects of the object or environment as well. In other words, aesthetic appreciation may have a variety of bases, including: science, emotions, formal properties, and so on. As long as aesthetic appreciation is understood as a heightened awareness of and pleasure in the object of appreciation, then, any basis which precipitates or directs this aware- ness and pleasure is a legitimate basis for the aesthetic appreciation of nature. This model, which I call the aesthetic-attention model, fulfills the broadly pragmatic ideal of providing an ample, variously applicable model for the aesthetic appreciation of nature.

Admittedly, with this model the question of *appropriate* appreciation is sidelined. The emphasis is on what it takes for the response to be aesthetic, and not more specifically on the proper basis and direction for aesthetic appreciation. Also, this model is not specific to the appreciation *of nature*. With the aesthetic- attention model there is no requirement that nature be appreciated as a distinct kind of thing, not even as a natural thing. Certainly there is no requirement that it be knowingly appreciated as a distinct kind of thing. Of course, a heightened awareness of an object may be informed by knowledge of the kind of thing the object is, but on the aesthetic-attention model a cognitively informed awareness is neither necessary nor a key to proper appreciation, it is simply a matter of opting to attend knowingly to a certain kind of thing.

7. Conclusion

Carlson's (and Dewey's) view(s) propose the correct mental and affective core for what an aesthetic experience is: a heightened awareness of and pleasure in some object or environment. However, for Carlson an appropriate heightened awareness must be a cognitively informed awareness. I have pointed out problems with this.

To reprise Mayeroff's critique of Dewey, quiescence has a contribution to make to human flourishing. Carlson draws upon Dewey's picture of artistic experience for his cognitive model of appreciation, wherein aesthetic awareness and pleasure are occasioned by a problem well solved, or, on Carlson's interpre- tation, by nature 'well-revealed'. But why also reject that aesthetic awareness and pleasure may be occasioned by quiescent experiences such as being moved by nature or being delighted with its formal properties? Carlson's answer is that for a heightened awareness to be deep and serious, it must be a cognitively informed awareness. I have argued against this. Awareness and pleasure which are characteristically noncognitive may be deep and serious in their own way.

Some, for example Budd, find it problematic that Carlson's model of appreciation for *nature* draws upon a model of *artistic* appreciation. Even though Carlson argues against models of appreciation which over-emphasize scenic nature, or treat nature as if it were art (e.g., the picturesque model of appreciation), still, Carlson's own model of appreciation is, as Budd points out, art-related insofar as it is norm-based. I am not troubled by an overlap between art and nature appreciation because I think that the appreciation of nature is free, though, not as Budd argues that it is free of norms, rather, that it is free in terms of options of bases for appreciation, which may include norm-based apprecition.

It is not Carlson's model itself which I find problematic. It is, in fact, a very attractive model of appreciation. What is problematic is the claim that it is the best model. This is an exclusionary position which is in conflict with the flourishing of the aesthetic appreciation of nature. As Robert Stecker has commented, a view which rules out as inappropriate or incorrect an entire range of appreciative experiences "... would, in the absence of powerful arguments, be implausible."[31] While Carlson presents a coherent, inherently valuable model of appreciation, he does not provide powerful arguments against others. A position which embraces the science-based model is desirable. But, a position which accommodates other models as well is most plausible. This, I have argued, is provided by the aesthetic-attention model.

NOTES

1. Allen Carlson, "Appreciation and the Natural Environment," *Journal of Aesthetics and Art Criticism* 37 (1979), pp. 267–275.

2. John Dewey, *Art as Experience* (1934) (New York: Perigee Trade, 1959), pp. 20–34.

3. Milton Mayeroff, "A Neglected Aspect of Experience in Dewey's Philosophy," *Journal of Philosophy* 60 (1963), pp. 146–153, see p. 148.

4. *Ibid.*, p. 146.

5. *Ibid.*, p. 147.

6. *Ibid.*, p. 152.

7. Beatrice Zedler, "The Quiet Dimension of Experience: Dewey as Poet," *Modern Schoolman* 56 (1979), pp. 349–355.

8. *Ibid.*, p. 352.

9. Dewey, *Art as Experience*, pp. 35–57.

10. Allen Carlson, "Nature and Positive Aesthetics," *Environmental Ethics* 6 (1984), pp. 5–34.

11. Malcolm Budd, *The Aesthetic Appreciation of Nature: Essays on the Aesthetics of Nature* (Oxford: Oxford University Press, 2002).

12. *Ibid.*, p. 91.

13. Nick Zangwill, "Formal Natural Beauty," *Proceedings of the Aristotelian Society* 101 (2001), pp. 363–376.

14. *Ibid.*, p. 210.

15. *Ibid.*, p. 214.

16. Noël Carroll, "On Being Moved by Nature: Between Religion and Natural History," in *Landscape, Natural Beauty and the Arts*, ed. Salim Kemal and Ivan Gaskel (Cambridge: Cambridge University Press, 1993), pp. 244–266.

17. *Ibid.*, p. 245

18. Mayeroff, "A Neglected Aspect of Experience in Dewey's Philosophy," p. 147.

19. Allen Carlson, "New Formalism and the Appreciation of Nature," *Journal of Aesthetics and Art Criticism* 62 (2004), pp. 363–376.

20. Glenn Parsons, "Freedom and Objectivity in the Aesthetic Appreciation of Nature," *British Journal of Aesthetics* 46 (2006), pp. 17–37, see p. 34.

21. Allen Carlson, "Budd and Brady on the Aesthetics of Nature," *Philosophical Quarterly* 55 (2005), pp. 106–113, see p. 107.

22. The phrase, "the nature of nature" is borrowed from Patricia Matthews, "Scientific Knowledge and the Aesthetic Appreciation of Nature," *Journal of Aesthetics and Art Criticism* 60 (2002), pp. 37–48, see p. 47.

23. Carroll, "On Being Moved by Nature: Between Religion and Natural History," p. 252.

24. Budd, *The Aesthetic Appreciation of Nature*, p. 139.

25. See especially: Carlson, "New Formalism and the Appreciation of Nature," and, Carlson, "Budd and Brady on the Aesthetics of Nature."

26. Budd, *The Aesthetic Appreciation of Nature*, pp. 139–40.

27. Allen Carlson, "Hargrove, Positive Aesthetics, and Indifferent Creativity," *Philosophy and Geography* 5 (2002), pp. 224–234, see p. 227.

28. Parsons, "Freedom and Objectivity in the Aesthetic Appreciation of Nature," p. 35.

29. *Ibid.*, p. 35.

30. Dewey found the notion of disinterestedness questionable. It implies a hands off approach to aesthetic experience, which runs counter to the hands on nature of his aesthetics. However, disinterested (not uninterested) appreciation is congruent with his notion of aesthetic experience as the heightened awareness of and pleasure in the object of appreciation. Carlson is more open to the notion of disinterestedness. He finds some traditional applications of disinterestedness questionable, but he agrees that the notion of disinterestedness itself distinguishes appreciation as aesthetic at all (see Carlson, "Appreciation and the Natural Environment").

31. Robert Stecker, "The Correct and the Appropriate in the Appreciation of Nature," *British Journal of Aesthetics* 37 (1997), pp. 393–402, see p. 394.

Rita Risser
Sessional Lecturer
Philosophy Department
University of British Columbia, Okanagan
Kelowna, British Columbia
Canada

Contemporary Pragmatism
Vol. 5, No. 1 (June 2008), 121–146

Editions Rodopi
© 2008

Pragmatism and Social Ethics: An Intercultural and Phenomenological Approach

Lenart Skof

This article deals with some intercultural and phenomenological uses of pragmatist thought. In the first part, early methods of comparative philosophy are linked to James's radical empiricism. The second part analyses Dewey's social philosophy, interpreted from the inter-cultural perspective and linked to James's philosophy. The third part argues for an enlargement of the uses of Deweyan social thought in the broader intercultural contexts. Finally, the phenomenology of breath is introduced and proposed as the basis for a new pragmatist social ethics of solidarity.

> A conception of human life and of its prospects has taken over the world. It is the most powerful religion of humanity today... At its extreme limit, it is the visionary conviction ... that all men and women are bound together by an invisible circle of love.
>
> R. M. Unger[1]

1.

From a methodological and epistemological point of view, perhaps one of the greatest imaginable differences existing within twentieth century philosophical thought is that between pragmatism and intercultural philosophy. Pragmatism is a distinctively American philosophy and an integral part of the Western philosophical (and scientific) tradition. Intercultural philosophy is a (relatively) new mode of thinking related to critical philosophical movements of the twentieth century. They appear to represent two opposite sides of philosophical discourse and worldview – pragmatism, an essentially (and historically) 'ethnocentric' philosophy of Western culture, and intercultural philosophy as its most natural adversary and rival.[2]

However, from the perspective of their practical results and importance for contemporary thought, a different story can be seen to emerge about pragmatism *and* intercultural philosophy – one pregnant with implicit as well as explicit interpretative possibilities. In his paper "Pragmatism and East-Asian Thought," Richard Shusterman already pointed out many roots of pragmatism that extend to Asian thought: Ralph Waldo Emerson and William James drew directly from Asian sources (Upanishads, Yoga, Buddhism, Vedanta); while John Dewey, during his visits to Japan and China, was fascinated and influenced by their cultures.[3]

According to one of the leading American pragmatist philosophers Cornel West, Emerson can be viewed as a forerunner to the entire tradition of American pragmatism. Emerson disregarded the philosophy of his time and rejected its epistemological problems (the "quest for certainty" and "search for foundations").[4] Being a fervent (but practically oriented) "mystic," Emerson intuitively drew from various Western and Eastern sources (the latter being predominantly Vedic/Upanishadic) in conceptualizing his worldview. Because of the nature of his eclecticism it is impossible to conclude how much of each tradition has actually entered his "proto-pragmatist" thought, but clearly there is a link to Indian thought in his most important notions about the soul.[5] Emerson influenced Charles Peirce and William James,[6] and John Dewey described the Emersonian worldview in terms of a historical, "European," Hegelian thinking.

Within the intercultural philosophy, on the other hand, the comparative philosopher P. Masson-Oursel offers us some interesting insights that point to its relation to the tradition of classical American pragmatism. It was P. Deussen who strove to describe anew the history of world philosophy (in his major work *Allgemeine Geschichte der Philosophie,* 1894–1917). Deussen, as a Schopenhauerian, was still unable to evade a great, 'classical' and Europeanized philosophical synthesis of Plato, Kant and Vedanta.

It was therefore P. Masson-Oursel's *Comparative Philosophy* that methodologically established a new line of thought in philosophy.[7] Masson-Oursel was both a radical Hegelian historicist and a radical Comtean positivist thinker, in the sense of being committed to the observation of specific facts rather than dogmas.[8] As a historicist, he inductively took in his *science historique* "the facts of philosophy from history,"[9] and as a positivist, he was convinced that there is not a single historical fact of society or civilization, be it large or small, that could not be objectively analyzed or interpreted in a thoroughly scientifically positive, i.e. non-ethnocentric way – "for there is no society without some civilization."[10] This was an important *nouveauté* in philosophy, a rarity even, for it was unusual for social and cultural anthropological writings of that time to give so much emphasis to the thought of the 'Other' when dealing with non-European thinking. This was long before the emergence of (postcolonial) African philosophy, as well as before the rise of intercultural philosophy. Methodologically, however, Masson-Oursel's aim to construct a positive comparative philosophy is not entirely unproblematic.

Masson-Oursel's study is an example of positivist philosophical thinking – a scientific method "pragmatically" committed to hypotheses, its major feature being scientific probability. Although he was convinced that no fully objective and anti-ethnocentrical philosophy is possible ("We are obliged to take Europe as our point of departure because we can only comprehend our neighbor relatively to ourselves, even though we learn not to judge him by ourselves"[11]), his major work, in which he criticizes subjectivist approaches as prejudicial, nevertheless reveals him as ultimately unable to anticipate the phenomeno-logical or hermeneutical method of Heidegger, Gadamer and, of course, that of intercultural philosophy. For him as a historicist (and as we will see later, a "radical empiricist"), a given fact (*phénoméne*; or, a *certitude de fait*) is simply taken from history and defined as a pure object of his comparative method, which is the science of the observer's mind for him. He says:

> There is not, and cannot be, other than positive method of so dealing with spiritual phenomena that the instrument of research neither alters them nor allows them to escape: it is to take hold of the phenomena in themselves, and not to apprehend them in terms of something else, and to find out what it is that, when reciprocally confronted, they have, so to speak, to say in criticism of each other....[12]

Underpinned with his 'positive notion', i.e. method of analogy (a proportion: *A* is to *B* as *Y* is to *Z*, including their individual environments or contexts), the facts are therefore any 'phenomena' that, being taken from 'history', can be analyzed within the framework of his comparative method. The term 'analogy' does not refer to a hermeneutical consciousness but is rather suggestive of the fact that this process is devoid of absolute truth ("But there is no truth that is not relative"[13]), that our science of the mind is therefore always unavoidably relative.

This Masson-Oursel's approach clearly resembles R. A. Mall's contemporary theory of analogical hermeneutics.[14] Mall's endeavor to embark on a way toward a theory of an analogous hermeneutics and toward a theory of understanding in intercultural philosophy reveals signs of philosophical doubts about the nature of the hermeneutic method, while it clearly deconstructs Masson-Oursel's pre-hermeneutic goal to fashion comparative philosophy as a pure and universal positive science of analogy. In Mall's words: "Every herme-neutics, therefore, has its own culturally sedimented roots and cannot claim universal and unconditional acceptance."[15] Comparative philosophy has there-fore its first critic in intercultural philosophy. But in the segment where Masson-Oursel designates his science as "radical empiricism," a genuine pragmatist criticism can be brought into this debate. Moreover, this also bears some consequences for contemporary comparative and intercultural philo-sophy.[16]

In his *Essays on Radical Empiricism*, James probably presents us with one of the most intriguing theories in the history of philosophy. Resembling Bergson and having had a strong impact on classical Husserlian phenomen-ology, James's thought in a way was already "phenomenological," and I also see his thinking in terms of a possible link with contemporary comparative and intercultural philosophy.[17] It is through his distinctively Jamesian (and Deweyan) pragmatist notion of *experience* – a notion that is absent (although mentioned) in Masson-Oursel, and one that transcends any uncritical and naive conception of radical empiricism – that this link is forged. Within the ambit of radical empiricism, taken "as a certain type of *weltanschauung*,"[18] all experience is a process in time (in Whitehead's sense). Critical of all trans-experimental tendencies, James deconstructs consciousness. Influenced by Locke and Berkeley, he writes: "I believe that 'consciousness', when once it has evaporated to this state of pure diaphaneity, is on the point of disappearing altogether."[19]

James's notion of pure experience as the sole primal material or matter in the world, and his notion of knowing (i.e. 'stream of thought') as a relation between experiences, open up a radically new perspective. It is impossible to construct a pure positive science as proposed by Comte and Masson-Oursel, since our knowing (comparative-analogous or relational) as the process itself is always a relation between experiences. Taken 'hermeneutically', James's thought, in its empiricist sense, is in fact even more radical than Mall's: at the beginning of the process, there is no fusion of horizons (*Horizont-verschmelzung*) and nor is there any analogy in the initial stage of the temporal experiential process, for "[m]y experiences and your experiences are 'with' each other in various external ways, but mine pass into mine, and yours pass into yours in a way in which yours and mine never pass into one another."[20] With the notion of intersubjectivity, which opens up a world of experiences by entering into other contexts, our shared worlds are a series of intersections where different mental contexts meet. Intersubjectivity is thus a designation for this process within the 'mosaic philosophy' of pure experience.[21]

But is there a comparative-intercultural potential in this strain of Jamesian thought? Toward the end of his first essay ("Does 'Consciousness' Exist?"), in a reply to his (imaginary) dualist critics, James surprises the reader with the following elaboration:

> I cannot help that, however, for I, too, have my intuitions and must obey them. Let the case be what it may in others, I am as confident as I am of anything that, in myself, the stream of thinking (which I recognize emphatically as a phenomenon) is only a careless name for what, when scrutinized, reveals itself to consist chiefly of the stream of my breathing. The "I think" which Kant said must be able to accompany all my objects, is the "I breathe" which actually does accompany them. There are other internal facts besides breathing (intracephalic muscular adjustments, etc., of which I have said a word in my larger *Psychology*), and these increase the assets of "consciousness," so far as the latter is subject to immediate perception; but breath, which was ever the original of "spirit," breath moving outwards, between the glottis and the nostrils, is, I am persuaded, the essence out of which philosophers have constructed the entity known to them as consciousness.[22]

In this 'anthropological' confession, James comes close to some of the most important features of contemporary comparative and intercultural thinking.

Giving prominence to the universal and anti-metaphysical (and anti-representational) anthropological phenomenon of *breath*, his philosophy can be seen to contribute vitally to contemporary intercultural *and* phenomenological thought.

Breath is arguably the only anthropological constant for human beings of the world, carrying both epistemological and ethical implications. Different macrocosmic and microcosmic designations for wind/breath (or wind/spirit) in the history of religions and philosophies (*mana, orenda, ka, ruah, prana, atman, aer, psyche, pneuma, anima, spiritus, ik', ki/qi*,etc.) point to a common physico-anthropological phenomenon of life and, more importantly, to our common physiological roots, which are not conceived as a substance of *human nature* but as a primal phenomenon prior to any philosophical theory.[23]

In Indian Upanishadic thought, breath (designated as *prana*; having meanings of both cosmic breath and expiration) is the primary epistemological 'phenomenon' of Indian philosophy: it is in breath or *prana* that our life dwells and is sustained, and it is *prana* that precedes the 'mind' (*manas*) or 'consciousness' (*vijñana*). Upanishadic thought also introduces the Vedantic notion of *advaita* (Upanishadic: *neti–neti*), i.e. nonduality.[24]

Thus James's intuitive and fully anti-Kantian designation of "I breathe" as the basis of a nondualist radical empiricism is clearly also in line with the ancient pre-philosophical thought of India and Greece.[25] According to Ogawa, 'breath' has an intercultural potential, for "all humanity is aware of this phenomenon."[26] Be it 'qi/ki' as 'breath/expiration/inspiration', 'pneuma' or 'prana' etc., they all point to our human, common, *and* communal relatedness.

To take this argument as the "old metaphysical idea concerning the relation between microcosmos and macrocosmos ... is not correct."[27] As a phenomenological phenomenon, *breath* is related to the coexistence of world and I (Ogawa relates it to Heidegger's "mood" [*Stimmung*], Schmitz's "Atmosphere" and K. Held's "Fundamental Mood" [*Grundstimmung*]), thus overcoming the dualist-substantialist thought: "[T]hese phenomena preceding all other moments of the lifeworld ... make it possible for human beings to be in the world."[28] Apart from its implications for phenomenology, breath as a primal cosmological-biological phenomenon also precedes all ethical (and social/political) reflection: it is 'breath' that provides the human community with its first and primal *experience* and act of *communication* (both in the pragmatic sense), i.e. of the *being-in-the-world(-with-others)* mode.

The following sections on Dewey and his democratic community will now consider some intercultural and ethical implications and an interpretation of the epistemologico-ethical, phenomenological and pragmatic intuitions we have so far discussed in relation to James.

2.

In 1951, John Dewey, alongside Sarvepalli Radhakrishnan and George Santayana, wrote the very first page for the first volume of *Philosophy East and*

West. The theme of their common concern was "On Philosophical Synthesis." It was Dewey who enabled, with his pragmatist understanding of all subsequent notions of interculturality, the journal's first appearance on the global philosophical scene:

> I think that the most important function your journal can perform in bringing about the ultimate objective of a 'substantial synthesis of East and West' is to help break down the notion that there is such a thing as a 'West' and 'East' that have to be synthesized. ... Some of the elements in Western cultures and Eastern cultures are so closely allied that the problem of 'synthesizing' them does not exist when they are taken in isolation. But the point is that none of these elements – in the East or the West – is in isolation. They are all interwoven in a vast variety of ways in the historico-cultural process. The basic prerequisite for any fruitful development of inter-cultural relations – of which philosophy is simply one constituent part – is an understanding and appreciation of the complexities, differences, and ramifying interrelationships both within any given country and among the countries, East and West, whether taken separately or together.[29]

Against the backdrop of postwar political conditions and under pressures of the political *blocs* of his time, Dewey – in accordance with his idea of democracy – clearly indicated the socio-ethical significance of the emerging intercultural philosophy in helping to constitute a better world community. Still, it is not an overinterpretation of his original words and intentions to propose that Dewey's short contribution inaugurates something far more crucial for contemporary intercultural thinking. Since the beginnings of African and Latin-American philosophy, the old distinction between East and West has become obsolete as a fundamental intercultural dichotomy, to be recently replaced by the North-South or even South-South axis. It was Dewey with his lectures in China who opened up, already in the early 1920s, a new philosophical space, to be later inhabited by intercultural philosophy. On the other hand, and in line with James's radical empiricism as already presented above, it is Dewey's notion of experience that also bears important consequences for comparative and intercultural philosophy. My argument for Dewey and interculturality (and, later in this paper, Dewey and phenomenology) will therefore proceed along two avenues: the first being an argument for the role of Deweyan communal idea of democracy in intercultural contexts, and the second being an argument for a phenomenologico-intercultural reconstruction of 'experience' as a constitutive part on the path toward some new modes of future social ethics.

What Larry Hickman proposed for pragmatism and its radical alternative method could also be valid for pragmatism and intercultural philosophy. To use a metaphor (borrowed from James who took it from the Italian pragmatist Giovanni Papini), the pragmatic method (in the original sense proposed by

Pierce) is like a corridor in a hotel. In other words, the proposal would render cultural differences relative under the pragmatic method precisely because different philosophers (as well as theologians and many others, of course) would have this corridor in common – they would all have to pass through it in order to get in or out of their 'rooms'.[30] It is important to acknowledge at this point that James did not "anticipate of privilege any special result. A method was offered as a method only – a ticket to ride wherever the method went."[31] To put it in a pragmatist way: "[T]he meaning of a concept is the difference it will make within and for our future experience."[32] But from the perspective of our understanding of James's *Essays on Radical Empiricism* it is the Deweyan notion of experience as part of his *reconstructive* work in philosophy that deserves our attention.[33]

Dewey's experiential form of evolutionary naturalism, with its effects on the lives of individuals as members of a democratic community, is conceived as a movement toward new communities of hope. His communally oriented reconstruction of experience opens up a new horizon for our *being-in-the-world*. It is a proposal loaded with historicity and responsibility. But we have to return to James to be able to fully acknowledge Dewey's contribution: his substitution of 'I think' for 'I breathe' was the first step in the process of reconstructing our *being-in-the-world*. But Jamesian notion of intersubjecitivity was not originally designed to be used in 'contemporary' philosophico-political contexts. It is therefore inappropriate to accuse James of 'individualistic' thinking (as has commonly been done in evaluating his pragmatism) and point to a lack of solidaristic elements in his philosophy; it was simply Dewey's specific situation in the changing world of the first decades of the twentieth century that demanded a new, solidaristic form of thinking.[34] For Dewey, the ordinary lived experience is a fully human mode of living, both reacting to and interacting with our surroundings. For "knowledge does not derive from some asomatic 'reason' but from embodied 'intelligence'."[35] It is this *somatic*, embodied anti-Cartesian and anti-Kantian mode of *being-in-the-world(-with-others)* suggested by Dewey that both follows and enlarges James's notion of radical empiricism. As such, it presents a new mode for our communal being, also due to the fact that our compassion, practical responsibility and care are always *for specific* beings and not for some asomatic individuals, even when these individuals have been invested with universal human rights.

I am inclined to say that this marks the pragmatic movement in its entirety (including Rorty's neopragmatism, for example). Indeed, an analysis of experience as a mode of the interpenetration of our lives and the environment we live in proceeds from the elementary biological phenomena such as breathing, eating etc. which, when taken in their 'integrity' and seen as 'constitutive' of our ordinary lives, clearly point to some metaphysical consequences. However, to avoid justified criticism of Dewey's 'metaphysical' tendencies of this kind (see Rorty's *Consequences of Pragmatism*[36]), it is necessary to avoid any integrative analyses of experience (which, according to Santayana, are *contradictio in termini* anyway; in addition, Santayana believes that "every phase of the ideal world emanates from the natural"[37]) but rather return to the phenomenal and anthropological value of 'I breathe' as already mentioned in reference to the different cultural contexts above, deriving from it its rich ethico-solidaristic potential. It is Dewey's interconnective account of experience that should be enlarged and read interculturally. It is therefore precisely through Dewey's social philosophy and its intercultural potentials that we can refrain from any metaphysically burdened notion of 'experience', that is to say, from any metaphysical bias that may lie in it, and pragmatically engage with the pressing issues of contemporary social and political thought, taken inter-culturally from the perspective of – for our purpose – Latin American, African and Asian social philosophy (poverty, justice/loyalty/solidarity, the idea of democracy, freedom etc.). The same criterion that we find in Peirce's, James's and Dewey's versions of pragmatism can therefore be used for an intercultural socio-ethical application of pragmatism: it is the difference it will make within and for the future experience of the poor and those who are worse off. Taken politically and ethically, new forms of solidaristic communal life are hoped for, i.e. a life rich in cooperative and jointly communicated experience.

In 1919 Dewey delivered a series of lectures at the Imperial University of Japan in Tokyo, which were rewritten and published as *Reconstruction in Philosophy* in 1920.[38] After receiving an invitation to visit China, he arrived in Shanghai in May 1919 and stayed there until July 1921. In 1920 the National Peking University granted him a doctorate *honoris causa*, and he was called a "Second Confucius." In the historical set of encounters between Western philosophers and non-Western environments – or with their cultural Others – this is probably one of the most influential examples for both parties, and is a genuine intercultural *experience* in its own right. In their book *The Democracy for the Dead*,[39] David Hall and Roger Ames present a rich potential of Dewey's philosophy in intercultural contexts, especially in Confucianism. In their pragmatic approach to China and its rich civilizational and cultural tradition, they follow a romantic approach – in the good pragmatic sense of an openness to alternatives. With its specific form of political organization, opposed to Western individualistic rights-based democratic tradition (i.e. the social contract tradition), China is for Hall and Ames a more communal 'rites-based society', and therefore also comparable to other non-Western alternative models of social organization.

With Dewey as "the chief American spokesman for communitarian democracy,"[40] there is clearly an intercultural potential in this encounter. And for our purpose, it also opens up possibilities for applying Dewey's social and political thought to other intercultural contexts. As I am arguing for a way toward new hopes for a betterment of democratic societies, especially those still subjected to various forms of poverty and unfreedom (freedom taken in the Deweyan, i.e. positive sense; in reference to different social and political contexts of Latin America, Africa and Asia/India), let us take our first and introductory example from Hall and Ames's book on Dewey and democracy in China.

For Dewey, freedom and democracy in their pragmatic sense are situated within the context of a certain culture: "The problem of freedom and of democratic institutions is tied up with the question of what kind of culture exists."[41] The idea of democracy "is not an alternative to other principles of associated life. It is the idea of community life itself."[42] In the first chapter of his *Freedom and Culture*, we are faced with a constitution of a communal 'human nature', i.e. of a primal human sociality that precedes any aprioristic (in the sense of an isolated individual in some imagined state of nature) and 'individualistic' account of the 'human condition', even when expressed in altruistic virtues (sympathy etc.). For Dewey, it is the fraternity (*fraternité*, later known as *solidarité*) that deserves rehabilitation as the basic form of sociality. Culture is defined as a complex body of customs and it is Dewey that warns us, in a genuine intercultural sense, against all universal consequences of Lockean (and related) liberal political theories: "The idea that mind and consciousness are intrinsically individual did not even occur to any one for much the greater part of human history."[43]

If democracy is allied with humanism, then some form of humanistic culture must accompany its reconstruction: it cannot depend upon political institutions alone but has to be expressed in the *attitudes* of human beings, pragmatically "measured by consequences produced in their lives."[44] It is Deweyan 'Great Community' that is herewith to be achieved. It is a community whose ideal is as far away from any collective claims as any other idea of involuntarily imposed 'liberty', and is therefore a community based on the idea of absolutely unrestrained private and public freedom. Therefore, communal social ethics does not imply any submission of our habits and lives to some form of institutionalized 'communal' freedom. As Dewey put it in his major work on political thought, *Public and Its Problems*, democracy is the idea of a communal life itself; it is not a rationality of a set of rational procedures but consists of (culturally conditioned) emotions and habits that underpin the attitudes of a given group *and* its individuals on their way toward a Great Community.

But what is the culture that would be compatible with Dewey's cause as defined within his 'humanistic' view of democracy? How is fraternity, or solidarity, to be achieved? Hall and Ames argue for an intercultural dialogue between pragmatism and Confucianism. There indeed are many "working connections" between Dewey and Confucius, as proposed by another proponent of an intercultural application of Dewey, Joseph Grange. Dewey's idea of 'growth' is related to *dao* as an experiential path to be taken; *de* is understood as attractive good and is compared to Dewey's idea of betterment; and finally, the central Confucian concept of *ren* as 'benevolence' and 'authoritative conduct' (to cite two among the many approximate translations) is analogous to Dewey's creation of oneself (through appropriate behavior) into a socially responsible human being.[45] This movement within both pragmatism and Confucianism is characterized by a few other features common to both: both Dewey and Confucius take that "the person is person-in-context. The notion of 'individuals' has as little relevance for American pragmatism as for Chinese culture. ... [T]he broader purposes of the community emerge from personal and communal goals," etc. (a communality not conceived as a form of collectivity).[46] Arguing for the implementation of the idea of democracy in China, the authors therefore hope for a new model of a pragmatic democratic community, which is to emerge from its encounter with Confucian culture:

> Our hope, therefore, is that the combination of Chinese and Western values and beliefs that emerges from future conversations will consist of elements of Chinese Confucianism and Western pragmatism.[47]

The issue of democracy in China is of course confronted with many other questions, starting with the ongoing discussion of human rights in China, which we cannot discuss here.[48] From the perspective of classical Western liberal interpretation, with its proposition of unconditional and universalistic human rights, it is difficult to imagine its full implementation within any democratic culture. But Hall and Ames are also skeptical of the use and efficiency of human rights within the rites-based social and political cultural environments of China. Given the communitarian context of Chinese culture, it is the notion of relatedness, setting communal 'cooperation' and 'responsibility' over 'freedom' and 'autonomy', that seems the more workable concept. But is this pragmatist-Confucian juncture a living option for a new (pragmatic) social philosophy and as such, an opportunity for an alternative development of the Deweyan idea of democracy? I would certainly argue that Dewey's idea of democracy is highly applicable even to some of the most pressing social issues of our present world, including China, but even more so, it is usable for the areas with high social inequality and poverty. We mean South America, Africa and India, for it is here that "suffering of the poor" becomes overmuch.[49] It therefore seems apt to now try and outline three alternative propositions for a pragmatic-intercultural dialogue on the Deweyan theme of 'freedom and democracy'.

3.

I will now outline, using three examples, a possible pragmatist model for intercultural social ethics. To return to our question, How is fraternity and solidarity to be achieved, when reflecting interculturally upon the Deweyan idea of Great Community? Our first example will refer to a "Maya democracy," as expounded in the liberation philosophy of the Argentinean-Mexican philosopher E. Dussel. His interpretation of communal solidarity as a "criterion of ethical validity"[50] can further our understanding of what kind of ethical thinking is needed to embark on an intercultural path toward Deweyan Great Community and its social hopes. At the same time, it will turn our attention to our preliminary remarks on the phenomenological-pragmatic importance of James's mode 'I breathe' for this mode of thinking. For Dussel, a process of ethical recognition of the oppressed Other as a person *precedes all discourse.*[51] He takes the following 'phenomenological' argument here, pointing to the denial of the most basic corporeal needs of human beings:

> A reason that precedes the beginning, that precedes the present, because my responsibility for the Other imposes itself before any decision, before any deliberation (before all argument or discourse).

> Our sons and daughters have no schools, no medicine, no clothing and no food; there is no roof under which to protect our poverty. ... Our children must work from the early age in order to get something to eat and water, and medicine. ... The terrible conditions of poverty endured by our people have but one common cause: lack of freedom and democracy. We believe that any improvement in the economic and social circumstances of our country's poor requires a truly authentic respect for the people's freedom and democratic will. ... Our voice will carry the voice of the good men and women who walk these worlds of pain and anger; and of the children and of the elderly who die of loneliness and neglect; and of the humiliated women; and of the small men.[52]

The extreme form of a larger solidarity with others as a mode of our communal ethical *being-in the-world* is further manifested in a slogan of the EZLN: *todo por todos, nada por nosotros* ("for everyone, everything, for ourselves, nothing").[53] Solidarity with others (those in similar situations of poverty and suffering) which is based on the politico-ethical recognition of basic corporeal needs is therefore a signpost for new socio-ethical thinking in a globalized world.

Citing Dussel's (Levinasian) argument with the communiqués of the EZLN, we come to the very core of Jamesian phenomenological-anthropological intuitions of the 'breath' phenomenon as well as to Deweyan idea of freedom and democracy, both in their primal anthropological-ethical sense. The claim for freedom and democracy as presented by the Maya is a question to be answered within the pragmatic mode of *being-in-the-world-with-others*, a mode that is replete with sensibilities for our most primal communal experience – communication and freedom. If we read Dewey in the intercultural and socio-ethical sense, achieving freedom does not take us only in the direction where the abstract individual is left free from interference of others (negative freedom), but also in the direction where one is always in the service of the oppressed, the neglected, the downtrodden – of specific children, women and men engulfed by poverty – where a person is free in the anthropologico-ethical sense of being in control over his or her life and being able to recognize this *sign of an ethical life* in another person. Dewey, in his most 'socialist' work from the 1930s

(*Liberalism and Social Action*) defined freedom as a concept not necessary in a society where suffering does not exist any more.

Our second example comes from contemporary African philosophy and political science. In the "Introduction" to a book on the idea of freedom and its local and global forms, R. H. Taylor says:

> Words for freedom, or what some would see in modern discourse as unfreedom, could be found in every language and culture. People knew what was not freedom because most African and Asian societies, like most early modern European societies, had ideas of social status and hierarchy which defined for individuals the limits of their freedom. People were designated as free or slave, as free or bondsman, as belonging to a particular caste or a class, in an elaborate hierarchy of social and political relationships.[54]

For a short outline of some of African ideas of freedom and communality, I will draw on the standard sources of comparative historical and political studies (Africa is taken to be a political and geographical concept), and point out the overarching commonalities in the nature of Africa's philosophical responses to Western colonial/postcolonial realities, and later the traditional Akan (ethno)philosophy as presented by K. Gyekye. Of course it was in the wake of the Atlantic slave trade era, followed by the colonial subjugation of the entire continent and, in the post-independence era, the struggle against the native authoritarian regimes (and today, against globalizing capitalism in Africa) that various *indigenous* responses were brought to bear on the question of unfreedom, and were expressed radically in those contexts. According to C. Young, the ultimate sources of unfreedom are therefore external to Africa.

We should also note, however, that on the other hand it was the Western idea of freedom that was contextualized and internalized in various ways in contem-porary Africa; that is to say, it was "syncretized with an indigenous heritage."[55] But in the debate whether ideas related to the concept of liberty (and democracy) can be found in *pre*colonial Africa, K. Gyekye sets forth his communitarianism-based arguments, which can also be closely related to intercultural applications of Dewey's social and political thought to Africa, and indeed can justify the pro-posed comparative approaches within the framework of Dewey's pragmatism. It is this thought that can be used in our discussion of contemporary issues of poverty and inequality in a 'globalized' Africa, and more broadly, within the social and political philosophy of Africana.[56] For Gyekye, African precolonial political forms were consensual and thus resembled Western democratic procedures.[57] It is by criticizing the consequences of a radical (even extreme) communitarian interpretation of J. Mbiti's statement "I am, because we are; and since we are, therefore I am" as implying a view that is too reductive and narrow for a sound and working definition of the self within a system, that Gyekye embarks on a way towards a moderate communitarianism, espousing autonomy of the individual assured in this process.

Another ethical criterion for a societal life, based on both individual and societal aspects of life in a community (global, in this case), can be found in contemporary African 'ubuntu ethics'. The path to social hope in ubuntu ethics is comprised of two basic principles: the first states that "to denigrate and disrespect the other human being is in the first place to denigrate and disrespect oneself only if it is accepted that oneself is a subject worthy of dignity and respect," and the second states that when one is confronted with a choice "between wealth and the preservation of the life of another human being, then one *should opt for the preservation of life*."[58] To return to Gyekye: as a sign of natural sociality of human beings, African moderate communitarianism can therefore provide a link to the pragmatic mode of *being-in-the-world-with-others,* a mode which, taken interculturaly, points to the priority of communal experience over individualism, yet strives to preserve a good sense of an active and thoroughly experiencing personhood in this process. For Gyekye "it is moderate communitarianism that, in the final analysis, adequately reflects the claims of both individuality and communality, both of which need to be recognized morally and functionally."[59]

It is in this sense that the 'communitarian' interpretation can help us conceive alternative ways in dealing with the contemporary political-ethical issues of the world, such as 'human rights', 'justice', poverty and various forms of social inequality. In this view, democracy and freedom demand both communality and individuality. In the traditional Akan 'democracy' (democracy is here widely understood as "the government of the people, by the people, and for the people"[60]), as presented by Gyekye and based on the 'political contract' (i.e. a contract that regards human beings as social by nature, as opposed to the social contract in the Enlightenment's political thought), we can find institutions and therewithin notable democratic elements as understood in the Western tradition. These are embodied in a series of positive procedures for arriving at political decisions which, according to Gyekye, are

> born of the pursuit of the social ideal or goal of solidarity – itself inspired by a belief in the identity of the interests of all the members of the community – and of the recognition of the political and moral values of equality, reciprocity and respect for the views of others.[61]

Irrespective of social status, these consensual 'democratic' procedures are clearly in line with Deweyan ideas of freedom and democracy, both aiming at greater social equality as a form of solidarity (*fraternité*) within any society. And it is with this 'pragmatist' message from the traditional Akan democracy and contemporary 'ubuntu ethics' that we have come to our final example.

Let us conclude with our third and final example of the intercultural use and application of Jamesian-Deweyan pragmatic philosophy. In modern India, we are faced with a different concept of both individuality and communality.

Established as early as in 1885, as the fundamental institution of Indian national will for future political self-determination against the British Raj, the Indian National Congress did not propose the concept of equal rights for all citizens or the concept of liberty as the basic right among the broadly conceived political rights of an individual. It was the "nation's collective right to self-determination" that defined the particular political form of freedom in Indian politics of that age.[62] For Isaiah Berlin, this conception of a 'national' freedom would be a clear example of an injustice. But in India, it is the conception of a double freedom for the individual *and* the community (of which the individual is a part, the other being a caste or national identity) that stands in opposition to the Western concepts of negative or positive freedom.[63]

Still, it is the ability to transfer a sectarian quest for 'freedom' within separate religious *and* communal identities into a "pursuit of egalitarian commitments,"[64] i.e. a healthy concept of freedom for the individual and for the public, as understood within the democratic vision and idea of Deweyan Great Community. Facing the old, culturally and metaphysically (and, of course, religiously) underpinned question of caste inequality and hierarchy (the *jati-varna* system of Indian society), it was the effort of the Founding Fathers of Indian Constitution that led India toward Western-type constitutional democracy. But in his speech on the occasion of the adoption of the Constitution in 1949, B. R. Ambedkar, being its chief architect, said:

> On the 26th of January 1950, we are going to enter into a life of contradictions. In politics we will have equality and in social and economic life we will have inequality. In politics we will be recognizing the principle one man one vote and one vote one value. In our social and economic life, we shall, by reason of our social and economic structure, deny the principle of one man one value.... How long shall we continue to deny equality in our social and economic life?[65]

These words could also be Dewey's, addressing his contemporaries in the United States' social and economic politics of the 1930s, or even class inequality and the social and political (lack of) opportunities of the disadvantaged in today's America. They reflect a genuine concern for the future of democratic life and social equality in India. The reason for his warning was a high rate of social inequality which – despite the reservation politics and positive discrimination originally provisioned in the Constitution for the untouchable castes of India or the so called 'Scheduled Castes' (and 'Scheduled Tribes') – has remained a well-preserved form of caste hierarchy even in today's Indian society (along with class and gender inequalities).

Issues in democratic freedoms, as identified in Indian constitution (fundamental rights, freedom of speech, equality before law etc.), are still obstructed by various anti-democratic practices and elementary negations of freedom – the latter as understood in the broader and positive Deweyan sense.

According to Amartya Sen, "these lacunae are among the major inadequacies in the use of democracy in India today."[66]

Prior to its first constitution, India knew reformers and social thinkers such as R. M. Roy or Rabindranath Tagore, whose ideas of freedom and social equality inspired political theorists and social movements in India. Tagore transformed the 'mukti' (as an ideal of otherworldly deliverance) to the worldly concept of social freedom, and Roy was the first to argue against the traditional notion of social inequality. But it was the nineteenth-century social revolutionary Jotirao Phule that inspired many contemporary social movements in India and is regarded as a forerunner of the contemporary Dalit groups and other anti-caste movements. Phule even dedicated his book on slavery (*Ghulamgiri*) to Abraham Lincoln, comparing Indian forms of slavery to European and American ones.

By providing his own understanding of the traditional Indian Brahmanic theories about the inborn social and ethical inequality between the untouchables and Shudras on the one hand and the other *dvija* castes on the other (Shudras and Ati-Shudras being kept out of this religious *and* social *rite de passage*), Phule proposed a new *ethical criterion* based on an inverted 'Aryan theory'.[67] Phule therefore ideally acknowledged a supposed pre-Aryan community based on the equality of all middle and low castes being destroyed by the intervention of Brahmanic caste ideology, in which, in his own understanding of this 'revolutionary' politics, we should opt for an anti-Brahmanic "True Religion of the Community."[68] This rationally constructed 'religion' based on the ethical criterion of equality resembles Dewey's idiosyncratic notion of *faith*, and it is this rationale that needs to be practically and pragmatically-democratically carried out.[69] Phule's and Ambedkar's ideas and their influence on contemporary democratic movements (such as the community-, i.e. caste-based Dalit movements)[70] are therefore in line with Dussel's Maya as well as African forms of 'democracy' as opposed to various institutional forms of exploitation and discrimination of those living in depressing social conditions of inequality and poverty.

4.

What ethical consequences and social sensibilities can now be inferred from these applications and enlargements of James's and Dewey's social thought to intercultural contexts? In his *Embodied Care*, Maurice Hamington argues for an analogy between 'breathing' and 'care': just like breathing is a basic and continuing process in our body, so "care, too, is so basic to human functioning that we can easily overlook it as a significant element in moral decision making."[71] We can agree to this point. But as I argued in previous sections of this article, it is the somatic phenomenon of breathing (being rich in intercultural potential) that actually precedes all ethical considerations and points to our communal relatedness. As a primal somatic phenomenon, breathing abides in our body. And it is in the body that our jointly communicated experience of *being-in-the-world*, with all its ethico-social consequences, originates.[72]

Let me bring in another pragmatist philosopher here – in her *Democracy and Social Ethics*, Dewey's friend and colleague Jane Addams suggests that our hopes for a larger democracy should be accompanied with care and experience, both stemming from the basic familiarity with the poor, immigrants and women of her time.[73] As a way of living in solidarity with others, her idea of democracy is also applicable to contemporary social ethics, working in different inter-cultural contexts. If "[b]arriers between groups of men had to be broken down, not so that all groups might be the same, but so that a sense of the community of all mankind might be maintained,"[74] then it is our social 'sensitivity', i.e. the enlargement of our ethico-social experiences, that will decide upon future cooperation between men and women of the world. For Dewey, experiencing is like breathing – "a rhythm of intakings and outgivings"[75] – and it is through our receptivity and giving that this ongoing process is being maintained. Sensitivity is our ability to *take in* these experiences, *seeing*, *feeling*, and *understanding* the lives of others, from our closest family circle to broader (global) communities. Being connected with others through every breath we take is, as it were, being connected to "everyone and everything."[76]

How can our natural bodily sensitivities become ethical sensitivities *for* the world, and as such accessible to the sphere of social ethics? I propose that, first, comparative philosophy can help us conceive a future social ethics as proposed from the viewpoint of pragmatist philosophy; and, second, that Merleau-Ponty's and related phenomenological analyses of the body/flesh can help us clear up this point, supporting both the pragmatic and the intercultural way to a social ethics.

On his introductory page in the *Philosophy East and West*, Dewey writes that "elements in Western cultures and Eastern cultures are so closely allied that the problem of 'synthesizing' them does not exist."[77] Likewise, Merleau-Ponty pointed to a need to think and philosophize interculturally and comparatively. In the chapter "The Orient and Philosophy," he is critically referring to both Hegel and Masson-Oursel, thus approaching in a genuine comparative fashion some major issues of intercultural understanding. Far from the usual Western pre-judicial reasoning of that time, Merleau-Ponty was firmly convinced that the West could learn from Eastern philosophies "to rediscover the relationship to being,"[78] and thus pledged for the process of reopening the rich possibilities of this intercultural encounter. Pointing to Husserl's late statement *der Traum ist ausgeträumt*, Merleau-Ponty declared: "Husserl has understood: our philo-sophical problem is to open up the concept without destroying it."[79]

As he embarked on a way toward a new phenomenological description of the lived body in his "Preface" to his *Phenomenology of Perception* ("What is Phenomenology?"), Merleau-Ponty described perception as *basic experience of the world*; later, he saw virtue (*virtù*) as "a principle of communion."[80] His phenomenological analyses of the body and perception resemble James's account of the 'mind' as a process that is never separate from body, and Dewey's evolutionary understanding of the lived experience as an ongoing flow of interactions between an organism and its environment. When referring to the psycho-physical vital body, Dewey refused to believe that "the universe [was] split into two separate and disconnected realms of existence, one psychical and the other physical..."[81] In her critical feminist approach to Merleau-Ponty, Shannon Sullivan, following Dewey, suggested a dynamic and interdependent view of organisms in their relations to environments. This (democratic) inter-dependency requires care, and is accompanied by an ongoing, inexhaustible transformation of our experiences. Dewey designates this process and the con-nection between inquiry and biological operations with the word "continuity."[82] Along with Dewey, Merleau-Ponty's philosophy is therefore an example of a nondualist and nonfoundationalist approach to the mind and body problem. And his 'ethics', like Dewey's – and unlike Levinasian or Heideggerian types of ethics – is characterized by "verticality rather than horizontality," therefore being symmetrical, communicative, *and* communitarian. It bears a rich demo-cratic potential.[83] And as we saw in Merleau-Ponty's comparative philosophical account, we can imagine this embodied ethics to be also working interculturally.

For Merleau-Ponty, alterity in our bodies is always already part of ipseity. The alterity does not represent any distinct form of humanity, ethnos, gender, or race. Although marked by an unavoidable locality and ethnocentrism, the process of bodily perception is always oriented toward strangers, the unknown, the other. The symbiosis and intercorporeality of me and others within our common and communal *being-in-the-world* – which therefore takes place in the body and later, in his *The Visible and the Invisible*, in 'flesh' – is a designation for this complex process of intertwining. It is a symbol of "the unity of the human *spirit*."[84] Moreover:

> My body is made of the same flesh as the world (it is perceived) ... this flesh of my body is shared by the world, the world reflects it...[85]

It is here that some very useful comparative possibilities open up. In Japan, the flow of *ki*-energy (i.e. our vital force) – like vital breath (*prana*) in India and *ik'* (one's breath and animacy, the living soul) in Mesoamerica among the Maya – is so closely related to breath that it can actually be identified with it: "Breath is a sign of life, without which the embodied *ego-cogito* can not sustain its life. In this sense, breath is closely related to *spiritus*, a *ki*-energy."[86] In his comparative philosophical reading of Merleau-Ponty's thought, S. Nagatomo introduced a new philosophy of the lived body, working beyond the West-East (or any other) dichotomy. On the basis of Merleau-Ponty's body intentionality and "intentional arc" (*l'arc intentionnel*), Nagatomo outlined an experiential moment of coming-together in an ethical way.[87] *Ki*-energy is a third term (*un troisieme terme*), reaching beyond the psychophysical nature. As *invisible* energy, it is the very condition of mutual inter-fusion of different *ki*-energies (i.e. different bodies, individuals). *Ki*-energy is recognized and maintained by breathing, by its voluntary and involuntarily performances. *Ki* is a "source out of which both the mental and the physical spring forth as phenomena."[88] As such, the phenomenon of breath is the basis for a social ethics, for it is the life of the community that emanates from it and is shared through it. In a Deweyan sense, breath is thus the fundamental mode of intercorporeal/intersubjective communication. It is the basic and rudimentary layer of solidaristic communal life.

My sensitivity to others as my 'twins in flesh' and my acknowledgment of their suffering (as well as their happiness) are therefore marked by our relatedness. Merleau-Ponty borrowed from Husserl the notion of *Einfühlung,* i.e. fellow-feeling and sympathy. Flesh as a conception of the body is a new *milieu* of this ongoing encounter, of this 'coming-together'. In his recent studies of 'saturated phenomena', i.e. "of the excess [*l'excès*] of intuition over the concept,"[89] J.-L. Marion states that for Descartes's *res cogitans*, the very act of feeling precedes other phenomena. The feeling body, in its unconditioned existence as *corpus et sensus*, has been primary in relation to other phenomena and experiences: "The ego only fixes itself when it takes flesh."[90] But it is breath, as a primal *bodily* phenomenon, that provides us with our first (somatic) experience: "[T]he person has a glimpse into this dimension of energy through his/her act of breathing..."[91] The body's intentionality therefore precedes consciousness. As "a rhythm of intakings and outgivings" (Dewey), my experiencing of the body actually originates in breath when, closing my eyes and forgetting about my senses, my sensitivity is first of all attuned to the muscular movements of my body (James).[92] As it originates in my breath (in phenomenological, anthropological, *and* ethical terms), perceiving, feeling and seeing another human being (or, likewise, any nonhuman animal) implies that I recognize her or him, that I have always already recognized her or his vital breath, the vital movements of the body. Thus I care for her or him. My sensitivity and solidarity is all attuned to the other's body. Somatically, *naturally*, I *feel* and I *know* that (s)he's alive, that (s)he's well.

In his study on pragmatism and phenomenology, Patrick Bourgeois says: "Perhaps phenomenology can untangle its roots and expand its scope in learning from pragmatism, and pragmatism can obtain a better and more clearly stated footing from phenomenology's penchant for descriptive attunement to lived experience as such."[93] In his reconstruction of the associated socio-political life, represented by the ideal of a democratic Great Community, Dewey referred to the attitudes of human beings. Our pragmatist question – *How is fraternity, or solidarity, to be achieved?* – can now be approached from the proximity of our primal ethical sensitivities as redescribed phenomenologically and inter-culturally, and be enlarged into a pragmatically conceived social ethics. For Dewey, habits as 'organic meanings' are pre-objective, and man is "a sense-giving being on a level of experience which is pre-reflective and pre-conscious, i.e., on that level of experience which is man's original access or opening to the world."[94] It is therefore on the level of habitual body that our ethical sensitivities are awakened and experienced, and the claim for freedom and democracy as socio-ethical forms of communal life shall be redescribed in an intercultural and pragmatic way when addressing the practical issues of poverty, inequality, and any form of injustice. In this, I hope, we can trace the roots of our social ethics as practical communality and, consequently, freedom – taken in the utopian (and eschatological) Deweyan (pragmatist) sense of a concept rendered unnecessary in a future democratic and solidaristic society where suffering does not exist anymore. And it is here that men and women of the world are bound together by an invisible, breath-like circle of love.

NOTES

1. Roberto Mangabeira Unger, *What Should the Left Propose?* (London and New York: Verso, 2005), pp. 100–101.

2. See for example Rorty's notions of cultural bias as regards our liberal democratic 'community' (among the most criticized formulations in his philosophy, besides his notions of contingency and liberal irony, is his "we liberals") and his criticism of anti-ethnocentrism. See his essay "On Ethnocentrism: A Reply to Clifford Geertz," in Rorty, *Objectivity, Relativism and Truth* (Cambridge, UK: Cambridge University Press, 1991). See also his critical correspondence with the comparative philosopher Anindita N. Balslev in Balslev, *Cultural Otherness: Correspondence with Richard Rorty* (Atlanta, Georgia: Scholars Press, 1991).

3. In *The Range of Pragmatism and the Limits of Philosophy*, ed. Richard Shusterman (Oxford: Blackwell, 2004), pp. 13–42, at pp. 16–17. About Dewey and interculturality see chap. 2 of my essay.

4. Cornel West, *The American Evasion of Philosophy: A Genealogy of Pragmatism*, (Madison: University of Wisconsin Press, 1989). For Emerson see chap. 1. In "Circles" (in Ralph W. Emerson, *Essays and Lectures* (New York: Literary Classics of the United States, 1983), pp. 403–414), Emerson writes: "Every ultimate fact is only the first of a new series" (p. 405). See also his notion of action and its primacy in the life of his "American Scholar."

5. Emerson developed his Over-Soul relying on the Indian (Upanishadic) 'Over-Soul' (*adhyatman*), in which through *inner* knowledge, to put it in Emersonian fashion, the micro- and macrocosmic principles of the world, bráhman and atman, abide in identity. See Frederic Ives Carpenter, *Emerson and Asia* (Cambridge, MA: Harvard University Press, 1930); Arthur Christy, *The Orient in American Transcendentalism: A Study of Emerson, Thoreau and Alcott* (New York: Octagon Books, 1932). On Emerson and Zen-Buddhism see Y. Kahutani, "Emerson, Whitman, and Zen Buddhism," *The Midwest Quarterly* 31 (1990), pp. 433–448; and Shoei Ando, *Zen and American Transcendentalism* (Tokyo: Hokuseido Press, 1970). See also Daniel J. Thottackara, *Emerson the Advaitin* (Bangalore, India: Asian Trading Corp, 1986); and Leyla Goren, "Elements of Brahmanism in the Transcendentalism of Emerson," *Emerson Society Quaterly* 34 Supplement (I. Quarter, 1964), pp. 34–37. For a bibliographic account of 'Orient' in transcendental periodicals see Roger C. Mueller's dissertation *The Orient in American Transcendental Periodicals (1835–1886)* (Minneapolis: University of Minnesota, 1969).

6. See West, *The American Evasion of Philosophy: A Genealogy of Pragmatism*, p. 249, n. 2.

7. Cit. after Paul Masson-Oursel, *Comparative Philosophy* (London: Kegan Paul, Trench, Trubner and Co., 1926). French orig.: *La philosophie comparée* (Paris: PUF, 1923). According to Wilhelm Halbfass's *India and Europe* (New York: State University of New York, 1990), p. 423, it was the Bengali philosopher Brajendra Nath Seal (1864–1938) who in his *Comparative Studies in Vaishnavism and Christianity* (1899) first used the term 'comparative philosophy'. Both Seal and Masson-Oursel were directly influenced by Auguste Comte. See also Masson-Oursel, "Objet et méthode de la philosophie comparée," *Revue de métaphysique et de morale* 19 (1911), pp. 541–548.

8. Gerald J. Larson and Eliot Deutsch mention Comte, Darwin, Marx, Müller, Tylor, Dilthey, Frazer, Freud, James, Durkheim, and Weber as forerunners of comparative philosophy. See *Interpreting Across Boundaries: New Essays In Comparative Philosophy* (Princeton, N.J.: Princeton University Press, 1988), "Introduction."

9. Masson-Oursel, *Comparative Philosophy*, p. 25.

10. *Ibid.*, p. 34.

11. *Ibid.*, p. 37.

12. *Ibid.*, p. 65.

13. *Ibid.*, p. 39.

14. Ram Adhar Mall, *Intercultural Philosophy* (Lanham, Md.: Rowman and Littlefield Publishers, 2000), chap. 2.

15. Mall, *Intercultural Philosophy*, p. 15. "Such a hermeneutics also leads to a healthy concept of comparative philosophy." (*Ibid.*, p. 17.)

16. For radical empiricism in Masson-Oursel see his *Comparative Philosophy*, at p. 60: "But, on the other hand, the only absolute rule on history is that radical empiricism that conditions our knowledge by respect for facts."

17. James, *Essays in Radical Empiricism* (Cambridge, MA: Harvard University Press, 1976). About James and his influences on Husserl see Herbert Spiegelberg, *The Phenomenological Movement*, 2 vols. (The Hague: Martinus Nijhoff, 1960).

18. James, *Essays in Radical Empiricism*, p. 22.

19. *Ibid.*, p. 3 ("Does 'Consciousness' Exist?").

20. *Ibid.*, p. 25 ("A World of Pure Experience").

21. See *ibid.*, p. 42. It is worth mentioning here that, according to Richard Bernstein, Peirce's triadic theory of signification (sign – another sign/first interpretant – second interpretant), and Royce's appropriation of it (as a process ad infinitum), also lead to, hermeneutically speaking, a construction of an (infinite) community of interpreters as already entailed in Peirce's theory. See Bernstein, "Community in the Pragmatic Tradition," in *The Revival of Pragmatism: New Essays on Social Thought, Law, and Culture*, ed. Morris Dickstein (Durham, N.C.: Duke University Press, 1998), pp. 141–156. According to Bernstein, "[i]nterpretation is essentially open to the future, and the process of interpretation requires a community of interpreters" (p. 145). About the ethico-political consequences of this thought for an intercultural community, see further.

22. James, *Essays in Radical Empiricism*, p. 19.

23. See for example Tadashi Ogawa, "Qi and Phenomenology of Wind," *Continental Philosophy Review* 31 (1998), pp. 321–335; Lenart Skof, "Il ruolo ed il significato degli elementi acqua, aria e terra nell'antica filosofia indiana e greca: uno studio comparativo," *Magazzino di filosofia* 5.13 (2004), pp. 123–137; Mechtilde Boland, *Die Wind-Atem Lehre in den älteren Upanishaden* (Münster, Germany: Ugarit Verlag, 1997).

24. See *Brhadaranyaka Upanishad* (BU). For a translation of all classical Upanishads with commentary see Patrick Olivelle, *Upanisads* (Oxford: Oxford University Press, 1998).

25. See the references on the Greek Presocratic thought in n. 23.

26. Ogawa, "Qi and Phenomenology of Wind," p. 324.

27. *Ibid.*, p. 325.

28. *Ibid.*, p. 326.

29. John Dewey, "On Philosophical Synthesis," *Philosophy East and West* 1 (1952), p. 3; in *The Later Works of John Dewey*, vol. 17, ed. Jo Ann Boydston (Carbondale: Southern Illinois University Press, 1991), p. 35. Among other major Western philosophers of that time, it was probably only Sartre that was capable of intercultural thinking of that kind (in his introduction to *Orphée Noir* in 1948).

30. James, *Pragmatism* (New York: Dover, 1995), p. 21. See Larry A. Hickman, "Pragmatism, Postmodernism, and Global Citizenship," in *The Range of Pragmatism and the Limits of Philosophy,* ed. Richard Shusterman (Malden, MA: Blackwell, 2004), pp. 63–79. Peirce wrote in his "How to Make Our Ideas Clear" (1878): "Consider what effects, which might conceivably have practical bearings, we conceive the object of our conception to have. Then, our conception of these effects is the whole of our conception of the object" (Charles S. Pierce, *Collected Papers*, vol. 5, ed. Charles Hartshorne and Paul Weiss (Cambridge, MA: Harvard University Press, 1935), p. 258).

31. James, *ibid.*, p. 66.

32. *Ibid.*, p. 68.

33. See Dewey, *Experience and Nature, The Later Works of John Dewey*, vol. 1, ed. Jo Ann Boydston (Carbondale: Southern Illinois University Press, 1988).

34. See James T. Kloppenberg, "Pragmatism: An Old Name for Some New Ways of Thinking?," in *The Revival of Pragmatism: New Essays on Social Thought, Law, and Culture*, pp. 83–127.

35. Raymond D. Boisvert, *John Dewey: Rethinking Our Time* (Albany: State University of New York Press, 1998), p. 10.

36. See Rorty's essay "Dewey's Metaphysics," in Rorty, *Consequences of Pragmatism: Essays, 1972–1980* (Minneapolis: University of Minnesota Press, 1982), pp. 72–89.

37. Dewey, *Experience and Nature*, p. 54.

38. *John Dewey, Lectures in China, 1919–1920,* ed. and trans. Robert W. Clopton and Twuin-chen Ou (Honolulu: University Press of Hawaii, 1973), p. 3. Dewey's lectures were translated from Chinese. Dewey intended to revise, expand and publish them, but "this intention was not carried out" (p. 2). For the process of bringing his lectures back to English, see "Introduction."

39. David L. Hall and Roger T. Ames, *The Democracy of the Dead: Dewey, Confucius, and the Hope for Democracy in China* (Chicago and Lasalle, Ill.: Open Court, 1999). See also Joseph Grange, *John Dewey, Confucius and Global Philosophy* (Albany: State University of New York Press, 2004).

40. *Ibid.*, p. 15.

41. Dewey, *Freedom and Culture*, in *The Later Works of John Dewey*, vol. 13, ed. Jo Ann Boydston (Carbondale: Southern Illinois University Press, 1988), p. 72.

42. Dewey, *Public and Its Problems*, in *The Later Works of John Dewey*, vol. 2, ed. Jo Ann Boydston (Carbondale: Southern Illinois University Press, 1975), p. 328.

43. Dewey, *Freedom and Culture*, in *The Later Works of John Dewey*, vol. 13, ed. Jo Ann Boydston (Carbondale: Southern Illinois University Press, 1988), p. 77.

44. *Ibid.*, p. 151.

45. Grange, *John Dewey, Confucius and Global Philosophy*, p. 22ff.

46. Hall and Ames, *The Democracy of the Dead: Dewey, Confucius, and the Hope for Democracy in China*, p. 184. See also p. 185f.

47. *Ibid.*, p. 186.

48. For the 'human rights' issue see *ibid.*, pp. 221–239 (chap. 11: "Communal Sources of Human Rights").

49. Jean-Luc Nancy, "The Future of Philosophy" (Interview with Benjamin C. Hutchens), in Hutchens, *Jean-Luc Nancy and the Future of Philosophy* (Montreal and Kingston: McGill-Queen's University Press, 2005), p. 166.

50. Enrique Dussel, *Beyond Philosophy: Ethics, History, Marxism, and Liberation Theology*, ed. E. Mendieta (Lanham, Md.: Rowman and Littlefield, 2003). See p. 173 (chap. "The 1994 Maya Rebellion in Chiapas"). Dussel refers to the communiques that the EZLN (*Zapatista* Army of National Liberation) made public in 1994 in their struggle for justice in Chiapas. It is Dussel's "criterion of ethical validity" that we are extending into our notion of a pragmatist-intercultural 'ethical criterion'.

51. *Ibid.*, pp. 172–173.

52. *Ibid.*, pp. 172–177.

53. See Scott Schaffer's *Resisting Ethics* (New York: Palgrave Macmillan, 2004), p. 207ff.

54. *The Idea of Freedom in Asia and Africa,* ed. Robert H. Taylor (Stanford, Cal.: Stanford University Press, 2002), p. 4.

55. See Crawford Young, "Ideas of Freedom in Africa," in *The Idea of Freedom in Asia and Africa*, pp. 9–39, at p. 12.

56. See for example *The Quest for Community and Identity*, ed. Robert E. Birt (Lanham, Md.: Rowman and Littlefield, 2002), especially chap. 5 ("Of the Quest for Freedom as Community") and chap. 6 (Lewis Gordon's paper "Sociality and Communality in Black: A Phenomenological Essay").

57. See Kwame Gyekye's chapter on "Democratic Elements in the Traditional Akan Political Practice," in Gyekye, *Tradition and Modernity: Philosophical Reflections on the African Experience* (New York and Oxford: Oxford University Press, 1997), pp. 124–133.

58. It is Ifeanyi A. Menkiti's interpretation that Gyekye is criticising. John Mbiti's statement is cited after Gyekye, *Tradition and Modernity: Philosophical Reflections on the African Experience*, p. 52. For a contemporary 'ubuntu ethics' see Mogobe B. Ramose's essays "The Philosophy of *ubuntu* and *ubuntu* as Philosophy," "The Ethics of *ubuntu*" and "Globalization and *ubuntu*," in *The African Philosophy Reader*, ed. Pieter H. Coetzee and Abraham P. J. Roux (London and New York: Routledge, 2003); for citations, see p. 644; *my emphasis*). Of course, it is the African ubuntu notion of "preservation of life" that resembles our mode 'I breathe' as the ethical criterion of pragmatic-intercultural thought, calling for an equal and fundamental justice for all subjects of any subjugation or denigration. For the argument I am making it is also important to notice that the Nguni (Bantu) word 'ubuntu' is etymologically related to 'umuntu', which denotes the human being as a *biological* being. See Ramose, "The Philosophy of *ubuntu* and *ubuntu* as Philosophy," p. 231.

59. Gyekye, *Tradition and Modernity*, p. 61.

60. *Ibid.*, p. 124.

61. *Ibid.*, p. 130.

62. Sunil Khilnani, *The Idea of India* (New York: Farrar, Straus and Giroux, 1999), p. 26. It is worth mentioning that, traditionally, the notion of 'individuality' in India was reserved for the renouncers (*sannyasin, sadhu*), living on the edge of society. For a democratic mind and its social life, this is clearly an example of a difficult, even "terrible freedom," being both an idea and ideal of an otherworldly type of freedom (see Sudipta Kaviraj, "Ideas of Freedom in Modern India," in *The Idea of Freedom in Asia and Africa*, pp. 97–142.

63. See Isaiah Berlin, *Political Ideas in the Romantic Age*, ed. Henry Hardy (Princeton, N.J.: Princeton University Press, 2006), chaps. 2 and 3: "The Idea of Freedom" and "Two Concepts of Freedom: Romantic and Liberal," see p. 155); see Kaviraj, "Ideas of Freedom in Modern India," p. 97. According to Angadipuram Appadorai, India knew an equivalent to the 'social contract' theory – it is in the canonical Buddhist *Digha Nikaya* and in *Jatakas* that we find a story about the origins of the society, when after a golden age of harmony, and after evil customs and sins had appeared, people chose the best among men and entered into an agreement with him. He was known as *Maha Sammata* (Appadorai, *Political Thoughts in India (400 B.C.–1980)* (Delhi, India: Khama Publishers, 2002), pp. 3–4).

64. Amartya Sen, *The Argumentative Indian* (New York: Farrar, Straus and Giroux, 2005), p. 38.

65. Bhimrao Ramji Ambedkar, "Speech on the Adoption of the Constitution," cit. after: *Democracy in India*, ed. Niraja Gopal Jayal (New Delhi: Oxford University Press, 2001), p. 24.

66. Sen, *The Argumentative Indian*, p. 36. For an extreme aspect of gender inequality in India see Sen's article "Missing Women," in *British Medical Journal* 304 (7 March 1992), and "Missing Women Revisited," in *British Medical Journal* 327 (6 December 2003).

67. For the 'ethical criterion' see Enrique Dussel and the Maya democracy; for the 'ethical criterion' as preservation of life see the contemporary Ramose's version of 'ubuntu ethics' in African philosophy, both in this chapter.

68. For Jotirao Phule's revolutionary theory see Gail Omvedt, "The Anti-caste Movement and the Discourse of Power," in *Democracy in India*, pp. 481–508. For a citation of Phule's "Sarvajanik Satya Dharma" principle see Omvedt, *Jotirao Phule and the Ideology of the Social Revolution in India* (New Delhi: Critical Quest, 2004), p. 6.

69. See Dewey's *A Common Faith*: "Faith in the continued disclosing of truth through directed cooperative human endeavor is more religious in quality than is any faith in a completed revelation" in *The Later Works of John Dewey*, vol. 9, ed. Jo Ann Boydston (Carbondale: Southern Illinois University Press, 1986), p. 18.

70. For a history of the Dalit and other anti-caste movements see Omvedt, "The Anti-caste Movement and the Discourse of Power," and the annotated bibliography.

71. Maurice Hamington, *Embodied Care: Jane Addams, Maurice Merleau Ponty and Feminist Ethics* (Urbana and Chicago: University of Illinois Press, 2004), p. 1. Hamington distinguishes 'care' from 'care ethics', arguing for "care as more than just another ethical theory" (p. 2).

72. The human body as the locus of ethics was analyzed by Arthur Schopenhauer. Schopenhauer developed his ethics from an originally biologico-anthropological phenomenon – the elusive, innermost, and obscure *feeling*. The innermost (i.e. the bodily) realm within us – that which is the closest to human beings, i.e. our bodily feelings and compassion stemming from them – all these are primal ethical phenomena for Schopenhauer. About bodily feelings and bodily ethics, see my paper on Schopenhauer,

"Metaphysical Ethics Reconsidered: Schopenhauer, Compassion and World Religions," in *Schopenhauer Jahrbuch* 87 (2006), pp. 101–117. Schopenhauer as a – still underestimated – predecessor of Nietzsche could also be of use in the recent debates concerning somatic sensations (i.e. critiques of Merleau-Ponty) as presented in Shusterman, "The Silent, Limping Body of Philosophy," in *The Cambridge Companion to Merleau-Ponty*, ed. Taylor Carman and Mark B. N. Hansen (Cambridge, UK: Cambridge University Press, 2005), pp. 151–180. For Schopenhauer's views see Volume I of his *The World as Will and Representation*, at § 67.

73. Jane Addams, *Democracy and Social Ethics* (New York: Macmillan, 1964), p. 13ff. It is worthwhile to mention that in her humanitarian pragmatist efforts, Addams was inspired by the social gospel movement. For her the criterion for a "social test" reaches beyond our personal and family relations, being: "did ye visit the poor, the criminal, the sick, and did ye feed the hungry" (p. 3).

74. Daniel Levine, *Jane Addams and the Liberal Tradition* (Madison: The State Historical Society of Wisconsin, 1971), p. 144. Already in her time, Addams's efforts in Hull House were referred to as 'cosmopolitan' (see Marilyn Fischer, "Jane Addams," in *A Companion to Pragmatism*, ed. John R. Shook and Joseph Margolis (Malden, MA; Oxford: Blackwell, 2006), p. 82). For Dewey and Addams about care and about the universal caring response as originating from their social ethics see M. Regina Leffers, "Pragmatists Jane Addams and John Dewey Inform the Ethic of Care," *Hypatia* 8.2 (Spring 1993), pp. 64–77.

75. Dewey, *Art as Experience*, in *The Later Works of John Dewey*, vol. 10, ed. Jo Ann Boydston (Carbondale: Southern Illinois University Press, 1987), p. 62.

76. Leffers, "Pragmatists Jane Addams and John Dewey Inform the Ethic of Care," p. 74. See Shusterman's attempt to develop a "somaesthetics" as a philosophical discipline and a way of cultivating the body in his *Performing Life: Aesthetic Alternatives for the Ends of Art* (Ithaca, N.Y.: Cornell University Press, 2000), – i.e. as a practice of cultivating the sentient body as "a key to better perception, action, virtue and happiness" ("Pragmatism and East-Asian Thought," p. 33). However, Shusterman refers to Asian (and other) meditational techniques (cultivation of the body etc.) and therefore does not proceed along a genuine phenomenological line of argument with all the ethical consequences I wish to develop here.

77. Dewey, "On Philosophical Synthesis," p. 3; in *The Later Works of John Dewey*, vol. 17, ed. Jo Ann Boydston (Carbondale: Southern Illinois University Press, 1991), p. 35.

78. Maurice Merleau-Ponty, "Everywhere and Nowhere," in *Signs*, trans. Richard C. McCleary (Evanston, Ill.: Northwestern University Press, 1964), p. 139. His essay was written in 1956.

79. *Ibid.*, p. 138.

80. Merleau-Ponty, "A Note on Machiavelli," in *ibid.*, p. 215.

81. Dewey, *Experience and Nature*, p. 205.

82. Shannon Sullivan, *Living Across and Through Skins: Transactional Bodies, Pragmatism and Feminism* (Bloomingtom: Indiana University Press, 2001). For Dewey see his *Logic: The Theory of Inquiry*, *The Later Works of John Dewey*, vol. 12, ed. Jo Ann Boydston (Carbondale: Southern Illinois University Press, 1986), p. 26. About Dewey and Merleau-Ponty see Mark Johnson, "Mind Incarnate: From Dewey to Damasio," *Daedalus* 135.3 (Summer 2006), pp. 46–54. In Merleau-Ponty's view, any form of political amelioration must be democratic and tend towards freedom in its essence.

83. About this point see Gary B. Madison's reconstructive exposition of Merleau-Ponty's 'communicative' ethics in "The Ethics and Politics of the Flesh," in *Merleau-Ponty's Later Works and Their Practical Implications: The Dehiscence of Responsibility* ed. Duane H. Davis (Amherst, N.Y.: Humanity Books, 2001), pp. 161–185: "For Merleau Ponty the 'other' is not some sort of transcendent, deus ex machina Other (*Sein als Solche, le visage de Dieu*) but is rather my equal, my 'double', my 'twin'" (p. 171). During his life, Merleau-Ponty did not develop an ethics, but his philosophy both implies and testifies to rich socio- and politico-ethical consequences.

84. Merleau-Ponty, *Signs*, p. 139 (my emphasis). James states in his *Essays on Radical Empiricism*: "... but breath, which was ever the original of 'spirit', breath moving outwards, between the glottis and the nostrils, is, I am persuaded, the essence out of which philosophers have constructed the entity known to them as consciousness. *That entity is fictitious, while thoughts in the concrete are fully real. But thoughts in the concrete are made of the same stuff as things are*" (James, *Essays in Radical Empiricism*, p. 19).

85. Merleau-Ponty, *The Visible and the Invisible,* trans. A. Lingis (Evanston, Ill.: Northwestern University Press, 1968), p. 248.

86. Shigenori Nagatomo, "Ki-Energy: Underpinning Religion and Ethics," *Zen Buddhism Today* no. 8 (October 1990), pp. 124–139. Note that Nagatomo's analogy of *ki* and *spiritus* is not arbitrary: the Latin *spiritus* ("a breath") is etymologically related to the Indo-European root **(s)peis-* ("to blow"), primarily being *energy* present in all living beings. For breath in Maya see Stephen Houston, David Stuart, and Karl Taube, *The Memory of Bones: Body, Being and Experience among the Classic Maya* (Austin, Tex.: University of Texas Press, 2006), p. 142ff. "[T]he ancient Maya believed that vitalizing forces resided in the breath and other exhalations..." (*ibid.*, p. 228). For comparative evidence from Africa see Z. S. Strother, "From Performative Utterance to Performative Object: Pende Theories of Speech, Blood Sacrifice, and Power Objects," *RES: Anthropology and Aesthetics* 37 (2000), pp. 49–71.

87. *Ibid.*, p. 126. For a brief presentation of Nagatomo's arguments on the "intentional arc" and its ethical consequences see *ibid.*, pp. 128ff.

88. *Ibid.*, p. 137.

89. Jean-Luc Marion, *In Excess: Studies of Saturated Phenomena*, trans. Robyn Horner and Vincent Berraud (New York: Fordham University Press, 2002), p. xxi.

90. *Ibid.*, p. 91. In Marion, 'the taking of flesh' points to a union *of the soul and the body*.

91. Nagatomo, *Attunement Through the Body* (Albany: State University of New York Press, 1992), p. 203. According to Indian Upanishadic thought, breathing (*prana*) preceedes all other vital functions, including our ability to speak. In an idiosyncratic Vedic plural form, *pranah* ('breaths') actually denotes a group of five vital powers/senses – thinking, speech, sight, hearing, and breathing. Breathing is the 'best' among them and these vital powers/sense faculties are thus named after him.

92. See James, *Essays in Radical Empiricism*, p. 19.

93. Patrick L. Bourgeois, "From Common Roots to a Broader Vision: A Pragmatic Thrust of European Phenomenology," *American Catholic Philosophical Quarterly* 70 (1996), pp. 381–397. For the citation see p. 383. For the related bibliography on pragmatism and phenomenology see *Notes* on pp. 381–397.

94. Victor Kestenbaum, *The Phenomenological Sense of John Dewey: Habit and Meaning* (Highlands, N.J.: Humanities Press, 1977), p. 4. For habits in Husserl, Dewey and Merleau Ponty see *ibid.*, p. 5ff.

Lenart Skof
Assistant Professor of Philosophy and Religion
Department of Philosophy
Faculty of Humanities
University of Primorska
Titov trg 5, 6000 Koper
Slovenia

Correspondence address:
Lenart Skof
Tomaziceva 40
1000 Ljubljana
Slovenia

Contemporary Pragmatism
Vol. 5, No. 1 (June 2008), 147–162

Editions Rodopi
© 2008

Semiosis, Dewey and Difference: Implications for Pragmatic Philosophy of Education

Andrew Stables

A fully semiotic perspective on living and learning draws on poststructuralism in seeing meaning and learning as deferred, and avoids mind-body substance dualism by means of collapsing the signal-sign distinction. This article explores the potential for, and constraints on the 'sign(al)' as a meaningful unit of analysis for universal application among the human sciences. It compares and contrasts this fully semiotic approach with the educational philosophy of John Dewey, concluding that if Dewey had problematized the signal-sign distinction, his legacy for education might have significantly different.

1. What is a sign(al)?

In the Western tradition (leaving aside, for example, Buddhist and Yogic conceptions of universal mind, which are not subject to Cartesian dualism[1]), traditionally a sign is conceived as different from a signal. A sign is generally understood as the intentional construct of a human, and therefore a minded being (the dominant, anthroposemiotic view), though there is a long minority tradition of seeing the world/universe as a series of divine signs, in which case God and humanity are seen as each minded (see Matthews on Augustine[2] and Skrbina on panpsychic thought in the Western tradition, including process philosophy[3]). There has been a much more recent interest in the possibilities of biosemiotic perspectives, whereby every living thing carries messages of survival value; on this account, DNA is a series of codes carrying 'what works' from history.[4] While several authors have pointed to the possibility of a pansemiotic perspective, embracing the non-living as well as the living, derived from Peirce, there has been little exploration of the implications of this, whereas conceptions of biosemiotics have influenced thinking about ecosemiotics, whereby the human – non-human nature relationship is understood in semiotic terms.[5]

Whether interaction is understood in terms of signs or signals is of some significance. Mind–matter/body dualism, as reinforced by Descartes and developed through modern science, has non-human entities effectively responding mechanically to signals, or prompts, without intention or awareness, with the possible exceptions (only recently acknowledged by scientists) of certain very limited aspects of animal behavior; even in the latter case (as in tool use, or evidence of limited memory), such behavior is not generally accepted as evidence of sign use, though some of the research evidence is challenging.[6] Such dualism therefore affects conceptions of the human, and, in turn, of learning theory, with cognitive approaches emphasizing the minded aspect of human living ('understanding'), and behaviorism the mechanical, and therefore more closely predictable ('behavior').[7] The most notable attempt in philosophy of education to overcome Cartesian dualism, that of John Dewey, will be the focus of consideration in the final section of this article, where it will be argued that the fully semiotic perspective both reinforces and develops that of Dewey, with significant consequences for his views on educational practice.

The neologism 'sign(al)' is intended to combine these perspectives under a post-Cartesian settlement. However, the sign(al) lacks precise definition. I construe it in *Living and Learning as Semiotic Engagement*[8] as like a punch, or a kick – i.e. as a prompt to action – and add in further articles[9] that the search for the sign(al) is problematic in terms of singularity and plurality. Also, as a unit of meaning, it is 'deferred' (after Derrida), and so is not precisely locatable in space-time (arguably *contra* Kant[10] but, perhaps, in sympathy with quantum theory, where normal expectations about quantity, time, and place break down at the most microcosmic level[11]).

The following pansemiotic account of the sign(al) draws on process philosophy (specifically Whitehead's *Process and Reality*[12]) and European poststructuralism (specifically Derrida).

Suppose that process creates (the effect of) substance (*via* duration), and that process is characterized at the most fundamental level by charged energy, and at the most sophisticated level by consciously-recognised events and experiences, experiences comprising our involvement in events. In taking the sign(al) to be that which moves us on (or moves something else on), it can be understood on either of these levels, either as a concatenation of charges (charged particles, or waves, or the effects of strings in a multidimensional universe, depending on one's approach to quantum physics), or as a (singular) charge. However, the paradox of the charged object, or subject, is that each singularity is, in fact, relational: dependent upon the tension between the positively and negatively charged poles, in traditional electromagnetic terms. As the structuralists and others have made clear, psychological and semantic objects exist in relation to their opposites. Furthermore, the charged (and relational) object is only an object by means of its encounter with a subject (itself relational). Thus the charges – sign(al)s, prompts, units of meaning – that constitute events and experiences are therefore always the results of collisions or relations of charged entities. This is a possible interpretation of Whitehead's conception of a 'nexus' of 'actual entities'.[13] We learn, therefore, through experiences, as experiences constitute personal reality. This is essentially a

Deweyan position, arrived at by an alternative route. Whitehead, like Dewey, has experience as firmly grounded in the present. Derrida, however, has experience and meaning as deferred.[14] At first sight, these positions seem incommensurable. However, if we put aside the issue of essential presence (which, after all, might be construed as little more than an argument about Plato; Whitehead regarded himself as an atypical interpreter of Plato), their accounts of experience bear a remarkable similarity little (if at all) explored in the literature. In their implications for education there may, however, be significant differences, that will be discussed below.

On the above set of process-oriented accounts, how do human beings (at least) learn and develop? Experiences are incremental. Each experience impacts on future experiences, *via* memory and conditioning. Whitehead refers to this as prehension: apprehension depends on prehension; Derrida refers to traces.[15] Dewey argues that perceptions determine stimulus as well as response.[16] On all these accounts, I am implicated in my experiences so learn to anticipate them, and such anticipation affects but never totally determines forthcoming experiences (see Bartlett's *schema* theory and related psychological accounts[17]). As my experiences mount, I re-classify. Life is thus a process of emergent patterning. While this patterning might be understood as either (cognitive) meaning-making or as (behavioral) conditioning – or, as Dewey prefers, as (conative) inclination towards action – it is clear both that the patterning an individual engages in is heavily influenced by that individual's culture (as meaning-making is always relational) and that it is unique to the individual (as an individual's context is always, to some degree, unique; as a being of relations, an individual is positioned within a culture). Thus there is no patterning without meaning and no meaning that is utterly predictable. So far, so Deweyan, except, it will be argued below, that outcomes lack the predictability on which Dewey's most influential educational philosophy partly depended.

Consider response to a flag consisting of black and white halves. The black half is a concatenation of charges, generally understood as wavelengths, that produce the effect of black; similarly the white. Although a viewer has generalised responses to black and white, her response to them as they constitute this flag is determined by a host of cultural influences, and by her (shifting) position *vis-à-vis* these. Conversely, this other responses to black and white may well be affected by her feelings relating to the flag. There is no need to remind an American readership, for example, of the contentiousness of the concepts, 'flag', 'black' and 'white'.

On the above account, the attempt to isolate the sign(al) precisely fails. The sign(al) is both the series of charges that produces the color effect and the flag in its cultural and historical context, as it affects the subject. However, whether it be small, large, singular or multiple, it remains the unit of meaning. It is a unit of analysis only insofar as we are prepared to abandon the concept of unit, for meaning cannot be broken down into units, or measured with respect to size or location. The basic 'unit' is perhaps best conceived as one of difference –

that which produces a charge – as Derrida and Deleuze,[18] among others, have posited, invoking a tradition that can be traced back to Heraclitus,[19] and not one of substance, following Western atomic theory from Leucippus and Democritus.[20]

The construal of a unit of meaning as a unit of difference puts this semiotic, pragmatic account of meaning making and purposeful activity at odds with the dominant pragmatist educational perspective – that of John Dewey, as expressed in his most influential writings on education – in one important respect.

2. Resonances with Dewey

The fully semiotic perspective outlined above, has the following implications for education:

(i) All human experience involves the modification of patterning whether or not it is subsequently credited as learning. Cognitive and behaviorist theories therefore offer inadequate accounts, the former by underplaying the importance of prior experience, the latter by underplaying the importance of context and the uniqueness of the individual position, and therefore the unpredictability of outcomes; in general, educational theory has a tendency to mystify and/or reify 'learning'.

(ii) All experience, including that which will be regarded as learning experience, involves tension and disruption of the known. The sign(al) operates as a prompt, a charge. Thus, just as learning can be either good or bad, so is teaching, tutoring or guidance equally interpretable as either positive identity development or more-or-less controlled identity disruption. Students must therefore expect to be challenged, upset or offended from time to time, and no educational practice or initiative will be uniformly universally received; it is not a case simply of building social progress towards pre-specified ends through shared activity.

(iii) Everything to do with teaching and learning is cultural practice. However, diversity of habituation ensures that experience is always varied, though the words used to describe it (for example) may not reveal the extent of the variation. People are thus more different than they seem to be, at least in their responses to particular situations; teaching, research and policy all need to recognise this variation. Furthermore, identity politics and multicultural education should no longer proceed on the assumption – conscious or implicit – that individuals are treatable simply as products of cultural, social and ethnic groups, taken either singly or in combination; as everyone is different, assumptions about 'greater' or 'lesser' difference according to group membership can have limited validity[21]; this problematizes conceptions of social justice.

(iv)   However, what we experience is experientially real, whatever the continuing doubts about its ontological status. We experience actual events. Events constitute the universe. Living, and therefore learning, really is experiential, and experience always holds the potential for learning.

(v)   Formal education does not enhance learning *per se*, but rather attempts to channel it in socially desirable directions. However, outcomes remain unpredictable: learners never quite learn what teachers teach, nor do they share the same assumptions about what constitutes (valuable) learning. Therefore, the conscious aims of the channelling are of limited validity; in this sense, education cannot be 'provided', and insofar as educational 'opportunities' can be provided, whether they will be received as opportunities, and how, cannot be adequately pre-specified.

(vi)   The unit of meaning is neither free-standing, of standard size, spatio-temporally locatable nor divisible. Meaning-events (experiences) cannot therefore be atomised: neither broken down nor reconstructed. Effective teaching, for example, cannot be identified in one context and transferred to another. The policy aim of evidence-based good practice in education and other fields of human relation is therefore poorly grounded: arguably part of a broader strategy to standardise the unstandardizable and to pre-specify inevitably unpredictable outcomes that is doomed to deliver less than its adherents promise[22]. Good teachers create rich experiences for students that come to be seen as having fulfilled social/cultural functions, as experienced by the individual student and by significant others: the more the emphasis on standardised, formal education, the more restricted the conception of the functions. Although created in liberal societies for quite opposite reasons, formal education in such societies can, under certain conditions, serve to inhibit rather than enhance experience. A good education, whether formal or informal, will leave the learners assured that they undergone a series of significant personal events that have promoted their (and, by implication, others') human flourishing.

Dewey was one of many important influences on the above work, though the semiotic approach draws on a variety of traditions. However, there are grounds for questioning whether this approach, notwithstanding its eclecticism, takes the debate beyond Dewey in any significant respect.

One possible response to this is that the semiotic approach provides an elaborated, or alternative conceptual framework into which (most of) Dewey's work fits very well, thus offering some new perspectives on Dewey, and suggesting possible future implications, as yet unrecognised. The alternative – to be expanded below –attempts to locate those aspects of Dewey's thought that are clearly resonant with, and those that clearly depart from that proposed in my book *Living and Learning as Semiotic Engagement* and elsewhere, offering tentative explanations for the key disjunctures.

The present argument does not attempt to draw on Dewey's full, and extremely wide, output, but rather focuses on a selection of texts representing expressions of his direct thinking about education and related aspects of his philosophy. The earliest (*The Reflex Arc Concept in Psychology*: henceforth *RAC*) dates from 1896; the latest (the Introduction to *The Use of Resources in Education*: henceforth *URE*), from 1952, when Dewey was in his nineties.[23] The principal focus, however, will be on *Democracy and Education*, first published in 1916[24] and Dewey's most extended and philosophically developed work with an explicitly educational focus.

Points (i)-(vi) above will now be considered specifically in relation to Dewey.

(i) A central element in Dewey is that of the conative, as opposed to cognitive or behavioural, nature of learning. In *RAC*, he points to the tendency of the still-young discipline of psychology to adopt discredited dualisms relating to mind and body. Rather:

> ... what is wanted is that sensory stimulus, central connections and motor responses shall be viewed, not as separate and complete entities in themselves, but as divisions of labor, function factors, within the concrete whole, now designated as the reflex arc. (Dewey, 1896: 2)[25]

Dewey's perspective here (and elsewhere) places emphasis on conation (broadly, the willingness and ability to act) rather than cognition or affect. As he points out a little further on in *RAC*,[26] a sound, for example, is not merely a stimulus but rather "an act ... of hearing." Each human act, which is an act of meaning, makes sense only in terms of expectations:

> From this point of view the discovery of the stimulus is the "response" to possible movement as "stimulus." We must have an anticipatory sensation, an image of the movements that may occur, together with their respective values, before attention will go to the seeing....[27]

To this extent, at least, Dewey concedes that there may be little, if anything, distinctive about 'learning' experiences *per se*, though he rarely makes this point explicitly in the texts under consideration. An exception occurs in *The School and Society* (hereafter *SS*):

> Learning? – certainly, but living primarily, and learning through and in relation to this living.[28]

Indeed, Dewey sometimes refers to life/living in a way that incorporates educational practice, and seems to leave little or no space for a distinct conception of learning. At the beginning of *Democracy and Education*, for example (Dewey, 1916 – hereafter *DE*), he states, "... all communication, and hence all social life, is educative."[29]

However, insofar as living is learning (and *vice versa*), it is always dependent on prior experience. Dewey is frequently critical of any educational scheme that regards the mind as independently able to make sense of a world it has not experienced. In *DE*, he stresses that

> ... the supposed original faculties of observation, recollection, willing, thinking etc. are purely mythological. There are no such ready-made powers waiting to be exercised and thereby trained.[30]

In *URE*, at the very end of his career, Dewey berates the progressive education movement (largely owing its existence to him) for confusing ideas with 'inherent essences'.[31]

On the uniqueness of individual response, however, Dewey is, particularly in his specifically educational writings, much more ambiguous. Throughout, but arguably most forcefully in his earlier writings, he combines a strong commitment to individual sense-making with an at least equally strong commitment to the school as cultural transmitter. "Through education," Dewey claims in *My Pedagogic Creed* (hereafter *PC*), "society can formulate its own purposes [and] organize its own means and resources *and can thus shape itself with definiteness and economy*" (my italics).[32] On examination, however, there is little evidence in any of Dewey's work of a definite set of desired or feasible outcomes. Rather, there are periodic reminders that people will make sense of things in their own ways. Indeed, in *Progressive Education and the Science of Education* (1928: *PSE*[33]), he promotes the experimental, 'laboratory' school on the grounds that "compared with traditional schools, [there is] a common emphasis upon respect for individuality and for increased freedom."[34] In fact, in the spirit of some of his later work rather than *PC*, he seems to have moved towards a more pluralistic, perhaps less naïve, conception of schooling, claiming in *PSE* that, "As the working operations of schools differ, so must the intellectual theories derived from those operations."[35]

As, for example, the extended discussion of 'vocationalism' in the latter stages of *DE* suggest, perhaps the real, and only identifiable clear aim of schooling is a commitment to lifelong learning. and Dewey can certainly be credited for raising awareness of this. On the other hand, he does make extremely strong claims for schools in *PC* and *SS* that barely take account of differential outcomes and pupil responses. At the opening of *SS* he asserts, "What the best and wisest parent wants for his own child, that must the community want for all its children,"[36] but Dewey's belief in the social construction of mind cannot extend to any sort of guarantee that everybody (even the 'best') will share the same values, or that schools can somehow ensure they are passed on. There is a hint of paternalism in the normative tones of 'best', 'wisest', 'must', and 'all'. The implication here is that the likes of Dewey know what is best for children as much as the most traditional didact.

There is some evidence of Dewey softening his line on this in later writings, though by then, it might be argued, the die had been cast in terms of schooling practices: the experimental school had had its day and the progressive schooling movement was well underway, much of it certainly not to Dewey's own satisfaction. In *DE*, Dewey notes, "The things with which a man *varies* are his genuine environment"[37], but there is no recanting of the lofty claims made in *PC* and *SS*. Perhaps the distinction between 'man' (*sic*) and child is carefully drawn here, or perhaps Dewey was simply not inclined to dwell on the contradiction between such acknowledgments of inevitable diversity and the earlier, simpler faith in schools. The nearest he comes to an acknowledgement of values dissonance in *DE* is in his insistence of the importance of that which schools do *not* pass on in his portrayal of them as selective environments.[38]

(ii)   Dewey tends to see education as always building on previous experience without ever, it seems, challenging it in uncomfortable ways, despite the emphasis on education as communication (particularly *DE*) and on individual liberty. The assumption is of education as an unqualified, and unproblematic, good. Students must undertake socially desirable tasks to which they will bring their prior expectations and because everyone (of good taste, anyway) wants the same thing, and intelligence is collective, neither prior experience nor subsequent evaluation will differ from the norm to the extent that ill-feeling will ensue. Rather, he tells in *CC* of "the race-experience which is embodied in that thing we call the curriculum,"[39] implying that the diverse backgrounds of many the citizens of his time had already been assimilated into a harmonious and homogeneous Americanism. Although Dewey defines experience in terms of 'trying' and 'undergoing',[40] he does not discuss the experience of schooling in terms even of challenge and difficulty, let alone potential incomprehension, unwillingness or disaffection. Rather, his naturalism leads him to stress – particularly in the earlier, more specifically educational texts – that all roads can lead to Damascus. When he writes in *SS* that "The children begin by imagining present conditions taken away until they are in contact with nature at first hand,"[41] he is quite at odds with a semiotic perspective, for language and cultural meaning do not constitute the bottom line for Dewey in any sense.

It is pertinent to note at this point that Dewey's relative interest in education seems to decline. In the extensive *Experience and Nature*[42] for example, neither 'education' nor 'school' deserves even an index entry, and there is no major work on education after *DE* (1916) until the very late and much less regarded *Education Today* (1940).[43] The rugged naturalism is undiminished in *EN*, however: Dewey dismisses those who see "qualities as always and only states of consciousness" as naïve dualistic cognitivists. Rather:

It is a reasonable belief that there would be no such thing as "consciousness" if events did not have a phase of brute and unconditioned "isness," of being just what they irreducibly are.[44]

(iii) Dewey's naturalism leads him to suggest that people are less different than they seem to be rather than the reverse. While many may have taken Dewey's prescriptions for active learning as pedagogically desirable for multicultural populations, Dewey does nothing to problematize them himself in this regard; indeed, he seems uninterested in cultural difference in his key writings on education, despite an evident interest in international affairs.[45] Interestingly, given the recent emphases on evidence-informed policy and practice on both sides of the Atlantic, Dewey promoted the use of multiple case studies to determine good practice in teaching and learning, writing of the need for "A series of constantly multiplying careful reports on conditions which experience has shown in actual cases to be favorable and unfavorable to learning."[46] In this, he promoted a belief in isolating and potentially transferring 'best practice' that characterises the contemporary policy scene but which is regarded with deep suspicion from a fully semiotic perspective.[47]

It is clear that Dewey did not see reality as significantly constructed by language, or semiotic interchange more broadly. His view, expressed in *DE*, of "life as a self-renewing process through action upon the environment,"[48] and education as enacted through communication, should not be confused with later perspectives on language *as* action, such as those of Austin, and the later Wittgenstein or Habermas.[49] There is no primacy of language in Dewey. For Dewey, things are invested with meaning (become signs as opposed to merely signals) because of collective human activity; they do not determine that activity. Consider the following from *EN* (italics in original):

Animals respond to certain stimuli.... Let us call this class the signalling reflexes.... Sub-human animals thus behave in ways which have no *direct* consequences of utility to the behaving animal.... Signaling acts evidently form the basic *material* of language ... [but] ... [t]he hen's activity is ego-centric; that of the human being is participative. The latter puts himself at the standpoint of a situation in which two parties share.... The character-istic thing about *B*'s understanding of *A*'s movement and sounds is that he responds to the thing from the standpoint of *A*.... To understand is to participate together, it is to make a cross-reference which, when acted upon, brings about a partaking in a common, inclusive undertaking.... The heart of language is not "expression" of something antecedent, much less expression of antecedent thought. It is communication; the establishment of co-operation in activity in which there are partners.... Primarily meaning is intent.[50]

Dewey's view of 'symbols' as "condensed substitutes of actual things and events"[51] does not have communicative activity grounded in sign systems, as would, for example, poststructuralist perspectives (given considerable latitude in the use of 'systems'). Perhaps as a legacy of the body-mind dualism he sought to escape, Dewey's system relies on an absolute qualitative difference between humans and other species that allows the former to engage in meaningful action which, while a response to some underlying reality, exploits language and other communicative tools without being dependent upon them. In this, he appears to replace the classical liberal belief in autonomous rational agency with one of collective rational agency. Whence this agency originates, other than as some mysterious force of nature, remains unclear. To Dewey, action invests meaning in language. His is not the direction that the mass of twentieth century philosophy and cultural theory would be able to follow.

(iv) Nevertheless, the still widely held claims that learning is experiential and that "we experience actual events" are entirely Deweyan and, indeed, have been formulated more clearly and effectively by Dewey than by anyone else. On this account, subjective experience is not merely a commentary on an objective world but contains within it both the means and the content of learning. Experience matters; indeed, it is all that really matters. What Dewey underplays, by contrast to many later perspectives, is the role of language and other semiotic systems in creating and defining that experience.

(v) However, this falls far short of an argument for any form of formal education, particularly as Dewey stresses in *DE* that "No thought, no idea, can possibly be conveyed as an idea from one person to another."[52] Neither is it an argument against formal education.

Dewey's strong advocacy of schools as the breeding grounds, or sites of renewal, of democratic societies is achieved by means of a combination of perspectives that, in most other systems, are at odds. In short, he manages to combine a belief in school as a place in which children can be taught to think for themselves (though compulsory schooling formed no part of the thinking of the early liberal contract theorists) with a happy acceptance of school as an institution for channelling activity to produce social coherence and positive compliance. Later, Marxist and post-Marxian theorists would understand this dynamic in terms of Ideological State Apparatus[53] or even symbolic violence[54]: hegemony "bought into" by a willing public. There is no sense of immanent critique in Dewey, however, who argues that purposeful human activity is individually liberating and socially cohesive at the same time, requiring no sense of liberation *from* social norms and practices. Dewey sees individual liberty as entirely compatible with community action in his best-known writings on education.

(vi) The implications for educational policy and practice from a fully semiotic perspective therefore seem quite at odds with those from Dewey in certain key respects, though each perspective can be construed as liberal-pragmatic and post-Cartesian, and each emphasises the primacy of human experience (rather than, say, structural measures or mere credentials). While the semiotic perspective sees schooling as deeply problematic (and educational largely insofar as it is problematic), Dewey assumes that both social aims and their implementation *via* schooling are largely unproblematic, given good pedagogy – itself relatively unproblematic. Dewey's philosophy is thus a one-size-fits-all prescription for thriving democracy in which the school as social institution is a site for cultural revivification.

3. Concluding remarks

There are therefore many defining parallels between Dewey's philosophy of education and a fully semiotic approach. Chief among these are the belief that mind, meaning and behavior are intextricably linked,[55] and the commitment to active involvement in education, such that it produces significant events for students.

The major point of departure concerns the recognition and valorisation of difference. Although Dewey depicts humans as inescapably relational, and communicative, the emphasis in his best known educational writings is on shared purpose and outcome; little or no account is taken of differences, however slight, in individual contexts of reception and response. Savery, for example, depicts Dewey as an "emergent naturalis[t]"[56] for whom natural events are cohesive and progressive and for whom (as for Hegel, an early influence), human dialogue has a synthetic and purely positive role. While, at the very end of his career, Dewey denied his position was 'holistic'[57] it nevertheless depends on a faith in the reality of historically verifiable events. By contrast, a fully semiotic perspective, while not necessarily fully relativistic, denies that what lies beyond the perceptual (broadly understood) is verifiable.

To Dewey, the value of educational activity is immediate and shared; on the semiotic account, it is deferred and shared in part. To Dewey, the school is a force for unquestionable good, provided that the pedagogy is right; on the semiotic account, schools, like activities, have no intrinsic value, but have potential as sites of valuable activity and will be variously received. To Dewey, problems are to be solved; on the semiotic account, problems are to be explored and reworked. To Dewey, everyone well educated will take the same values from school; on the semiotic account, everyone will take something different from school (or from whatever alternative experiences to schooling they may have).

For Dewey, therefore, there is not a great gulf between political and comprehensive liberalism, as later formulated by Rawls[58]: school, for example, can respect individual liberty simultaneously with insisting on shared activity and compliance, not merely because its members find points of contact between differing belief systems, but because society (educated society, at least) will share commitment to a set of values to be transmitted. On the semiotic account, religious and other cultural differences belie the possibility of all adult members of the broader community agreeing what values and practices to pass on. This implies that the educational value of schooling comes not from integration and the standardisation of best practice (although rules of engagement must be agreed on the 'political' level), but rather from the exploration and juxtaposition of many kinds of difference, without expectation of complete resolution. This further implies preference for a system of schooling characterised by competing models and a degree of internal inconsistency.

These differences arise from different attempts to counteract substance dualism. In *Experience and Nature* (1925), Dewey developed the substantive concept 'body-mind'. He did not problematize the process-oriented signal-sign distinction, though it would have been a logical corollary for him to have done so and if he had, his educational legacy might have been significantly different.

In summary, while the fully semiotic approach to education shares most aspects of Dewey's philosophical scheme, the degree to which it differs is sufficient to suggest a widely differing, much more pluralistic approach to education as public policy.

NOTES

1. See, for example, http://www.vajranatha.com/teaching/DzogchenChinese.htm accessed on 14 November 2006.

2. Gareth Matthews, *Augustine* (Oxford: Blackwell, 2005).

3. David Skrbina, *Panpsychism in the West* (Cambridge, MA: MIT Press, 2005).

4. Claus Emmeche, "The Biosemiotics of Emergent Properties in a Pluralist Ontology," in *Semiosis, Evolution, Energy: Towards a Reconceptualisation of the Sign*, ed. E. Taborsky (Aachen: Shaker Verlag, 1999), 89–108.

5. Timo Maran, "Where Do Your Borders Lie? Reflections on the Semiotical Ethics of Nature," in *Beyond Wild Nature: Transatlantic Perspectives on Ecocriticism*, ed. Catrin Gersdorf and Sylvia Mayer (Amsterdam: Rodopi, 2006).

6. See, for example, the work of the Language Research Center at Georgia State University, for increasing evidence of the similarities in cognitive processing between, in particular, children and other primates (see http://www2.gsu.edu/~wwwlrc/research-main.htm). See also Jane Goodall's work on chimpanzee language and tool use and other aspects of animal intelligence (see http://www.janegoodall.org/jane/cv.asp, accessed 14 November 2006.

7. I acknowledge the huge range of both behaviorist and cognitivist approaches, and the attendant areas of overlap. See, for example, www.iep.utm.edu/b/behavior.htm (accessed 14 November 2006). However, my concern is not principally with the sophistication of the arguments at the 'leading edges' of psychology and neuroscience so much as with the popular understandings of these terms (e.g. by teachers) which bear the legacies of crude concepts of stimulus-response conditioning (classical and operant) on the one hand, and of the mind as private, inner, sometimes spiritual space on the other.

8. Andrew Stables, *Living and Learning as Semiotic Engagement: A New Theory of Education* (Lewiston, N.Y.: Mellen, 2005). Themes are further developed in Stables, "Sign(al)s: Living and Learning as Semiotic Engagement," *Journal of Curriculum*

Studies 38 (2006), pp. 373–387; "Semiosis and the Myth of Learning," in *Proceedings of International Network of Philosophers of Education 10th Biennial Conference: Philosophical Perspectives on Educational Practice in the 21st Century* (Malta: Allied Newspapers, 2006); "From Semiosis to Social Policy: The Less Trodden Path," *Signs Systems Studies* 34.1 (2006), pp. 121–134; Stables and S. Gough, "Towards a Semiotic Theory of Choice and of Learning," *Educational Theory* 56 (2006), pp. 271–285.

9. "As we cannot be sure about whether mind and matter are really separate, we cannot be sure of the validity of dividing signs from signals, hence my rather clumsy neologism, the sign(al) – and, if this makes sense, then the statement 'living is semiotic engagement' is, potentially, a foundational statement for a post-foundational age. That is to say, we could usefully begin our studies of all sorts of things in the human sphere with a realization that messages – be they laws, political ideologies, teachers' explanations or even medicines or physical punishments – are received and acted upon differently by people and are always understood in the light of their previous experience. They are all things we inevitably make sense of in ways that are both common and unique to some extent." Stables, *Living and Learning as Semiotic Engagement*, p. 375.

10. Immanuel Kant, *Critique of Pure Reason* (Basingstoke, UK: Macmillan, 1933).

11. For an introduction to quantum theory, see Alastair Rae, *Quantum Physics: A Beginner's Guide* (Oxford: Oneworld, 2006). Although Albert Einstein famously remarked that "God does not play dice," events at the quantum (subatomic) level seem subject to laws only of probability not of certainty. David Bohm wrote, "The quantum theory, as it is now constituted, presents us with a very great challenge, if we are at all interested in such a venture, for in quantum physics there is no consistent notion at all of what the reality may be that underlies the universal constitution and structure of matter." Bohm, *Wholeness and the Implicate Order* (London and New York: Routledge, 1980), xv.

12. Alfred North Whitehead, *Process and Reality* (New York: Free Press, 1929).

13. "One of his categories of existence is that of 'Nexus' (*Process* 22). A nexus consists (roughly speaking, in actual entities *interrelated* through their prehensions of one another." John Lango, "Whitehead's Category of Nexus of Actual Entities," *Process Studies* 29 (2000), pp. 16–42, at p. 16.

14. Jacques Derrida, "Différance," in *Margins of Philosophy* (Chicago: University of Chicago Press, 1982), pp. 3–27.

15. While Derrida insists that the trace has no obvious existence – it is that (more or less) that the deferral of meaning leaves behind and that thus haunts future meanings, in some way – the same might be said of Whitehead's prehensions, for all the latter's strong sense of presence. Jacques Derrida, *Of Grammatology* (Baltimore, Md.: John Hopkins University Press, 1976).

16. See John Dewey, "The Reflex Arc Concept in Psychology," *Psychological Review* 3 (1896), pp. 357–370, and Dewey, "Perception and Organic Action," *Journal of Philosophy, Psychology and Scientific Methods* 9 (1912), pp. 645–669.

17. For example, F. C. Bartlett, *Thinking* (New York: Basic Books, 1958).

18. For example, Gilles Deleuze and Felix Guattari, *What Is Philosophy?* (New York: Columbia University Press, 1991).

19. "On those stepping into rivers staying the same other and other waters flow." Heraclitus, undated fragment, quoted from the Internet Encyclopedia of Philosophy at http://www.utm.edu/research/iep/h/heraclit.htm, accessed 27 January 2006.

20. Giorgio Carboni's *The Necklace of Democritus* (1999), tells us: "The atomic theory of matter was first proposed by Leucippus, a Greek philosopher who lived in the 5th century before Christ. At this time the Greeks were trying to understand the way matter is made. According to Anassagora, it is possible to subdivide matter in smaller and smaller parts, and he proposed that this process can be continued with no limit. In Anassagora's view, you can always divide a bit of substance into two parts, and each of these parts is also divisible into two parts, and so on – no matter how small each part gets there is no problem dividing it again into even smaller parts. But according to Leucippus, eventually you arrive at small particles which can not be further subdivided. Leucippus called these indivisible particles *atoms*. Leucippus's atomic theory was further developed by his disciple, *Democritus*, (the subject of our story) who concluded that infinite divisibility of a substance belongs only in the imaginary world of mathematics and should not be applied to physics because he believed that in the real world matter is composed of discrete particles." This quotation is from the online publication at http://www.funsci.com/fun3_en/democritus/democritus.htm, accessed on 15 November 2006.

21. This is a claim with radical educational consequences, particularly in countries that recognise affirmative action/positive discrimination. For a fuller exposition of the justification and possible implications of this non-deterministic view, see Stables, "Multiculturalism and Moral Education: Individual Positioning, Dialogue and Cultural Practice," *Journal of Moral Education* 34 (2005), pp. 185–197.

22. Andrew Stables, "School as Imagined Community in Discursive Space: A Perspective on the School Effectiveness Debate," *British Educational Research Journal* 29 (2003), pp. 895–902.

23. John Dewey, "The Reflex Arc Concept in Psychology," and Martin Dworkin, *Dewey on Education: Selections* (New York: Teachers College Press, 1959).

24. John Dewey, *Democracy and Education* (New York: Macmillan, 1916).

25. Dewey, "The Reflex Arc Concept in Psychology," p. 2.

26. *Ibid.*, p. 4.

27. *Ibid.*, p. 7.

28. John Dewey, *The School and Society* (Chicago: University of Chicago Press, 1915).

29. Dewey, *Democracy and Education*, p. 5.

30. *Ibid.*, p. 62.

31. Dworkin, *Dewey on Education: Selections*, p. 133.

32. John Dewey, "My Pedagogic Creed," *The School Journal* 54 (1897), pp. 77–80, quoted from http://www.infed.org/archives/e-texts/e-dew-pc.htm, accessed on 16 November 2006.

33. Dworkin, *Dewey on Education: Selections*.

34. Dworkin, *Dewey on Education: Selections*, p. 115.

35. *Ibid.*, pp. 116–117.

36. Dewey, *The School and Society*, p. 7.

37. Dewey, *Democracy and Education*, p. 11.

38. *Ibid.*, p. 20.

39. Dworkin, *Dewey on Education: Selections*, p. 53.

40. Dewey, *Democracy and Education*, p. 139.

41. Dworkin, *Dewey on Education: Selections*, p. 61.

42. John Dewey, *Experience and Nature* (La Salle, Ill.: Open Court, 1925).

43. John Dewey, *Education Today* (New York: Putnam, 1940).

44. Dewey, *Experience and Nature*, p. 74.

45. John Dewey, *Impressions of Soviet Russia and the Revolutionary World, Mexico-China-Turkey* (New York: The New Republic, 1929).

46. Dworkin, *Dewey on Education: Selections*, p. 125.

47. Andrew Stables, "School as Imagined Community in Discursive Space: A Perspective on the School Effectiveness Debate," *British Educational Research Journal* 29 (2003), pp. 895–902.

48. Dewey, *Democracy and Education*, p. 2.

49. J. L. Austin, *How To Do Things With Words* (Oxford: Oxford University Press, 1975); Jürgen Habermas, *Theory of Communicative Action* (Cambridge, UK: Polity, 1984); and Ludwig Wittgenstein, *Philosophical Investigations* (Oxford: Blackwell, 1967).

50. Dewey, *Experience and Nature*, p. 147.

51. *Ibid.*, p. 71.

52. Dewey, *Democracy and Education*, p. 159.

53. Louis Althusser, *Lenin and Philosophy and Other Essays* (London: NLB, 1971).

54. Pierre Bourdieu, R. Nice, T. Bottomore, and Jean-Claude Passeron, *Reproduction in Education, Society and Culture* (London: Sage, 1990).

55. "In sum, mind appears in the conduct of the individual when outcomes are anticipated and thus become controlling factors in the present ordering of events and activities.... Meanings relate to behaviors." John L. Childs, "The Educational Philosophy of John Dewey," in *The Philosophy of John Dewey*, ed. P. A. Schilpp (La Salle, Ill.: Open Court, 1951), pp. 417–444, at p. 425.

56. William Savery, "The Significance of Dewey's Philosophy," in *The Philosophy of John Dewey*, ed. P. A. Schilpp (La Salle, Ill.: Open Court, 1951), pp. 479–514, at p. 498. Also: "The criterion of the value of the school curriculum is the extent to which it creates a desire for continued growth and supplies means for making the desire effective in fact." (Dewey, *Democracy and Education*, p. 53).

57. Schilpp, *The Philosophy of John Dewey*, p. 570.

58. John Rawls, *Political Liberalism* (New York: Columbia University Press, 1993).

Andrew Stables
Professor of Education and Philosophy
Department of Education
University of Bath
Bath, BA2 7AY
United Kingdom

Contemporary Pragmatism
Vol. 5, No. 1 (June 2008), 163–172

Editions Rodopi
© 2008

Book Reviews

Cheryl Misak, ed. *New Pragmatists*. Oxford: Clarendon Press, 2007.
Pp. 195. Cloth ISBN 0-1992-7997-7.

"New" is a difficult term to employ with precision, as it could denote something qualitatively distinct from something previous, or it could merely mean the latest in a serial ordering of similar units. Cheryl Misak's edited collection, *New Pragmatists*, appears to be "new" in more of the former sense, as it involves many distinguished contributors, many of whom do not call the study of classical pragmatism their home. Many are involved in important debates in contemporary epistemology and metaphysics, thus rendering their engagement with pragmatism to be a "new" way to address many of these issues. I am positive that this collection will spur much discussion, and it is an encouraging sign to see such individuals grapple with the ongoing tradition of American pragmatism. I will sketch out some of the issues addressed in the eight interesting essays comprising this volume, followed by one concern I have about this collection as a whole.

Jeffrey Stout begins the collection with his essay, "On Our Interest in Getting Things Right: Pragmatism without Narcissism." Stout's point is to answer the "critics of pragmatism" who have "long charged that it fails to do justice to the objective dimension of human inquiry" (7). The way he goes about this, like many in the current volume, is by using the "neo-pragmatist" Richard Rorty as an argumentative foil. Rorty exemplifies the narcissistic sort of pragmatist, an individual who sees the worth of pragmatism lying solely in its unabashed anthropocentrism. Stout discusses the important human-centeredness that he is concerned with in regard to Rorty – that of all norms of truth and justification. The Rortian story, of course, is that all of these are reducible to some sort of communal agreement or solidarity. Stout wishes to defend against such a move, and thus turns to an admirable distillation of recent work by Bjørn Ramberg on Rorty and the subject of norms of truth discourse. Ramberg is applauded largely because he (according to Stout's account) gets Rorty to admit that *some* discourse (viz., "realist" discourse) aims at "getting things right." Stout finds this point to be absolutely essentially to building up a "new" pragmatism that takes objectivity seriously, yet retains its falliblist sensibilities. According to Stout's argument, pragmatism must take account of the human interest in getting things right (a truth interest, so to speak), which entails two points: (1) the norms that guide this interest and give it specific direction in cases of inquiry are themselves fallible, and (2) these norms are not reducible to communal agreement (18). Like an archer using various "virtues" or skills of archery to hit the goal of the target, Stout argues that inquirers evaluate issues of justification and assertion based upon a guiding norm of truth. If the archer fails to hit her target, she is disappointed; if an inquirer senses that despite agreement, she is missing something about a particular issue of inquiry, she too feels disappointed. Stout's ultimate point, one he shares with Robert Brandom, is that there is a sensed and justifiable difference that inquirers realize between applying a concept and applying it rightly. The last case concerns our interest in getting it *right*, not just getting it in an agreeable fashion (viz., Rorty's position).

The next two contributions are unusual, but for different reasons. The second essay is quite unique –Ian Hacking's chapter explains why he is *not* a pragmatist. Through an elaborate discussion of whose lectures he attended, what pragmatists he read and didn't read, and many of the works he has written, we learn that Hacking does not want to be called a pragmatist; instead, many of the themes in his work (viz., fallibilism) are shared with pragmatism, but are not attributable to pragmatism as a tradition. Hacking ends his contribution by stating the conclusion his biographical sketch has been pointing to – "Some of the theses favored by pragmatists, neo-pragmatists, or new pragmatists, arise from and seem natural in many other contemporary perspectives" (47–48). The third chapter by Arthur Fine is unusual not so much because it disavows pragmatism, but because it does not seem to substantively engage the pragmatist tradition. Fine does an admirable job discussing the perceived threats of relativism, especially in regard to knowledge claims and justificatory practices. He sums up the threat by pointing out that the overriding fear is that relativism will render the change from our present practices to future practices chaotic and without reasonable direction. The assumption here, according to Fine, is that "reasonableness" is said to depend on invariant standards or norms. While this is an interesting discussion of scientific method, fallibism, and a reasonable relativism, it does not seem to be very "pragmatic" – here and there, a quotation or phrase from Dewey is dropped, but there is no sustained discussion of Dewey's conception of instrumentalism, experimentalism, or his notion of experience. Instead of a new *pragmatist* take on relativism such as the work of Joseph Margolis, Fine's piece seems to be a discussion of relativism simply in light of scientific practice. This is interesting, of course, but it is not uniquely pragmatist in its orientation or analysis.

The fourth chapter, entitled "Pragmatism and Deflationism," comes from Cheryl Misak and concerns a possible response to deflationary accounts of truth. Misak's piece is interesting in that she takes the theory of truth proffered by Charles S. Peirce seriously as a potential antidote to current reductions of truth; instead, she believes that a Peircian account of truth accommodates naturalistic tendencies to start in the midst of human practices (viz., inquiry), while maintaining a meaningful role for the property of truth. Misak considers the deflationary and prosententialist positions, agreeing with the urge to say the heart of inquiry is not only assertability, but also continued assertability. This, she says, seems to be the centerpiece of Peirce's account of inquiry: inquirers hold beliefs not because of their current satisfactory status, but also because they lead the inquirers to expect continued future assertability. The difference seems to be one of temperament. The deflationist wants nothing to do with the predicate "is true," whereas Misak argues that the pragmatist wants to keep this, although as a move internal to a specific kind of inquiry. This is what she calls a focus on "what-is-true" that proceeds from the practice of inquiry itself in some specific domain (say, science or mathematics), and not an actual definition of "truth" in general. Thus, "The pragmatist will say that truth is proper assertion, but different discourses have different standards for proper assertion" (86). On such an account, there is room for the predicate "is true," and it serves as a meaningful term in the actual practices of inquiry. Misak ends her chapter with a tantalizing link to the realism/anti-realism debate. Certain practices of inquiry (viz. science) seem to hint at a strong sort of indefeasibility, even if it is a regulative ideal of the end of inquiry (as in Peirce's case). Misak points out that only here does the realism/anti-realism debate emerge – *after* a ground-up account of our practices of inquiry and truth-seeking. The debate concerns the acceptability of that sort of ideal of defeasibility, but doesn't dispute the heuristic value (according to Misak) of a Peircian way of "getting leverage on the project of truth by exploring its connections with practice" (88). Misak's discussion aptly touches on a theme common to many of the writings in this book – the connection of standards of assertability and truth to the processes of inquiry, all the while resisting foundational norms of truth.

David Macarthur and Huw Price's piece, "Pragmatism, Quasi-realism, and the Global Challenge," comprises the fifth chapter of this volume. This piece serves as a detailed and intricate analysis of the putatively anti-pragmatist position of Simon Blackburn on language, and how such a position eventually collapses into the authors' form of pragmatism. This latter form is what they call "pragmatic quietism," which eschews metaphysical views, commitments, and vocabularies. It is interesting that no references to Peirce, James, Dewey, or Rorty appear in the bibliography, and Dewey and Rorty are only mentioned in two footnotes; the authors' use of "pragmatism," then, must be taken as being of a benignly idiosyncratic sort. In explicating their form of pragmatism, Macarthur and Price make it clear that their view still allows for theoretical analyses of language and its use in assertion; what is rejected is the way of talking about assertion that sees it as *solely* and *homogenously* descriptive or representational. Instead, they marshal a variety of arguments to show that their brand of quietism on representational issues escapes the problems that Blackburn's account would fall into if it resists the pressures to become a global account of language. Thus, the authors ultimately conclude that Blackburn's quasi-realism must, at some point, become a global account, and that such an account is close to what they call pragmatic quietism. Such a view accounts for the unity among language uses, as well as for the differences since they "begin with pragmatic differences, differences among the kinds of things that the assertions in question *do*" (115).

Their position is "quietist" toward metaphysical vocabulary insofar as it involves a "rejection of that vocabulary for the purposes of philosophical theory" (116). They conclude their interesting piece with two divergent readings of Wittgenstein's quietism, but they leave it to the reader to fully explore the value of each of these ways of taking this important figure.

The sixth contribution is the first (and only) piece in this collection to address the issue of new pragmatism and ethics in a sustained manner. David Bakhurst explores the relation of ethical particularism to what can be called "pragmatist ethics" (largely stemming from John Dewey's writings). The position of ethical particularism, as enunciated by proponents such as Jonathan Dancy and John McDowell, holds that "sound moral judgment issues from the exercise of a sensibility that transcends codification into rules or principles" (122). Bakhurst notices that this view of moral sensibility and ability is close to the views of habituated moral behavior resident in the classical pragmatists (and their expositors). He thus sets out to see if a productive dialogue can be had between the ethical particularists and the pragmatists. The first problem comes from the realist proclivities of the particularist – the moral agent is responding aptly to moral features of the situation, whereas pragmatists such as Rorty find that pragmatic approaches to ethics are thoroughly anthropocentric in their sources of value. Bakhurst believes that Dewey's form of pragmatic ethics can better meet the concerns of ethical particularism, as Dewey places values as part of the situation humans find themselves in (thus toning down Rorty's anthropocentrism). Of course, this situation is largely social, and involves our acting and reacting in light of other agents. Dewey thereby holds a way of connecting particularism with pragmatism – pragmatism allows input from principles as moral guide (though there are still problems with this reading of the usefulness of principles), and allows for a useful analogy between moral and aesthetic activity. Concerning this latter issue, Bakhurst points out that moral responsiveness and aesthetic responsiveness are similar in that they are each non-codifiable ways of responding to a given situational whole. Additionally, he aptly notes that the jazz musician responds not only to "facts" of her (social) musical situation, but also to the creations of others in the ensemble (viz., the sounds issuing from the others). The pragmatist approach to ethics, with its emphasis on social "facts" and one's responsiveness to them, supplements the personal-focus of ethical particularism.

Terry Pinkard's chapter, tantalizingly titled "Was Pragmatism the Successor to Idealism?," is both captivating and slightly disappointing. It is captivating insofar as it serves as a vivid presentation of the conflict between Kant and Hegel over the status and source of normativity. It is disappointing in that it couches this disagreement in the "Hegelianism" of Dewey and other pragmatists, but never fundamentally answers the question contained in the title. After a detailed and enlightening examination of Hegel's take on interest, freedom, and normativity, Pinkard returns to pragmatism in the final few pages of the piece, largely focusing on whether Robert Brandom's appropriation of

Hegel is more akin to the thought of Fichte than Hegel. The final page considers the interesting question – was Hegel a pragmatist? The answer is – perhaps. Pinkard seems to leave it up to the reader to decide what commitments pragmatism has toward the source of interests and freedom, and then to answer the question on their own. If they find that pragmatism emphasizes "the *realization* of our own freedom" (166) over a historical progression, then Hegel would be a pragmatist. If one sees pragmatism as holding to freedom and interest in a more Kantian fashion (as pre-existing), then Hegel would not be a pragmatist. While these moves cover all the options, a deeper discussion of pragmatist sources could complement Pinkard's reading of Hegel and decisively answer his question as to the link between Hegel and the American pragmatists.

The final contribution is from Danielle Macbeth, entitled "Pragmatism and Objective Truth." Macbeth starts with Peirce's "pragmatic maxim" and addresses its coherence with a workable notion of objectivity. After discussing Sellars and McDowell on the various ways of interacting with the world, Macbeth argues that there are two sorts of concepts at play – what she calls modern mathematical concepts (such as those used in modern physics) and sensory concepts (such as the color red). Ultimately, Peirce's pragmatic maxim, which Macbeth links to an inferential web that comprises the "view from nowhere" (190), fails to account for the more sensory type of concept. Macbeth states that "The pragmatist maxim, while it is indeed an insight into meaning, is not an insight into meaning *überhaupt*. It is an insight into the meaning only of distinctively modern mathematical concepts; and such concepts, I have argued, are intelligible only as an essentially late fruit of our ongoing sensory experience of the world as we first find it" (190). Thus, the pragmatist account of meaning should be scaled back to one of what could be called, following Sellars and McDowell, the "scientific" view of the world. Macbeth's reading of modern mathematical concepts as exhausting Peirce's notion of concept is an interesting, albeit potentially arguable, analysis and deserves further attention from those interested in Peirce's ambitious project in epistemology.

Overall, Cheryl Misak has done an admirable job assembling some important philosophers on a topic that is not over-studied in modern philosophical circles. Pragmatism as a whole definitely will be benefited from the attention given to it by these "new pragmatists," as well as from the time given to the reading of their work as a whole. I must register one reservation with the "new" way of reading pragmatism and its importance that is enshrined in this volume. More precisely, I want to draw attention to what is left out of all these essays – the important pragmatist theme of *meliorism*. This is the position taken by James and Dewey (some would also include Peirce, as well) that recognizes the present situation as incomplete and able to be improved. Thus, a meliorative effort in philosophy goes beyond a mere fallibilism because it focuses on (1) actual ends to be achieved and devotes serious attention to (2) the ways such ends can actually be instantiated. In the discussion of truth, realism, fallibilism, and so on in the current volume, the pragmatist approach of analyzing philosophical issues with the goal of improving actual, lived experience is missing. One must never forget that the early pragmatists, especially James and Dewey, were integrally involved in theorizing and writing not just for other philosophers, but for the larger purpose of improving life. Why did James practice and study so many meliorative somatic techniques, or use his 1906 presidential address to the American Philosophical Association to plead for a disciplined study of the "energies of men" and how they can be improved? Why did Dewey not only write about art and education, but also administratively take part in the Barnes Foundation and the Laboratory School?

Even the one essay in this collection that addresses moral issues in a sustained matter lacks this melioritive focus – like the contributions dealing with epistemological/metaphysical issues, it focuses on giving a *descriptive* theoretical account of some human practice (viz., moral judgment). The missing alternative is to give attention to ways of *changing* or *reconstructing* human practices or habits. Other "new pragmatists," such as Richard Shusterman, would approach this issue differently, perhaps giving the bulk of their attention to what ends should be aimed at in the production moral inquirers and how we can effectively produce such habits in individuals. This is the melioristic voice that is missing from the current volume; any current revival of pragmatism would be greatly enhanced if it were to include such a voice. *New Pragmatists* serves as an interesting, if incomplete, start to elaborating on what pragmatism has to contribute to modern philosophical discussions.

Scott R. Stroud
University of Texas at Austin

Romand Coles and Stanley Hauerwas. *Christianity, Democracy, and the Radical Ordinary: Conversations between a Radical Democrat and a Christian.* Eugene, Oregon: Cascade Books, 2008. Pp. xii + 366. Paperback ISBN 978-1-55635-297-3.

For some of us "cotemporary pragmatists" who do philosophical theology and political philosophy, Jeffrey Stout's *Democracy and Tradition* was a book that had to be written. It put in conversation those who defend a "secular democracy" (think Jürgen Habermas, John Rawls, and Richard Rorty) with those who defend a Christian "traditionalism" in contemporary philosophy and theology (think Stanley Hauerwas, Alasdair MacIntyre, and John Milbank). Of these philosophers and theologians, Stanley Hauerwas is now officially the first one to respond to Stout in book-length form – though he had some help in doing it. In *Christianity, Democracy, and the Radical Ordinary*, Romand Coles (a political theorist at Duke University) and Stanley Hauerwas (*the* theological ethicist at Duke University, Duke Divinity School, and Duke Law School) offer us timely reflections on the relation between contemporary Christian theology and contemporary democratic political theory. These timely reflections are worth the ride and the ticket price for what they call their "conversations between a radical democrat and a Christian."

Coles is not only concerned with contemporary democratic political theory but with ordinary lives and "radical democracy." Coles and Hauerwas find themselves in conversation because Coles thinks that some of the best exemplars of his understanding of "radical democracy" are found in actual Christian churches and communities. For example, the Christian churches that Charles Marsh writes about in his *The Beloved Community* – like Martin Luther King's church in Birmingham, Alabama – exemplify what a "radical democracy" looks like, for Coles, because they practice the politics of both "generosity" and "receptivity." Radical democratic communities practice the politics of "generosity" by being the church, being the body of Christ for the world, and giving in "excess" of what God has given them. And radical democratic communities practice the politics of "receptivity" by being challenged by other communities and traditions through argument and making explicit their differences and disagreements, through encountering the "other" and receiving the "other," and with the kind of "wild patience" that requires a sacrifice of attempting to control history and the world.

Though it is not a self-description, Coles is a deeply pragmatic thinker in that his political *theories* are determined by the actual *practices* of *real* communities. Coles is not a Christian, which becomes an interesting issue in *Christianity, Democracy, and the Radical Ordinary*, but he takes Christian churches and communities seriously in ways analogous to how William James took Christian believers and their convictions seriously throughout his work. Coles works within the tradition of democratic political theory, but his use of democracy stays close to the ground and thus is much closer to that of John Dewey than John Rawls. And, like any good pragmatist ought to do, Coles does not partake in polemics against those with whom he disagrees but rather offers a "rational reconstruction" (Jürgen Habermas's phrase) of the arguments of his opponents. In doing so, he brings his readers into sympathy with his opponents as much as with those for whom he agrees.

What is Hauerwas's role in this conversation? As a fond reader of Hauerwas's work, I found this book to be one of his most important and insightful because Hauerwas is *fully engaged with* and *vulnerable to* someone who is "outside the church." The reason for this engagement and vulnerability is that Hauerwas seems to trust Coles in ways he seems not to trust other critics of his work. Perhaps the reason for this trust is exactly Coles's practice of "rational reconstruction" when it comes to Hauerwas's arguments and thought. Coles does not seek to *stick* labels on Hauerwas like "sectarian" or "traditionalist" but rather puts questions to Hauerwas about his logic, reasoning, and thought patterns. That is, Coles forces Hauerwas to reflect on his *habits of thinking* rather than simply on his conclusions to his arguments or titles to his books. (Some critics of Hauerwas attack him especially for the subtitle to his book *After Christendom?*, which is *How the Church Is to Behave If Freedom, Justice, and a Christian Nation Are Bad Ideas* – a criticism to which Hauerwas continually responds by saying that this subtitle is not his own but rather an editor's and thus critics ought to read the book instead of the cover!)

Perhaps more importantly for Hauerwas's trust of Coles is that Coles does not tell Hauerwas that he quit being Christian or even that he should have a lower ecclesiology or a less determinate view of the Christian tradition. In fact, at one place in the book, Coles even suggests that Hauerwas take Jesus even more seriously in his work and allow others to wash the feet of the church as Jesus allowed others to wash his feet. It is in this practice of foot-washing and service that Coles finds a good example of what the politics of "generosity" and "receptivity" are: both the willingness to serve others through washing their feet ("generosity") *and* the willingness to be served by others by inviting them to wash your feet ("receptivity"). Coles thinks Hauerwas accounts well for how the church washes the feet of each other and the world but not of how the world can wash the feet of the church. Hauerwas, according to Coles therefore, accounts for "generosity" but not "receptivity."

Hauerwas is a deeply pragmatic thinker in his own right, especially in his "bottom-up" approach to Christian ethics and theology. For Hauerwas, ethics and theology start from the ground – that is, with *actual* practices and *real* people who embody the virtues. Hauerwas does not think that the life of the church depends on some external criteria or justification but rather on what Christians actually *do* as part of the life of the church. No where is this conviction more evident than in his most recent anthology, edited with Samuel Wells, entitled *The Blackwell Companion to Christian Ethics*. Every essay in that anthology addresses an "ethical question" by first talking about a Christian practice that helps make sense or might help make sense of that particular "ethical question." Therefore, it is a particular practice that makes sense of a general question and not the other way around. Gerald Schlabach, for example, addresses the question of "peace and war" through the practice of the Eucharist and what it might mean for Christians who take the Eucharist at the same time across the globe each week to have to kill one another for the sake of their particular countries; what ought to be more determinate for a baptized believer and soldier: breaking bread and taking the wine together, or following the command from one's country to kill those who might also break bread and take wine?

Coles puts some good questions to Hauerwas and his followers. Coles does not challenge the "bottom-up" approach (for it is this very approach that Coles finds attractive in Hauerwas's work) but rather the assumption that the interior life of the church is enough for ethical and theological engagements with the "other." It *is* enough, according to Coles, on one level: the level of "generosity." The interior life of the church rightly forms Christians to be the body of Christ for the world. But it *is not* enough, according to Coles, on the level on "receptivity." Following Jesus rightly and being in full accord with the gospel, according to Coles, ought to *decenter* the Christian and the life of the church. But the contributors to the *Blackwell Companion to Christian Ethics* do not assume or discuss this "*decentering*" of the life of the church. Rather, they work in a way that creates a social imaginary for the Christian that all one needs one finds in the interior life of the church rather than *at its borders*. In response to Schlabach's article, for example, Coles says that his "sense is that this imaginary constitutes the borders between church and world in a way that *makes the border secondary to an interior volume* that is at the center and that *only prepares for* rather than *is itself partly constituted by the borders themselves*" (212). In other words, Hauerwas and his followers in *The Blackwell Companion to Christian Ethics* lack this kind of "receptivity" that requires engagement with others at the church-world border, because it is at *this* border – not in an interior space or volume of the church that excludes and is protected from others – where the church finds its identity.

The strength of this book is that neither Coles nor Hauerwas talks about Christian theology or "radical democracy" in the clouds but rather talks about what actual people are doing. The weakness of the book, if there is one, is that the "conversation" between Coles and Hauerwas in the final chapter is too "nice." Though they make some differences and disagreements clear, they both work too hard to "clean up" those differences and disagreements in ways that they criticize "liberalism" for forcing all of us to do. For example, if Coles can say "That's wonderful" to Hauerwas's claim that Christians "do not have to triumph over others, *because* God has triumphed" and that it is *only* "in the light of *that* triumph do we [Christians] believe it possible to live with patience that makes nonviolence not only possible but necessary" (343), then why is Coles not a Christian? I am not trying to *make* Coles sound like he *is* a Christian with my question, but I – perhaps with other interested readers, both Christian and non-Christian – want to hear how someone can say "That's wonderful" to the claim that it is *only* because of God's triumph over others that Christians live with patience and therefore it is only *because of God* that nonviolence is both possible and necessary. Hauerwas is not referring to some generic God but the God who is God in three persons: the God who sent his Son and Spirit to the world. If Coles thinks that claim is "wonderful," then Coles needs to explain how his *wonder* is a wonder that does not entail the kind of participation and practice required of those claims about God. With such an explanation, Coles would be making his disagreement with Hauerwas about why he is not a Christian more direct and explicit.

I return now to my argument that this book is Hauerwas's book-length response to Jeffrey Stout's *Democracy and Tradition*. Hauerwas's response to Stout is that he is willing to take radical democracy seriously if radical democracy necessarily includes the politics of "generosity" and "receptivity," as

Coles outlines it. For Hauerwas, that means that defenders of democracy – like Coles and Stout – need to be receptive of the Church on the Church's terms.

Hauerwas, therefore, shows that he can *fully engage with* and even *be vulnerable to* a "radical democrat" that attempts to talk with Hauerwas on Hauerwas's own ecclesial terms. Coles does that *kind of talking*, talk on someone else's terms, better than anyone I have read in awhile. Coles thus *textually displays* his politics of "generosity" and "receptivity" and gets Hauerwas – the alleged Christian "sectarian" and "traditionalist" – to practice the same kind of politics. In this sense, then, *Christianity, Democracy, and the Radical Ordinary* is an academic performance of the politics of "generosity" and "receptivity" between a political theorist and a Christian theological ethicist.

Jacob Goodson
University of Virginia